Bloom's Major Literary Characters

Nick Adams

King Arthur

George F. Babbitt

Elizabeth Bennet

Leopold Bloom

Sir John Falstaff

Huck Finn

Frankenstein

Jay Gatsby

Hamlet

Hester Prynne

Raskolnikov and Svidrigailov

Bloom's Major Literary Characters

Huck Finn

Edited and with an introduction by
Harold Bloom
Sterling Professor of the Humanities
Yale University

CHELSEA HOUSE
P U B L I S H E R S
A Haights Cross Communications Company
Philadelphia

©2004 by Chelsea House Publishers, a subsidiary of Haights Cross Communications.

 A Haights Cross Communications ◥ Company

Introduction © 2004 by Harold Bloom.

Printed and bound in the United States of America.

10 9 8 7 6 5 4 3 2 1

Library of Congress Cataloging-in-Publication Data applied for.

Huck Finn / edited and with a introduction by Harold Bloom.
        p. cm. — (Bloom's major literary characters)
Includes bibliographical references (p.) and index.
   ISBN 0-7910-7883-3
  1. Twain, Mark, 1835–1910. Adventures of Huckleberry Finn. 2. Twain, Mark, 1835–1910—Characters—Huckleberry Finn. 3. Finn, Huckleberry (Fictitious character) 4. Boys in literature. [1. Twain, Mark, 1835–1910. Adventures of Huckleberry Finn.] I. Bloom, Harold. II. Major literary characters. PS1305.H829 2003 813'.4—dc22

                                 2003024086

Contributing editor: Pamela Loos

Cover design by Keith Trego

Cover: Huck Finn, © Ewing Galloway/Index Stock Imagery, Inc.

Layout by EJB Publishing Services

Chelsea House Publishers
1974 Sproul Road, Suite 400
Broomall, PA 19008-0914

www.chelseahouse.com

Contents

HAROLD BLOOM

The Analysis of Character

"Character," according to our dictionaries, still has as a primary meaning a graphic symbol, such as a letter of the alphabet. This meaning reflects the word's apparent origin in the ancient Greek character, a sharp stylus. *Charactēr* also meant the mark of the stylus' incisions. Recent fashions in literary criticism have reduced "character" in literature to a matter of marks upon a page. But our word "character" also has a very different meaning, matching that of the ancient Greek *ēthos*, "habitual way of life." Shall we say then that literary character is an imitation of human character, or is it just a grouping of marks? The issue is between a critic like Dr. Samuel Johnson, for whom words were as much like people as like things, and a critic like the late Roland Barthes, who told us that "the fact can only exist linguistically, as a term of discourse." Who is closer to our experience of reading literature, Johnson or Barthes? What difference does it make, if we side with one critic rather than the other?

Barthes is famous, like Foucault and other recent French theorists, for having added to Nietzsche's proclamation of the death of God a subsidiary demise, that of the literary author. If there are no authors, then there are no fictional personages, presumably because literature does not refer to a world outside language. Words indeed necessarily refer to other words in the first place, but the impact of words ultimately is drawn from a universe of fact. Stories, poems, and plays are recognizable as such because they are human utterances within traditions of utterances, and traditions, by achieving authority, become a kind of fact, or at least the sense of a fact. Our sense that literary characters, within the context of a fictive cosmos, indeed are fictional personages is also a kind of fact. The meaning and value of every character in a successful work of literary representation depend upon our ideas of persons in the factual reality of our lives.

Literary character is always an invention, and inventions generally are indebted to prior inventions. Shakespeare is the inventor of literary character as we know it; he reformed the universal human expectations for the verbal imitation of personality, and the reformation appears now to be permanent and uncannily inevitable. Remarkable as the Bible and Homer are at representing personages, their characters are relatively unchanging. They age within their stories, but their habitual modes of being do not develop. Jacob and Achilles unfold before us, but without metamorphoses. Lear and Macbeth, Hamlet and Othello severely modify themselves not only by their actions, but by their utterances, and most of all through *overhearing themselves*, whether they speak to themselves or to others. Pondering what they themselves have said, they will to change, and actually do change, sometimes extravagantly yet always persuasively. Or else they suffer change, without willing it, but in reaction not so much to their language as to their relation to that language.

I do not think it useful to say that Shakespeare successfully imitated elements in our characters. Rather, it could be argued that he compelled aspects of character to appear that previously were concealed, or not available to representation. This is not to say that Shakespeare is God, but to remind us that language is not God either. The mimesis of character in Shakespeare's dramas now seems to us normative, and indeed became the accepted mode almost immediately, as Ben Jonson shrewdly and somewhat grudgingly implied. And yet, Shakespearean representation has surprisingly little in common with the imitation of reality in Jonson or in Christopher Marlowe. The origins of Shakespeare's originality in the portrayal of men and women are to be found in the *Canterbury Tales* of Geoffrey Chaucer, insofar as they can be located anywhere before Shakespeare himself, Chaucer's savage and superb Pardoner overhears his own tale-telling, as well as his mocking rehearsal of his own spiel, and through this overhearing he is emboldened to forget himself, and enthusiastically urges all his fellow-pilgrims to come forward to be fleeced by him. His self-awareness, and apocalyptically rancid sense of spiritual fall, are preludes to the even grander abysses of the perverted will in Iago and in Edmund. What might be called the character trait of a negative charisma may be Chaucer's invention, but came to its perfection in Shakespearean mimesis.

The analysis of character is as much Shakespeare's invention as the representation of character is, since Iago and Edmund are adepts at analyzing both themselves and their victims. Hamlet, whose overwhelming charisma has many negative components, is certainly the most comprehensive of all literary characters, and so necessarily prophesies the labyrinthine complexities of the will in Iago and Edmund. Charisma, according to Max Weber, its first codifier, is primarily a natural endowment, and implies a primordial and idiosyncratic power over nature, and so finally over death. Hamlet's uncanniness is at its most suggestive in the scene of his long dying, where the audience, through the mediation of Horatio, itself is compelled to meditate upon suicide, if only because outliving the prince of Denmark scarcely seems an option.

Shakespearean representation has usurped not only our sense of literary character, but our sense of ourselves as characters, with Hamlet playing the part of the largest of these usurpations. Insofar as we have an idea of human disinterestedness, we tend to derive it from the Hamlet of Act V, whose quietism has about it a ghostly authority. Oscar Wilde, in his profound and profoundly witty dialogue, "The Decay of Lying," expressed a permanent insight when he insisted that art shaped every era, far more than any age formed art. Life imitates art, we imitate Shakespeare, because without Shakespeare we would perish for lack of images. Wilde's grandest audacity demystifies Shakespearean mimesis with a Shakespearean vivaciousness: "This unfortunate aphorism about art holding the mirror up to Nature is deliberately said by Hamlet in order to convince the bystanders of his absolute insanity in all art-matters." Of *Hamlet*'s influence upon the ages Wilde remarked that: "The world has grown sad because a puppet was once melancholy." "Puppet" is Wilde's own deconstruction, a brilliant reminder that Shakespeare's artistry of illusion has so mastered reality as to have changed reality, evidently forever.

The analysis of character, as a critical pursuit, seems to me as much a Shakespearean invention as literary character was, since much of what we know about how to analyze character necessarily follows Shakespearean procedures. His hero-villains, from Richard III through Iago, Edmund, and Macbeth, are shrewd and endless questers into their own self-motivations. If we could bear to see Hamlet, in his unwearied negations, as another hero-villain, then we would judge him the supreme analyst of the darker recalcitrances in the selfhood. Freud followed the pre-Socratic Empedocles, in arguing that character is fate, a frightening doctrine that maintains the fear that there are no accidents, that overdetermination rules us all of our lives. Hamlet assumes the same, yet adds to this argument the terrible passivity he manifests in Act V. Throughout Shakespeare's tragedies, the most interesting personages seem doom-eager, reminding us again that a Shakespearean reading of Freud would be more illuminating than a Freudian exegesis of

Shakespeare. We learn more when we discover Hamlet in the Freudian Death Drive, than when we read *Beyond the Pleasure Principle* into *Hamlet*.

In Shakespearean comedy, character achieves its true literary apotheosis, which is the representation of the inner freedom that can be created by great wit alone. Rosalind and Falstaff, perhaps alone among Shakespeare's personages, match Hamlet in wit, though hardly in the metaphysics of consciousness. Whether in the comic or the modern mode, Shakespeare has set the standard of measurement in the balance between character and passion.

In Shakespeare the self is more dramatized than theatricalized, which is why a Shakespearean reading of Freud works out so well. Character-formation after the passing of the Oedipal stage takes the place of fetishistic fragmentings of the self. Critics who now call literary character into question, and who proclaim also the death of the author, invariably also regard all notions, literary and human, of a stable character as being mere reductions of deeper pre-Oedipal desires. It becomes clear that the fortunes of literary character rise and fall with the prestige of normative conceptions of the ego. Shakespeare's Iago, who wars against being, may be the first deconstructionist of the self, with his proclamation of "I am not what I am." This constitutes the necessary prologue to any view that would regard a fixed ego as a virtual abnormality. But deconstructions of the self are no more modern than Modernism is. Like literary modernism, the decentered ego came out of the Hellenistic culture of ancient Alexandria. The Gnostic heretics believed that the psyche, like the body, was a fallen entity, mechanically fashioned by the Demiurge or false creator. They held however that each of us possessed also a spark or pneuma, which was a fragment of the original Abyss or true, alien God. The soul or psyche within every one of us was thus at war with the self or pneuma, and only that sparklike self could be saved.

Shakespeare, following after Chaucer in this respect, was the first and remains still the greatest master of representing character both as a stable soul and a wavering self. There is a substance that endures in Shakespeare's figures, and there is also a quicksilver rendition of the unsettling sparks. Racine and Tolstoy, Balzac and Dickens, follow in Shakespeare's wake by giving us some sense of pre-Oedipal sparks or drives, and considerably more sense of post-Oedipal character and personality, stabilizations or sublimations of the fetish-seeking drives. Critics like Leo Bersani and René Girard argue eloquently against our taking this mimesis as the only proper work of literature. I would suggest that strong fictions of the self, from the Bible through Samuel Beckett, necessarily participate in both modes, the sublimation of desire, and the persistence of a primordial desire. The mystery of Hamlet or of Lear is intimately invested in the tangled mixture of the two modes of representation.

Psychic mobility is proposed by Bersani as the ideal to which deconstructions of the literary self may yet guide us. The ideal has its pathos, but the realities of literary representation seem to me very different, perhaps destructively so. When a novelist like D. H. Lawrence sought to reduce his characters to Eros and the Death Drive, he still had to persuade us of his authority at mimesis by lavishing upon the figures of *The Rainbow* and *Women in Love* all of the vivid stigmata of normative personality. Birkin and Ursula may represent antithetical and uncanny drives, but they develop and change as characters pondering their own pronouncements and reactions to self and others. The cost of a non-Shakespearean representation is enormous. Pynchon, in *The Crying of Lot 49* and *Gravity's Rainbow*, evades the burden of the normative by resorting to something like Christopher Marlowe's art of caricature in *The Jew of Malta*. Marlowe's Barabas is a marvelous rhetorician, yet he is a cartoon alongside the troublingly equivocal Shylock. Pynchon's personages are deliberate cartoons also, as flat as comic strips. Marlowe's achievement, and Pynchon's, are beyond dispute, yet they are like the prelude and the postlude to Shakespearean reality. They do not wish to engage with our hunger for the empirical world and so they enter the problematic cosmos of literary fantasy.

No writer, not even Shakespeare or Proust, alters the available stock that we agree to call reality, but Shakespeare, more than any other, does show us how much of reality we could encounter if only we retained adequate desire. The strong literary representation of character is already an analysis of character, and is part of the healing work of a literary culture, which implicitly seeks to cure violence through a normative mimesis of ego, *as if it were stable*, whether in actuality it is or is not. I do not believe that this is a social quest taken on by literary culture, but rather that we confront here the aesthetic essence of what makes a culture *literary*, rather than metaphysical or ethical or religious. A culture becomes literary when its conceptual modes have failed it, which means when religion, philosophy, and science have begun to lose their authority. If they cannot heal violence, then literature attempts to do so, which may be only a turning inside out of the critical arguments of Girard and Bersani.

I conclude by offering a particular instance or special case as a paradigm for the healing enterprise that is at once the representation and the analysis of literary character. Let us call it the aesthetics of being outraged, or rather of successfully representing the state of being outraged. W. C. Fields was one modern master of such representation, and Nathanael West was another, as was Faulkner before him. Here also the greatest master remains Shakespeare, whose Macbeth, himself a bloody outrage, yet retains our imaginative sympathy precisely because he grows increasingly outraged as he experiences the equivocation of the fiend that lies like truth. The double-natured promises and the prophecies of the weird sisters finally induce in Macbeth an apocalyptic version of the stage actor's anxiety at missing cues, the horror of a phantasmagoric stage fright of missing one's time, of always reacting too late. Macbeth, a veritable monster of solipsistic inwardness but no intellectual, counters his dilemma by fresh murders, that prolong him in time yet provoke him only to a perpetually freshened sense of being outraged, as all his expectations become still worse confounded. We are moved by Macbeth, however estrangedly, because his terrible inwardness is a paradigm for our own solipsism, but also because none of us can resist a strong and successful representation of the human in a state of being outraged.

The ultimate outrage is the necessity of dying, an outrage concealed in a multitude of masks, including the tyrannical ambitions of Macbeth. I suspect that our outrage at being outraged is the most difficult of all our affects for us to represent to ourselves, which is why we are so inclined to imaginative sympathy for a character who strongly conveys that affect to us. The Shrike of West's *Miss Lonelyhearts* or Faulkner's Joe Christmas of *Light in August* are crucial modern instances, but such figures can be located in many other works, since the ability to represent this extreme emotion is one of the tests that strong writers are driven to set for themselves.

However a reader seeks to reduce literary character to a question of marks on a page, she will come at last to the impasse constituted by the thought of death, her death, and before that to all the stations of being outraged that memorialize her own drive towards death. In reading, she quests for evidences that are strong representations, whether of her desire or her despair. Such questings constitute the necessary basis for the analysis of literary character, an enterprise that always will survive every vagary of critical fashion.

Editor's Note

My introduction applies the principles of my series essay on "The Analysis of Character" to the ways in which Huck exemplifies freedom.

Lionel Trilling praises Huck (and Mark Twain), for giving us "the very voice of unpretentious truth," while T.S. Eliot gives us a hymn to the River, returning to his own youth.

For Leslie Fiedler, the wonder and terror of childhood fuse in Huck's story, after which Richard Poirier demonstrates how deeply Huck is embedded in the conventions he seeks to evade.

Millicent Bell, analyzing Huck's own imagination, gives us a fresh perspective upon the vagabond in America, while Roy Harvey Pearce judges that Huck, whose quest is to survive, cannot survive in society or outside it, and so stands as a witness to his own truth.

I prefer Harold Beaver to all other critics on Huck, and here he meditates upon Huck's refusal of violence, after which Andrew Jay Hoffman nevertheless regards Huck's wise passivity as a heroism.

Moral heroism in Huck is the theme of David E.E. Sloane, while Tom Quirk concludes this volume by praising the "realistic urgency" of the novel.

HAROLD BLOOM

Introduction

Huck Finn seeks freedom; that is the judgment of Leo Marx and of most good critics of *Adventures of Huckleberry Finn*. What critics disagree about is the nature of Huck's longed-for freedom. Is it freedom *for* something, or primarily freedom *from* many things—society, family, respectability, daily reality, growing up, and ultimately dying?

Huck's family consists of a dangerous, indeed murderous father, who might always turn up again, somehow. Obviously, freedom in the first place must mean freedom from such a deathly father, and continuous motion, like that of the great river, is the best way of evading the father, and so the very best place to be is on the raft. But freedom for Huck does not mean solitude—Huck is neither a god nor a beast, and he is afraid of being alone, as most of us are. That must be why Jim is the perfect companion for him, particularly when Jim is in flight, a flight that in itself already is as much freedom as Jim so far has known.

But Huck is not a Kerouac beatnik on the road, just going for the sake of going. Huck is not a drifter, but more accurately a shrewd and kindly observer, who does not value his own freedom above the reality of other people, as say Thoreau did. Indeed, one accurate way of seeing Huck is to ponder the difference between Huck and Jim on the raft and Thoreau at Walden Pond. Thoreau's greatest pride is in economic freedom above all things, and so in getting his values right. He will not pay a jot more for

anything than what it is worth. But Huck is always willing to overpay—up to
a point—and with the currency of his leisure and his concern, including his
capacity for compassion and affection.

Huck overpays for the friendship of Tom Sawyer, which is one way of
explaining why the book ends so lamely, and perhaps he overpays also for
most of his adventures, since he is morally superior to everyone he
encounters, except for Jim. If the theme of the book is the search for
freedom, and the book's major image is the river, then the theme and the
image only superficially fit one another. The river is not in itself free,
anymore than Walden Pond is—the river must move, and the pond must stay
fixed in place. Perhaps the book after all is not just about freedom, but about
the limits of freedom as well.

Yet that is the book, and not the literary character, Huck Finn. Huck's
central dilemma defines the spiritual uniqueness of our country, for if Huck
fears solitude, nevertheless he is driven to crave it. There are two crucial
tenets in what I think must be called *the* American Religion, of which
Emerson was the theologian, and Mark Twain the authorized Fool, or
national storyteller. One is that no American feels free if she is not alone; the
other is that every American passionately believes that she is no part of the
Creation. Huck, no theologian, implicitly identifies himself with what
preceded Creation, and so with what must regard all Creation, however
beautiful, as a kind of Fall, since Creation introduces death and time into a
Fullness beyond them. The superstitions that govern Huck, and his teacher,
Jim, ultimately take their authority from the river, itself not free and yet
somehow an emblem of freedom. It is as though the Fullness of the original
Abyss takes its final representation in the river, and in those whom the river
instructs.

Huck's superstitions (and Jim's, and Twain's, for that matter) are not at
all African-American, but go back to the Thracian, shamanistic origins of
Western folk-religion, to what can be regarded as Orphic traditions. As befits
an American Orphic, Huck's Orphism bears a marked difference from the
ancient variety, The emphasis is not upon the survival of an occult self, but
upon survival plain and simple, upon the continuity of the self. That is the
burden of the justly famous final paragraph of the book:

> Tom's most well, now, and got his bullet around his neck on a
> watch-guard, for a watch, and is always seeing what time it is, and
> so there ain't nothing more to write about, and I am rotten glad
> of it, because if I'd a knowed what a trouble it was to make a book
> I wouldn't a tackled it and ain't agoing to no more. But I reckon
> I got to light out for the Territory ahead of the rest, because Aunt

Sally she's going to adopt me and sivilize me and I can't stand it.
I been there before.

The bullet indeed is rightly a timepiece, in Huck's vision, and the identity of bullet and watch is part of our discomfort with culture, our discontent with supposed civilization. It is one of the poems of our climate, Walt Whitman's, that Huck joins in reckoning that he must light out for the Territory ahead of the rest of us. Lighting out upon the open road is the largest American lie against time, and Huck is the grandest of our deliberate liars, lying always, as he says, even just to keep in practice. Nietzsche warned that incessant lying is the most exhausting of modes, and one of the darknesses of Huck's character is how exhausted he so perpetually impresses us as having become. Unlike Twain, Huck is neither a humorist nor a misanthrope, as T. S. Eliot sensibly noted. Unlike Eliot, Huck does not aver that mankind cannot bear very much reality. I cannot recall many major literary characters who resign themselves to bearing as much reality as Huck does, since his capacity for fellow-feeling is well-nigh infinite.

Some critics have interpreted Huck's quest as being not for freedom, but for family. We can smile at the prospect of a fully domesticated Huck, while granting that the boy's fierce loneliness generates much of his marvelous pathos. Yet Huck's lies defend him against all fixed identity, because identity is not to be trusted. As the son of a murderous father, Huck evades identity and loves without trust, and so without expecting to be loved in return. The trope of fatherhood is allied for Huck with the murderousness of time, the universe of death. In turning to the river, and to Jim, Huck abandons any quest for family and chooses instead an origin that will also be an end, a fullness that has little to do with nature, and has much in common with Whitman's retrievements out of the night.

V. S. Pritchett once observed that Tom Sawyer was imaginative, but that Huck was not: "Huck never imagines anything except fears." Empirically, Pritchett may have been right, yet Huck's anxieties are considerably more impressive and moving than Tom's imaginary adventures, and Huck is clearly the more imaginative creation. He is like Whitman's Real Me or Me Myself, "both in and out of the game, and watching and wondering at it." His status as observer may be the product of estrangement or repression, but his observations have the curious authority of an anxiety that nevertheless does not seek to appropriate for itself. A good-hearted anxiety ought to be an oxymoron, but is not when we consider the character of Huck. That in turn leads to the question most central to judging Huck as a character: do we think of him as a boy, or as an ageless consciousness?

I cannot conceive of Huck Finn other than as he is, and aging could not change him. He need neither unfold nor develop, for there is nothing immature in him. His affections are fully formed, and would never abandon him. The Hamlet of Act I and of Act V are different men, yet we do not feel a contradiction between them, because the later Hamlet is the severely purged and purified form of the earlier. Huck is already his final self, even as a boy. What cannot alter in Huck is his will, which is both relatively unconditioned and wholly benign. One sees why Hemingway found his Nick Adams in Huck, and why Jake Barnes and the other major Hemingway protagonists are versions of Huck. Like their vagabond precursor, they are too pure in will to be violated by any experience. Huck will not sour or darken, even though he will never trust anyone, with the single and saving exception of Jim, and the more dubious instance of Tom Sawyer.

A wholly secular being, Huck nevertheless incarnates the American religion of reliance upon what is best and oldest in the self. History falls away before that spark of the best and oldest, because the spark takes no stock in dead people, which was Huck's reaction to Moses. Huck's concern is with the living, and with what is alive within the living. He is more Hemingway than Hemingway could be, because he begins with what Hemingway studies as nostalgia, and recovers only by the ascesis of his style. Huck is the image of freedom most central to American literary culture. The image represents loneliness and wildness, as well as freedom, and how could Huck not be lonely, being as he is a kind of originary daemon? A dead mother and a murderous father are less central to Huck than we can imagine. At his center there is a spark of an earlier Orphic existence, and he incarnates ancient truths that he himself cannot know, and that as Americans we relearn from him.

LIONEL TRILLING

Huckleberry Finn

In 1876 Mark Twain published *The Adventures of Tom Sawyer* and in the same year began what he called "another boys' book." He set little store by the new venture and said that he had undertaken it "more to be at work than anything else." His heart was not in it—"I like it only tolerably well as far as I have got," he said, "and may possibly pigeonhole or burn the MS when it is done." He pigeonholed it long before it was done and for as much as four years. In 1880 he took it out and carried it forward a little, only to abandon it again. He had a theory of unconscious composition and believed that a book must write itself; the book which he referred to as "Huck Finn's Autobiography" refused to do the job of its own creation and he would not coerce it.

But then in the summer of 1887 Mark Twain was possessed by a charge of literary energy which, as he wrote to Howells, was more intense than any he had experienced for many years. He worked all day and every day, and periodically he so fatigued himself that he had to recruit his strength by a day or two of smoking and reading in bed. It is impossible not to suppose that this great creative drive was connected with—was perhaps the direct result of—the visit to the Mississippi he had made earlier in the year, the trip which forms the matter of the second part of *Life on the Mississippi*. His boyhood and youth on the river he so profoundly loved had been at once the happiest and

From *The Liberal Imagination*. © 1940 by Lionel Trilling.

most significant part of Mark Twain's life; his return to it in middle age stirred memories which revived and refreshed the idea of *Huckleberry Finn*. Now at last the book was not only ready but eager to write itself. But it was not to receive much conscious help from its author. He was always full of second-rate literary schemes and now, in the early weeks of the summer, with *Huckleberry Finn* waiting to complete itself, he turned his hot energy upon several of these sorry projects, the completion of which gave him as much sense of satisfying productivity as did his eventual absorption in *Huckleberry Finn*.

When at last *Huckleberry Finn* was completed and published and widely loved, Mark Twain became somewhat aware of what he had accomplished with the book that had been begun as journeywork and depreciated, postponed, threatened with destruction. It is his masterpiece, and perhaps he learned to know that. But he could scarcely have estimated it for what it is, one of the world's great books and one of the central documents of American culture.

Wherein does its greatness lie? Primarily in its power of telling the truth. An awareness of this quality as it exists in *Tom Sawyer* once led Mark Twain to say of the earlier work that "it is *not* a boys' book at all. It will be read only by adults. It is written only for adults." But this was only a manner of speaking, Mark Twain's way of asserting, with a discernible touch of irritation, the degree of truth he had achieved. It does not represent his usual view either of boys' books or of boys. No one, as he well knew, sets a higher value on truth than a boy. Truth is the whole of a boy's conscious demand upon the world of adults. He is likely to believe that the adult world is in a conspiracy to lie to him, and it is this belief, by no means unfounded, that arouses Tom and Huck and all boys to their moral sensitivity, their everlasting concern with justice, which they call fairness. At the same time it often makes them skillful and profound liars in their own defense, yet they do not tell the ultimate lie of adults: they do not lie to themselves. That is why Mark Twain felt that it was impossible to carry Tom Sawyer beyond boyhood—in maturity "he would lie just like all the other one-horse men of literature and the reader would conceive a hearty contempt for him."

Certainly one element in the greatness of *Huckleberry Finn*, as also in the lesser greatness of *Tom Sawyer*, is that it succeeds first as a boys' book. One can read it at ten and then annually ever after, and each year find that it is as fresh as the year before, that it has changed only in becoming somewhat larger. To read it young is like planting a tree young—each year adds a new growth ring of meaning, and the book is as little likely as the tree to become dull. So, we may imagine, an Athenian boy grew up together with the *Odyssey*. There are few other books which we can know so young and love so long.

The truth of *Huckleberry Finn* is of a different kind from that of *Tom Sawyer*. It is a more intense truth, fiercer and more complex. *Tom Sawyer* has the truth of honesty—what it says about things and feelings is never false and always both adequate and beautiful. *Huckleberry Finn* has this kind of truth, too, but it has also the truth of moral passion; it deals directly with the virtue and depravity of man's heart.

Perhaps the best clue to the greatness of *Huckleberry Finn* has been given to us by a writer who is as different from Mark Twain as it is possible for one Missourian to be from another. T. S. Eliot's poem, "The Dry Salvages," the third of his *Four Quartets*, begins with a meditation on the Mississippi, which Mr. Eliot knew in his St. Louis boyhood:

I do not know much about gods; but I think that the river
Is a strong brown god ...

And the meditation goes on to speak of the god as

almost forgotten
By the dwellers in cities—ever, however, implacable,
Keeping his seasons and rages, destroyer, reminder of
What men choose to forget. Unhonoured, unpropitiated
By worshippers of the machine, but waiting, watching and
waiting.[1]

Huckleberry Finn is a great book because it is about a god—about, that is, a power which seems to have a mind and will of its own, and which to men of moral imagination appears to embody a great moral idea.

Huck himself is the servant of the river-god, and he comes very close to being aware of the divine nature of the being he serves. The world he inhabits is perfectly equipped to accommodate a deity, for it is full of presences and meanings which it conveys by natural signs and also by preternatural omens and taboos: to look at the moon over the left shoulder, to shake the tablecloth after sundown, to handle a snakeskin, are ways of offending the obscure and prevalent spirits. Huck is at odds, on moral and aesthetic grounds, with the only form of established religion he knows, and his very intense moral life may be said to derive almost wholly from his love of the river. He lives in a perpetual adoration of the Mississippi's power and charm. Huck, of course, always expresses himself better than he can know, but nothing draws upon his gift of speech like his response to his deity. After every sally into the social life or the shore, he returns to the river with relief and thanksgiving; and at each return, regular and explicit as a chorus in a

Greek tragedy, there is a hymn of praise to the god's beauty, mystery, and strength, and to his noble grandeur in contrast with the pettiness of men.

Generally the god is benign, a being of long sunny days and spacious nights. But, like any god, he is also dangerous and deceptive. He generates fogs which bewilder, and contrives echoes and false distances which confuse. His sand bars can ground and his hidden snags can mortally wound a great steamboat. He can cut away the solid earth from under a man's feet and take his house with it. The sense of the danger of the river is what saves the book from any touch of the sentimentality and moral ineptitude of most works which contrast the life of nature with the life of society.

The river itself is only divine; it is not ethical and good. But its nature seems to foster the goodness of those who love it and try to fit themselves to its ways. And we must observe that we cannot make—that Mark Twain does not make—an absolute opposition between the river and human society. To Huck much of the charm of the river life is human: it is the raft and the wigwam and Jim. He has not run away from Miss Watson and the Widow Douglas and his brutal father to a completely individualistic liberty, for in Jim he finds his true father, very much as Stephen Dedalus in James Joyce's *Ulysses* finds his true father in Leopold Bloom.[2] The boy and the Negro slave form a family, a primitive community—and it is a community of saints.

Huck's intense and even complex moral quality may possibly not appear on a first reading, for one may be caught and convinced by his own estimate of himself, by his brags about his lazy hedonism, his avowed preference for being alone, his dislike of civilization. The fact is, of course, that he is involved in civilization up to his ears. His escape from society is but his way of reaching what society ideally dreams of for itself. Responsibility is the very essence of his character, and it is perhaps to the point that the original of Huck, a boyhood companion of Mark Twain's named Tom Blenkenship, did, like Huck, "light out for the Territory," only to become a justice of the peace in Montana, "a good citizen and greatly respected."

Huck does indeed have all the capacities for simple happiness he says he has, but circumstances and his own moral nature make him the least carefree of boys—he is always "in a sweat" over the predicament of someone else. He has a great sense of the sadness of human life, and although he likes to be alone, the words "lonely" and "loneliness" are frequent with him. The note of his special sensibility is struck early in the story: "Well, when Tom and me got to the edge of the hilltop we looked away down into the village and could see three or four lights twinkling where there were sick folks, maybe; and the stars over us was sparkling ever so fine; and down by the village was the river, a whole mile broad, and awful still and grand." The identification of the lights as the lamps of sick-watches defines Huck's character.

His sympathy is quick and immediate. When the circus audience laughs at the supposedly drunken man who tries to ride the horse, Huck is only miserable: "It wasn't funny to me ...; I was all of a tremble to see his danger." When he imprisons the intending murderers on the wrecked steamboat, his first thought is of how to get someone to rescue them, for he considers "how dreadful it was, even for murderers, to be in such a fix. I says to myself, there ain't no telling but I might come to be a murderer myself yet, and then how would I like it." But his sympathy is never sentimental. When at last he knows that the murderers are beyond help, he has no inclination to false pathos. "I felt a little bit heavy-hearted about the gang, but not much, for I reckoned that if they could stand it I could." His will is genuinely good and he has no need to torture himself with guilty second thoughts.

Not the least remarkable thing about Huck's feeling for people is that his tenderness goes along with the assumption that his fellow men are likely to be dangerous and wicked. He travels incognito, never telling the truth about himself and never twice telling the same lie, for he trusts no one and the lie comforts him even when it is not necessary. He instinctively knows that the best way to keep a party of men away from Jim on the raft is to beg them to come aboard to help his family stricken with smallpox. And if he had not already had the knowledge of human weakness and stupidity and cowardice, he would soon have acquired it, for all his encounters forcibly teach it to him—the insensate feud of the Grangerfords and Shepherdsons, the invasion of the raft by the Duke and the King, the murder of Boggs, the lynching party, and the speech of Colonel Sherburn. Yet his profound and bitter knowledge of human depravity never prevents him from being a friend to man.

No personal pride interferes with his well-doing. He knows what status is and on the whole he respects it—he is really a very *respectable* person and inclines to like "quality folks"—but he himself is unaffected by it. He himself has never had status, he has always been the lowest of the low, and the considerable fortune he had acquired in *The Adventures of Tom Sawyer* is never real to him. When the Duke suggests that Huck and Jim render him the personal service that accords with his rank, Huck's only comment is, "Well, that was easy so we done it." He is injured in every possible way by the Duke and the King, used and exploited and manipulated, yet when he hears that they are in danger from a mob, his natural impulse is to warn them. And when he fails of his purpose and the two men are tarred and feathered and ridden on a rail, his only thought is, "Well, it made me sick to see it; and I was sorry for them poor pitiful rascals, it seemed like I couldn't ever feel any hardness against them any more in the world."

And if Huck and Jim on the raft do indeed make a community of saints, it is because they do not have an ounce of pride between them. Yet this is not perfectly true, for the one disagreement they ever have is over a matter of pride. It is on the occasion when Jim and Huck have been separated by the fog. Jim has mourned Huck as dead, and then, exhausted, has fallen asleep. When he awakes and finds that Huck has returned, he is overjoyed; but Huck convinces him that he has only dreamed the incident, that there has been no fog, no separation, no chase, no reunion, and then allows him to make an elaborate "interpretation" of the dream he now believes he has had. Then the joke is sprung, and in the growing light of the dawn Huck points to the debris of leaves on the raft and the broken oar.

> Jim looked at the trash, and then looked at me, and back at the trash again. He had got the dream fixed so strong in his head that he couldn't seem to shake it loose and get the facts back into its place again right away. But when he did get the thing straightened around he looked at me steady without ever smiling, and says:
>
> "What do dey stan' for? I'se gwyne to tell you. When I got all wore out wid work, en wid de callin' for you, en went to sleep, my heart wuz mos' broke bekase you wuz los', en I didn' k'yer no mo' what became er me en de raf'. En when I wake up en fine you back agin, all safe en soun', de tears come, en I could a got down on my knees en kiss yo' foot, I's so thankful. En all you wuz thinkin' 'bout wuz how you could make a fool uv ole Jim wid a lie. Dat truck dah is *trash*; en trash is what people is dat puts dirt or de head er dey fren's en makes 'em ashamed."
>
> Then he got up slow and walked to the wigwam, and went in there without saying anything but that.

The pride of human affection has been touched, one of the few prides that has any true dignity. And at its utterance, Huck's one last dim vestige of pride of status, his sense, of his position as a white man, wholly vanishes: "It was fifteen minutes before I could work myself up to go and humble myself to a nigger; but I done it, and I warn't sorry for it afterwards either."

This incident is the beginning of the moral testing and development which a character so morally sensitive as Huck's must inevitably undergo. And it becomes an heroic character when, on the urging of affection, Huck discards the moral code he has always taken for granted and resolves to help Jim in his escape from slavery. The intensity of his struggle over the act suggests how deeply he is involved in the society which he rejects. The satiric brilliance of the episode lies, of course, in Huck's solving his problem not by doing "right" but by doing "wrong." He has only to consult his conscience, the conscience of a Southern boy in the middle of the last century, to know that he ought to return Jim to slavery. And as soon as he makes the decision according to conscience and decides to inform on Jim, he has all the warmly gratifying emotions of conscious virtue. "Why, it was astonishing, the way I felt as light as a feather right straight off, and my troubles all gone.... I felt good and all washed clean of sin for the first time I had ever felt so in my life, and I knowed I could pray now." And when at last he finds that he cannot endure his decision but must sacrifice the comforts of the pure heart and help Jim in his escape, it is not because he has acquired any new ideas about slavery—he believes that he detests Abolitionists; he himself answers when he is asked if the explosion of a steamboat boiler had hurt anyone, "No'm, killed a nigger," and of course finds nothing wrong in the responsive comment, "Well, it's lucky because sometimes people do get hurt." Ideas and ideals can be of no help to him in his moral crisis. He no more condemns slavery than Tristram and Lancelot condemn marriage; he is as consciously *wicked* as any illicit lover of romance and he consents to be damned for a personal devotion, never questioning the justice of the punishment he has incurred.

Huckleberry Finn was once barred from certain libraries and schools for its alleged subversion of morality. The authorities had in mind the book's endemic lying, the petty thefts, the denigrations of respectability and religion, the bad language, and the bad grammar. We smile at that excessive care, yet in point of fact *Huckleberry Finn* is indeed a subversive book—no one who reads thoughtfully the dialectic of Huck's great moral crisis will ever again be wholly able to accept without some question and some irony the assumptions of the respectable morality by which he lives, nor will ever again be certain that what he considers the clear dictates of moral reason are not merely the engrained customary beliefs of his time and place.

We are not likely to miss in *Huckleberry Finn* the subtle, implicit moral meaning of the great river. But we are likely to understand these moral implications as having to do only with personal and individual conduct. And since the sum of individual pettiness is on the whole pretty constant, we are likely to think of the book as applicable to mankind in general and at all times and in all places, and we praise it by calling it "universal." And so it is; but like many books to which that large adjective applies, it is also local and particular. It has a particular moral reference to the United States in the period after the Civil War. It was then when, in Mr. Eliot's phrase, the river was forgotten, and precisely by the "dwellers in cities," by the "worshippers of the machine."

The Civil War and the development of the railroads ended the great days when the river was the central artery of the nation. No contrast could be more moving than that between the hot, turbulent energy of the river life of the first part of *Life on the Mississippi* and the melancholy reminiscence of the second part. And the war that brought the end of the rich Mississippi days also marked a change in the quality of life in America which, to many men, consisted of a deterioration of American moral values. It is of course a human habit to look back on the past and to find it a better and more innocent time than the present. Yet in this instance there seems to be an objective basis for the judgment. We cannot disregard the testimony of men so diverse as Henry Adams, Walt Whitman, William Dean Howells, and Mark Twain himself, to mention but a few of the many who were in agreement on this point. All spoke of something that had gone out of American life after the war, some simplicity, some innocence, some peace. None of them was under any illusion about the amount of ordinary human wickedness that existed in the old days, and Mark Twain certainly was not. The difference was in the public attitude, in the things that were now accepted and made respectable in the national ideal. It was, they all felt, connected with new emotions about money. As Mark Twain said, where formerly "the people had desired money," now they "fall down and worship it." The new gospel was, "Get money. Get it quickly. Get it in abundance. Get it in prodigious abundance. Get it dishonestly if you can, honestly if you must."[3]

With the end of the Civil War capitalism had established itself. The relaxing influence of the frontier was coming to an end. Americans increasingly became "dwellers in cities" and "worshippers of the machine." Mark Twain himself became a notable part of this new dispensation. No one worshiped the machine more than he did, or thought he did—he ruined himself by his devotion to the Paige typesetting machine, by which he hoped to make a fortune even greater than he had made by his writing, and he sang the praises of the machine age in *A Connecticut Yankee in King Arthur's Court*. He associated intimately with the dominant figures of American business enterprise. Yet at the same time he hated the new way of life and kept bitter memoranda of his scorn, commenting on the low morality or the bad taste of the men who were shaping the ideal and directing the destiny of the nation.

Mark Twain said of *Tom Sawyer* that it "is simply a hymn, put into prose form to give it a worldly air." He might have said the same, and with even more reason, of *Huckleberry Finn*, which is a hymn to an older America forever gone, an America which had its great national faults, which was full of violence and even of cruelty, but which still maintained its sense of reality, for it was not yet enthralled by money, the father of ultimate illusion and lies.

Against the money-god stands the river-god, whose comments are silent—sunlight, space, uncrowded time, stillness, and danger. It was quickly forgotten once its practical usefulness had passed, but, as Mr. Eliot's poem says, "The river is within us...."

In form and style *Huckleberry Finn* is an almost perfect work. Only one mistake has ever been charged against it, that it concludes with Tom Sawyer's elaborate, too elaborate, game of Jim's escape. Certainly this episode is too long—in the original draft it was much longer—and certainly it is a falling off, as almost anything would have to be, from the incidents of the river. Yet it has a certain formal aptness—like, say, that of the Turkish initiation which brings Molière's *Le Bourgeois Gentilhomme* to its close. It is a rather mechanical development of an idea, and yet some device is needed to permit Huck to return to his anonymity, to give up the role of hero, to fall into the background which he prefers, for he is modest in all things and could not well endure the attention and glamour which attend a hero at a book's end. For this purpose nothing could serve better than the mind of Tom Sawyer with its literary furnishings, its conscious romantic desire for experience and the hero's part, and its ingenious schematization of life to achieve that aim.

The form of the book is based on the simplest of all novel-forms, the so-called picaresque novel, or novel of the road, which strings its incidents on the line of the hero's travels. But, as Pascal says, "rivers are roads that move," and the movement of the road in its own mysterious life transmutes the primitive simplicity of the form: the road itself is the greatest character in this novel of the road, and the hero's departures from the river and his returns to it compose a subtle and significant pattern. The linear simplicity of the picaresque novel is further modified by the story's having a clear dramatic organization: it has a beginning, a middle, and an end, and a mounting suspense of interest.

As for the style of the book, it is not less than definitive in American literature. The prose of *Huckleberry Finn* established for written prose the virtues of American colloquial speech. This has nothing to do with pronunciation or grammar. It has something to do with ease and freedom in the use of language. Most of all it has to do with the structure of the sentence, which is simple, direct, and fluent, maintaining the rhythm of the word-groups of speech and the intonations of the speaking voice.

In the matter of language, American literature had a special problem. The young nation was inclined to think that the mark of the truly literary product was a grandiosity and elegance not to be found in the common speech. It therefore encouraged a greater breach between its vernacular and its literary language than, say, English literature of the same period ever allowed. This accounts for the hollow ring one now and then hears even in the work of our best writers in the first half of the last century. English writers of equal stature would never have made the lapses into rhetorical excess that are common in Cooper and Poe and that are to be found even in Melville and Hawthorne.

Yet at the same time that the language of ambitious literature was high and thus always in danger of falseness, the American reader was keenly interested in the actualities of daily speech. No literature, indeed, was ever so taken up with matters of speech as ours was. "Dialect," which attracted even our serious writers, was the accepted common ground of our popular humorous writing. Nothing in social life seemed so remarkable as the different forms which speech could take—the brogue of the immigrant Irish or the mispronunciation of the German, the "affectation" of the English, the reputed precision of the Bostonian, the legendary twang of the Yankee farmer, and the drawl of the Pike County man. Mark Twain, of course, was in the tradition of humor that exploited this interest, and no one could play with it nearly so well. Although today the carefully spelled-out dialects of nineteenth-century American humor are likely to seem dull enough, the subtle variations of speech in *Huckleberry Finn*, of which Mark Twain was justly proud, are still part of the liveliness and flavor of the book.

Out of his knowledge of the actual speech of America Mark Twain forged a classic prose. The adjective may seem a strange one, yet it is apt. Forget the misspellings and the faults of grammar, and the prose will be seen to move with the greatest simplicity, directness, lucidity, and grace. These qualities are by no means accidental. Mark Twain, who read widely, was passionately interested in the problems of style; the mark of the strictest literary sensibility is everywhere to be found in the prose of *Huckleberry Finn*.

It is this prose that Ernest Hemingway had chiefly in mind when he said that "all modern American literature comes from one book by Mark Twain called *Huckleberry Finn*." Hemingway's own prose stems from it directly and consciously; so does the prose of the two modern writers who most influenced Hemingway's early style, Gertrude Stein and Sherwood Anderson (although neither of them could maintain the robust purity of their model); so, too, does the best of William Faulkner's prose, which, like Mark Twain's own, reinforces the colloquial tradition with the literary tradition. Indeed, it may be said that almost every contemporary American writer who deals conscientiously with the problems and possibility of prose must feel, directly or indirectly, the influence of Mark Twain. He is the master of the style that escapes the fixity of the printed page, that sounds in our ears with the immediacy of the heard voice, the very voice of unpretentious truth.

NOTES

1. Copyright 1943 by T. S. Eliot, reprinted by permission of Harcourt, Brace and Company.

2. In Joyce's *Finnegan's Wake* both Mark Twain and Huckleberry Finn appear frequently. The theme of rivers is, of course, dominant in the book; and Huck's name suits Joyce's purpose, for Finn is one of the many names of his hero. Mark Twain's love of and gift for the spoken language make another reason for Joyce's interest in him.

3. *Mark Twain in Eruption*, edited by Bernard De Voto, p. 77.

T.S. ELIOT

An Introduction to Huckleberry Finn

*T*he *Adventures of Huckleberry Finn* is the only one of Mark Twain's various books which can be called a masterpiece. I do not suggest that it is his only book of permanent interest; but it is the only one in which his genius is completely realized, and the only one which creates its own category. There are pages in *Tom Sawyer* and in *Life on the Mississippi* which are, within their limits, as good as anything with which one can compare them in *Huckleberry Finn*; and in other books there are drolleries just as good of their kind. But when we find one book by a prolific author which is very much superior to all the rest, we look for the peculiar accident or concourse of accidents which made that book possible. In the writing of *Huckleberry Finn* Mark Twain had two elements which, when treated with his sensibility and his experience, formed a great book: these two are the Boy and the River.

Huckleberry Finn is, no doubt, a book which boys enjoy. I cannot speak from memory: I suspect that a fear on the part of my parents lest I should acquire a premature taste for tobacco, and perhaps other habits of the hero of the story, kept the book out of my way. But *Huckleberry Finn* does not fall into the category of juvenile fiction. The opinion of my parents that it was a book unsuitable for boys left me, for most of my life, under the impression that it was a book suitable only for boys. Therefore it was only a few years ago that I read for the first time, and in that order, *Tom Sawyer* and *Huckleberry Finn*.

From *The Adventures of Huckleberry Finn*, by Samuel L. Clemens. Published in 1950 by The Cresset Press.

Tom Sawyer did not prepare me for what I was to find its sequel to be. *Tom Sawyer* seems to me to be a boys' book, and a very good one. The River and *the* Boy make their appearance in it; the narrative is good; and there is also a very good picture of society in a small mid-Western river town (for St. Petersburg is more Western than Southern) a hundred years ago. But the point of view of the narrator is that of an adult observing a boy. And Tom is the ordinary boy, though of quicker wits, and livelier imagination, than most. Tom is, I suppose, very much the boy that Mark Twain had been: he is remembered and described as he seemed to his elders, rather than created. Huck Finn, on the other hand, is the boy that Mark Twain still was, at the time of writing his adventures. We look at Tom as the smiling adult does: Huck we do not look at—we see the world through his eyes. The two boys are not merely different types; they were brought into existence by different processes. Hence in the second book their roles are altered. In the first book Huck is merely the humble friend—almost a variant of the traditional valet of comedy; and we see him as he is seen by the conventional respectable society to which Tom belongs, and of which, we feel sure, Tom will one day become an eminently respectable and conventional member. In the second book their nominal relationship remains the same; but here it is Tom who has the secondary role. The author was probably not conscious of this when he wrote the first two chapters: *Huckleberry Finn* is not the kind of story in which the author knows, from the beginning, what is going to happen. Tom then disappears from our view; and when he returns, he has only two functions. The first is to provide a foil for Huck. Huck's persisting admiration for Tom only exhibits more clearly to our eyes the unique qualities of the former and the commonplaceness of the latter. Tom has the imagination of a lively boy who has read a good deal of romantic fiction: he might, of course, become a writer—he might become Mark Twain. Or rather, he might become the more commonplace aspect of Mark Twain. Huck has not imagination, in the sense in which Tom has it: he has, instead, vision. He sees the real world; and he does not judge it he allows it to judge itself.

Tom Sawyer is an orphan. But he has his aunt; he has, as we learn later, other relatives; and he has the environment into which he fits. He is wholly a social being. When there is a secret band to be formed, it is Tom who organizes it and prescribes the rules. Huck Finn is alone: there is no more solitary character in fiction. The fact that he has a father only emphasizes his loneliness; and he views his father with a terrifying detachment. So we come to see Huck himself in the end as one of the permanent symbolic figures of fiction; not unworthy to take a place with Ulysses, Faust, Don Quixote, Don Juan, Hamlet and other great discoveries that man has made about himself.

It would seem that Mark Twain was a man who—perhaps like most of us—never became in all respects mature. We might even say that the adult side of him was boyish, and that only the boy in him, that was Huck Finn, was adult. As Tom Sawyer grown up, he wanted success and applause (Tom himself always needs an audience). He wanted prosperity, a happy domestic life of a conventional kind, universal approval, and fame. All of these things he obtained. As Huck Finn he was indifferent to all these things; and being composite of the two, Mark Twain both strove for them, and resented their violation of his integrity. Hence he became the humorist and even clown: with his gifts, a certain way to success, for everyone could enjoy his writings without the slightest feeling of discomfort, self-consciousness or self-criticism. And hence, on the other hand, his pessimism and misanthropy. To be a misanthrope is to be in some way divided; or it is a sign of an uneasy conscience. The pessimism which Mark Twain discharged into *The Man That Corrupted Hadleyburg* and *What is Man?* springs less from observation of society, than from his hatred of himself for allowing society to tempt and corrupt him and give him what he wanted. There is no wisdom in it. But all this personal problem has been diligently examined by Mr. Van Wyck Brooks; and it is not Mark Twain, but *Huckleberry Finn*, that is the subject of thus introduction.

You cannot say that Huck himself is either a humorist or a misanthrope. He is the impassive observer: he does not interfere, and, as I have said, he does not judge. Many of the episodes that occur on the voyage down the river, after he is joined by the Duke and the King (whose fancies about themselves are akin to the kind of fancy that Tom Sawyer enjoys) are in themselves farcical; and if it were not for the presence of Huck as the reporter of them, they would be no more than farce. But, seen through the eyes of Huck, there is a deep human pathos in these scoundrels. On the other hand, the story of the feud between the Grangerfords and the Shepherdsons is a masterpiece in itself: yet Mark Twain could not have written it so, with that economy and restraint, with just the right details and no more, and leaving to the reader to make his own moral reflections, unless he had been writing in the person of Huck. And the *style* of the book, which is the style of Huck, is what makes it a far more convincing indictment of slavery than the sensationalist propaganda of *Uncle Tom's Cabin*. Huck is passive and impassive, apparently always the victim of events; and yet, in his acceptance of his world and of what it does to hum and others, he is more powerful than his world, because he is more *aware* than any other person in it.

Repeated readings of the book only confirm and deepen one's admiration of the consistency and perfect adaptation of the writing. This is a style which at the period, whether in America or in England, was an innovation, a new discovery in the English language. Other authors had achieved natural speech in relation to particular characters—Scott with characters talking Lowland Scots, Dickens with cockneys: but no one else had kept it up through the whole of a book. Thackeray's Yellowplush, impressive as he is, is an obvious artifice in comparison. In *Huckleberry Finn* there is no exaggeration of grammar or spelling or speech, there is no sentence or phrase to destroy the illusion that these are Huck's own words. It is not only in the way in which he tells his story, but in the details he remembers, that Huck is true to himself. There is, for instance, the description of the Grangerford interior as Huck sees it on his arrival; there is the list of the objects which Huck and Jim salvaged from the derelict house:

> We got an old tin lantern, and a butcher-knife without any handle, and a bran-new Barlow knife worth two bits in any store, and a lot of tallow candles, and a tin candlestick, and a gourd, and a tin cup, and a ratty old bedquilt off the bed, and a reticule with needles and pins and beeswax and buttons and thread and all such truck in it, and a hatchet and some nails, and a fish-line as thick as my little finger, with some monstrous hooks on it, and a roll of buckskin, and a leather dog-collar, and a horseshoe, and some vials of medicine that didn't have no label on them; and just as we was leaving I found a tolerable good curry-comb, and Jim he found a ratty old fiddle-bow, and a wooden leg. The straps was broke off of it, but barring that, it was a good enough leg, though it was too long for me and not long enough for Jim, and we couldn't find the other one, though we hunted all round.
>
> And so, take it all round, we made a good haul.

This is the sort of list that a boy reader should pore over with delight; but the paragraph performs other functions of which the boy reader would be unaware. It provides the right counterpoise to the horror of the wrecked house and the corpse; it has a grim precision which tells the reader all he needs to know about the way of life of the human derelicts who had used the house; and (especially the wooden leg, and the fruitless search for its mate) reminds us at the right moment of the kinship of mind and the sympathy between the boy outcast from society and the negro fugitive from the injustice of society.

Huck in fact would be incomplete without Jim, who is almost as notable a creation as Huck himself. Huck is the passive observer of men and events, Jim the submissive sufferer from them; and they are equal in dignity. There is no passage in which their relationship is brought out more clearly than the conclusion of the chapter in which, after the two have become separated in the fog, Huck in the canoe and Jim on the raft, Huck, in his impulse of boyish mischief, persuades Jim for a time that the latter had dreamt the whole episode.

> '... my heart wuz mos' broke bekase you wuz los', en I didn' k'yer no mo' what become er me en de raf'. En when I wake up en fine you back agin', all safe en soun', de tears come en I could a got down on my knees en kiss' yo' foot, I's so thankful. En all you wuz thinkin' 'bout wuz how you could make a fool uv ole Jim wid a lie. Dat truck dah is *trash*; en trash is what people is dat puts dirt on de head er dey fren's en makes 'em ashamed.' ...
>
> It was fifteen minutes before I could work myself up to go and humble myself to a nigger—but I done it, and I warn't ever sorry for it afterwards, neither.

This passage has been quoted before; and if I quote it again, it is because I wish to elicit from it one meaning that is, I think, usually overlooked. What is obvious in it is the pathos and dignity of Jim, and this is moving enough; but what I find still more disturbing, and still more unusual in literature, is the pathos and dignity of the boy, when reminded so humbly and humiliatingly, that his position in the world is not that of other boys, entitled from time to time to a practical joke; but that he must bear, and bear alone, the responsibility of a man.

It is Huck who gives the book style. The River gives the book its form. But for the River, the book might be only a sequence of adventures with a happy ending. A river, a very big and powerful river, is the only natural force that can wholly determine the course of human peregrination. At sea, the wanderer may sail or be carried by winds and currents in one direction or another; a change of wind or tide may determine fortune. In the prairie, the direction of movement is more or less at the choice of the caravan; among mountains there will often be an alternative, a guess at the most likely pass. But the river with its strong, swift current is the dictator to the raft or to the steamboat. It is a treacherous and capricious dictator. At one season, it may move sluggishly in a channel so narrow that, encountering it for the first time at that point, one can hardly believe that it has travelled already for hundreds of miles, and has yet many hundreds of miles to go; at another season, it may obliterate the low Illinois shore to a horizon of water, while in its bed it runs with a speed such that no man or beast can survive in it. At such times, it carries down human bodies, cattle and houses. At least twice, at St. Louis, the western and the eastern shores have been separated by the fall of bridges, until the designer of the great Eads Bridge devised a structure which could resist the floods. In my own childhood, it was not unusual for the spring freshet to interrupt railway travel; and then the traveller to the East had to take steamboat from the levee up to Alton, at a higher level on the Illinois shore, before he could begin his rail journey. The river is never wholly chartable; it changes its pace, it shifts its channel, unaccountably; it may suddenly efface a sandbar, and throw up another bar where before was navigable water.

It is the River that controls the voyage of Huck and Jim; that will not let them land at Cairo, where Jim could have reached freedom; it is the River that separates them and deposits Huck for a time in the Grangerford household; the River that reunites them, and then compels upon them the unwelcome company of the King and the Duke. Recurrently we are reminded of its presence and its power.

> When I woke up, I didn't know where I was for a minute. I set up and looked around, a little scared. Then I remembered. The river looked miles and miles across. The moon was so bright I could a counted the drift-logs that went a-slipping along, black and still, hundreds of yards out from shore. Everything was dead quiet, and it looked late, and *smelt* late. You know what I mean— I don't know the words to put it in.

> It was kind of solemn, drifting down the big still river, laying on our backs looking up at the stars, and we didn't ever feel like talking loud, and it warn't often that we laughed, only a little kind of a low chuckle. We had mighty good weather as a general thing, and nothing ever happened to us at all, that night, nor the next, nor the next.
>
> Every night we passed towns, some of them away up on black hillsides, nothing but just a shiny bed of lights, not a house could you see. The fifth night we passed St. Louis, and it was like the whole world lit up. In St. Petersburg they used to say there was twenty or thirty thousand people in St. Louis, but I never believed it till I see that wonderful spread of lights at two o'clock that still night. There warn't a sound there; everybody was asleep.

We come to understand the River by seeing it through the eyes of the Boy; but the Boy is also the spirit of the River. *Huckleberry Finn*, like other great works of imagination, can give to every reader whatever he is capable of taking from it. On the most superficial level of observation, Huck is convincing as a boy. On the same level, the picture of social life on the shores of the Mississippi a hundred years ago is, I feel sure, accurate. On any level,

Mark Twain makes you see the River, as it is and was and always will be, more clearly than the author of any other description of a river known to me. But you do not merely see the River, you do not merely become acquainted with it through the senses: you experience the River. Mark Twain, in his later years of success and fame, referred to his early life as a steamboat pilot as the happiest he had known. With all allowance for the illusions of age, we can agree that those years were the years in which he was most fully alive. Certainly, but for his having practised that calling, earned his living by that profession, he would never have gained the understanding which his genius for expression communicates in this book. In the pilot's daily struggle with the River, in the satisfaction of activity, in the constant attention to the River's unpredictable vagaries, his consciousness was fully occupied, and he absorbed knowledge of which, as an artist, he later made use. There are, perhaps, only two ways in which a writer can acquire the understanding of environment which he can later turn to account: by having spent his childhood in that environment—that is, living in it at a period of life in which one experiences much more than one is aware of; and by having had to struggle for a livelihood in that environment—a livelihood bearing no direct relation to any intention of writing about it, of *using* it as literary material. Most of Joseph Conrad's understanding came to him in the latter way. Mark Twain knew the Mississippi in both ways: he had spent his childhood on its banks, and he had earned his living matching his wits against its currents. Thus the River makes the book a great book. As with Conrad, we are continually reminded of the power and terror of Nature, and the isolation and feebleness of Man. Conrad remains always the European observer of the tropics, the white man's eye contemplating the Congo and its black gods. But Mark Twain is a native, and the River God is his God. It is as a native that he accepts the River God, and it is the subjection of Man that gives to Man his dignity. For without some kind of God, Man is not even very interesting.

Readers sometimes deplore the fact that the story descends to the level of *Tom Sawyer* from the moment that Tom himself reappears. Such readers protest that the escapades invented by Tom, in the attempted "rescue" of Jim, are only a tedious development of themes with which we were already too familiar—even while admitting that the escapades themselves are very amusing, and some of the incidental observations memorable.[1] But it is right that the mood of the end of the book should bring us back to that of the beginning. Or, if this was not the right ending for the book, what ending would have been right?

In *Huckleberry Finn* Mark Twain wrote a much greater book than he could have known he was writing. Perhaps all great works of art mean much more than the author could have been aware of meaning: certainly,

Huckleberry Finn is the one book of Mark Twain's which, as a whole, has this unconsciousness. So what seems to be the rightness, of reverting at the end of the book to the mood of *Tom Sawyer*, was perhaps unconscious art. For Huckleberry Finn, neither a tragic nor a happy ending would be suitable. No worldly success or social satisfaction, no domestic consummation would be worthy of him; a tragic end also would reduce him to the level of those whom we pity. Huck Finn must come from nowhere and be bound for nowhere. His is not the independence of the typical or symbolic American Pioneer, but the independence of the vagabond. His existence questions the values of America as much as the values of Europe; he is as much an affront to the "pioneer spirit" as he is to "business enterprise"; he is in a state of nature as detached as the state of the saint. In a busy world, he represents the loafer; in an acquisitive and competitive world, he insists on living from hand to mouth. He could not be exhibited in any amorous encounters or engagements, in any of the juvenile affections which are appropriate to Tom Sawyer. He belongs neither to the Sunday School nor to the Reformatory. He has no beginning and no end. Hence, he can only disappear; and his disappearance can only be accomplished by bringing forward another performer to obscure the disappearance in a cloud of whimsicalities.

Like Huckleberry Finn, the River itself has no beginning or end. In its beginning, it is not yet the River; in its end, it is no longer the River. What we call its headwaters is only a selection from among the innumerable sources which flow together to compose it. At what point in its course does the Mississippi become what the Mississippi *means*? It is both one and many; it is the Mississippi of this book only after its union with the Big Muddy—the Missouri; it derives some of its character from the Ohio, the Tennessee and other confluents. And at the end it merely disappears among its deltas: it is no longer there, but it is still where it was, hundreds of miles to the North. The River cannot tolerate any design, to a story which is its story, that might interfere with its dominance. Things must merely happen, here and there, to the people who live along its shores or who commit themselves to its current. And it is as impossible for Huck as for the River to have a beginning or end— a *career*. So the book has the right, the only possible concluding sentence. I do not think that any book ever written ends more certainly with the right words:

> But I reckon I got to light out for the Territory ahead of the rest, because Aunt Sally she's going to adopt me and civilize me, and I can't stand it. I been there before.

NOTE

1. e.g. "Jim don't know anybody in China."

LESLIE A. FIEDLER

Huckleberry Finn:
Faust in the Eden of Childhood

III

*H*uckleberry Finn is, then, essentially a book about a marginal American type, who only wants to stay alive; but who does not find this very easy to do, being assailed on the one side by forces of violence, which begrudge him the little he asks, and on the other, by forces of benevolence, which insist that he ask for more. Against the modesty and singleness of his purpose, everything else is measured and weighed: religion, the social order, other men. Huck exists on a sub-moral level; for he cannot afford, in his minimal economy, the luxury of living by the moral codes of the Widow Douglases of his small-town world. Such codes assume a standard of security, if not actual prosperity, to which he does not even aspire: "She told me what she meant—I must help other people, and do everything I could for other people and look out for them all the time, and never think about myself…. I went out in the woods and turned it over in my mind a long time, but I couldn't see no advantage in it—except for the other people; so that at last I reckoned I wouldn't worry about it any more, but just let it go." Huck has not yet fallen, manages to live still without that "moral sense," which his last avatar, the young devil in *The Mysterious Stranger*, describes as the blight of mankind.

Yet Huck is not, of course, a devil or even a savage, only a semi-barbarian; and having grown up on the edge of civilization, he has always

---

From *Love and Death in the American Novel.* © 1960 by Criterion Books, Inc.

known, even before his brief indoctrination by Miss Watson, the ethical precepts of her world. No more free-thinker than savage, he not only knows, but, in an abstract way, believes in these codes, by which he could not survive for an instant in the lawless sub-society which he inhabits. There is, therefore, a constant disjunction in his mind (very like irony—and exploited by Twain for irony's sake) between what he considers he *ought* to do, and what he is aware that he *must* do; and it is this disjunction which underlies the moral crisis of the book. Huck begins with such minor crimes as lying and cussing, smoking and petty theft; and, indeed, the first is so habitual a reflex that he scarcely knows what to do at a point where apparently only telling the truth can help him.

> I reckon a body that ups and tells the truth when he is in a tight place is taking considerable many resks, though I ain't had no experience, and can't say for certain ... and yet here's a case where I'm blest if it don't look like the truth is better and actuly safer than a lie.... I never seen nothing like it.

These lines are spoken by Huck in the Wilks episode, when Twain's own reality-principle is being sold out to sentimentality; but they reflect still the basic set which distinguishes the juvenile pariah from the Good Bad Boy.

There is occasionally a certain bravado about Huck in his relationship to the world of morality, which he can neither abide nor disavow. When, for instance, Miss Watson (to whom "scrunching up" or yawning during lessons is a sin punishable in hell) tells Huck about the "bad place," he says he wishes he were there; and is considerably cheered to learn that Tom is likely to end up there, too. A moment later, however, he is in a state of depression and terror, imagining that he hears the voice of a ghost that "can't rest easy in its grave," seeing evil omens everywhere and performing his own rites of exorcism. "I got up and turned around in my tracks three times and crossed my heart every time." One must assume that he is beset by similar feelings of guilt and despair after his later nonchalant declaration: "Well, then, says I, what's the use you learning to do right when it's troublesome to do right and ain't no trouble to do wrong, and the wages is just the same? ... So I reckoned I wouldn't bother no more about it, but after this always do whichever comes handiest at the time."

Huck had just made the first decisive move toward stealing Jim out of slavery, and feels that he has graduated at last from petty crimes to major ones. It never enters his head for a moment that protecting Jim against recapture is anything but *wrong*; for he has no abolitionist ideas and questions the justice of slavery no more than did Aristotle. He considers, however, that as an outcast he has little to lose; and is only overcome with horror when the Good Bad Boy Tom seems about to become his accomplice. His whole world of values is momentarily threatened, and only re-establishes itself when he learns that Jim has been all along free and Tom has known it: "... I couldn't ever understand before ... how he could help a body set a nigger free with his bringing up." Huck believes in the equality of the races as little as he does in abolition; and when, after his long association with Jim, he is asked by Aunt Sally whether anyone was hurt in a steamboat accident, he answers blandly, "No'm, killed a nigger." There is no intended irony either in Huck's comment about Tom or in his response to Aunt Sally; Twain may *use* them ironically, but this must not mislead us. If Huck lies, runs, and hides for Jim's sake, even as he has lied, run, and hid for his own, this is not because he thinks he is acting in behalf of some higher moral code, but because he has extended his area of self-interest to a family of two. He loves Jim quite literally as himself, and is willing to go to hell for him, even as he was willing to go there for the sake of "scrunching" a little or cussing or smoking.

There is no irony, either, in the self-reproach, the acceptance of his own damnation which Huck finally speaks; whatever games Twain may be playing with his declaration, Huck quite simply believes it:

> ... something inside of me kept saying, There was the Sunday-school, you could 'a' gone to it; and if you'd 'a' done it they'd 'a' learnt you there that people that acts as I'd been acting about that nigger goes to the everlasting fire.
>
> It made me shiver. And I about made up my mind to pray, and see if I couldn't try to quit being the kind of boy I was and be better ... but deep down in me I knowed it was a lie, and He knowed it. You can't pray a lie—I found that out.

His attempted prayer a failure, Huck tries to write a letter to Miss Watson, telling her where Jim is, and thus putting things right with his conscience; but though doing it makes him feel "washed clean of sin for the first time," his love for Jim returns. He remembers not some abolitionist slogan or moral tag about the equal rights of all mankind, only how Jim "would always call me honey, and pet me, and do everything he could think of for me ..." and he decides not to send the letter.

> ... I studied a minute, sort of holding my breath, and then says to myself: "All right, then I'll *go* to Hell"—and tore it up.
>
> It was awful thoughts and awful words, but they was said. And I let them stay said; and never thought no more about reforming.

I shoved the whole thing out of my head, and said I would take
up wickedness again, which was in my line, being brung up to it,
and the other warn't.

At this point, the Faustian theme is improbably reborn in the midst of
comedy and nostalgia. Lionel Trilling compares Huck at the moment of his
decision to a courtly lover submitting to eternal torment for the sake of his
beloved; but he seems more Faust than Lancelot: one with Ahab and Pierre
and Hester and Ethan Brand. To be sure, Twain is toying with the theme,
evading final responsibility; for he knows that the most genteel post-Civil-
War reader, secure in a world without slavery, will see Huck, not as a Satanic
and hybristic rebel, setting the promptings of his own ignorant heart over the
law of the land and the teaching of his church—but as a moral hero! Yet in
Huck, for an instant at least, the marginal loafer, the uncommitted idler is
revealed as the American Faust; the dark side turned up of what *Huckleberry
Finn*'s first reviewer called "the ruffianism that is one result of the
independence of Americans." Yet the revelation is made in so witty and
charming and ambiguous a way, that the same reviewer has described Huck's
terrible decision as "most instructive and amusing."

Twain has a further duplicitous device, which is quite simply to make
his shiftless Faustian drifter a boy, a child with, he keeps assuring us, a truly
virtuous heart. Not only does Twain shrug off the issues, social and moral,
involved in a life based on lying and stealing with the implicit comment that
"Boy will be boys!"; but he further confounds confusion by identifying his
juvenile pariah with the sentimental stereotypes of the child as Noble Savage
and the child as victim of society. Huck is, whatever his other faults, the most
nonviolent of American fictional children, more like Oliver Twist than Tom
Sawyer, who is his companion. Unlike Tom, he never fights with his fists; and
though he takes up a rifle once against his delirious father, who has
threatened him with a knife, he does not fire it. He never quite shoots even
in self-defense; and during the Grangerford feud, for instance, finds a perch
in a tree and merely watches, trembling, the foolish bravery of others. He
runs, hides, equivocates, dodges, and, when he can do nothing else, suffers.
Though admiring critics speak of him sometimes as "manly" or
"courageous," he is actually timid almost to the point of burlesque—the anti-
type of the foolhardy Tom. To be sure, aboard the *Walter Scott*, he whips up
courage enough to eavesdrop on the quarreling crooks by reminding himself
of what Tom Sawyer would have done ("and I says to myself, Tom Sawyer
wouldn't back out now, and I won't either"); but more customarily, discretion
is the whole of his valor. He is quite frank about his fears, telling us over and

over: "I warn't feeling very brash, there warn't much sand in my craw"; "I was too scared"; "Well, I catched my breath and most fainted"; "It made me so sick I most fell out of the tree." And when the lynch mob, after which he has tagged along, breaks and runs before the defiance of Colonel Sherburn, Huck observes in self-mockery, "I could 'a' stayed if I wanted to, but I didn't want to."

He has, indeed, the right to be afraid, for he has no effective protectors. A "motherless boy," his father is his worst enemy; and he is, by the time he enters the scene, incapable of paying the price of membership in a respectable household, immune to "civilization." Moreover, his civilizers prove strangely unable to defend him; for when his own origins rise against him (he is, after all, the child of ignorance and drunkenness and violence), the polite community, disabled by sentimentality and a commitment to legal process, stands helplessly by. Not only do the half-world, which bred him, and the genteel community, which tried to adopt him, betray him; but Nature herself, to which he flees as a final refuge, proves a treacherous parent, offering, along with moments of joy and calm, times of terror in storm and fog. No wonder Huck is a strangely melancholy child—not only possessed by a sense of alienation ("lonesome" is almost his favorite adjective), but obsessed by, more than half in love with death.

From the first, the reader is made aware of Huck's dark preoccupations: "I felt so lonesome I most wished I was dead.... I heard an owl ... who-whooing about somebody that was dead, and a whippoorwill and a dog crying about somebody who was going to die." And, indeed, he plays dead in order to survive, rigs a scene of murder to persuade his Pap (who has taken him for the angel of death!) and the world that he is beyond their reach: "They won't ever hunt the river for anything but my dead carcass. They'll soon get tired of that, and won't bother no more about me." Afterwards, he seems a ghost to everyone who knew him; and even at the moment just before what he calls his rebirth ("it was like being born again") at the Phelps farm, his original melancholia returns:

> there was them kind of faint dronings of bugs and flies in the air
> that makes it seem so lonesome and like everybody's dead and
> gone ... it makes a body wish *he* was dead, too, and done with it
> all.... When I got a little ways I heard the dim hum of a spinning-
> wheel wailing along up and sinking along down again; and then I
> knowed for certain I wished I was dead—for that is the
> lonesomest sound in the whole world.

"Lonesome" and "dead": the two words are inextricably linked; and they rise in Huck's mind at the moment just before he leaves and just as he is about to re-enter the matriarchal world—which is all the civilization he knows.

"Hannibal" is Mark Twain's name for the world of belongingness and security, of school and home and church, presided over by the mothers. There are men on the upper levels of this respectable world (Judge Thatcher, for instance, self-important and pompous), but they are not, in *Huckleberry Finn*, presented as its rulers or its conscience. Tom, of course, has no father at all, is responsible only to Aunt Polly; while Huck is found at the book's start in the all-female household of the Widow Douglas and the old maid, Miss Watson. "I never seen anybody but lied one time or another," Huck remarks at the outset, "without it was Aunt Polly, or the widow, or maybe Mary." These are the super-ego figures of the book, these husbandless mothers or fatherless daughters who cannot lie, only love. But the kindly widow is given a dour double in Miss Watson, as if to reveal the threat always lurking beneath matriarchal tenderness: the rigid piety, the petty discipline, the belief in soap—the love of money! Miss Watson, we remember, tempted by a slave-trader's generous offer, plans to sell her nigger, Jim, down the river and away from his family! The world of mothers, after all, believes not only in Providence and cleanliness and affection, but in slavery, too. Yet it is the best of all conceivable worlds to Mark Twain.

Into it all girls are inducted, apparently, simply by being born; for there are, in Mark Twain's Hannibal, no bad girls only good ones, marriage with whom means an initiation into piety and conformity, the end of freedom. But as long as childhood lasts, Twain's boys are granted a special immunity from the codes of the mothers. Those mothers do not, of course, openly announce this privilege, only secretly hope that, against their avowed wishes, their sons will rebel, be properly "misch*ee*vous." The boy who conforms too soon, the Good Good Boy represented by Sid Sawyer, is despised a little by the mothers themselves, who prefer the Good Bad Boy, Tom—and long to convert into his image the juvenile pariah with the heart of gold, Huck Finn. There are no Bad Bad Boys in Twain's legendary town, no vicious delinquents beyond all hope of reform; such a thing is as impossible as a vicious woman! Even outside of his fiction, in personal reminiscence, Twain could not bring himself to grant that Huck's sisters had been prostitutes.

Evil he can imagine only in terms of a fully adult male, a Bad Father— like Injun Joe in *Tom Sawyer* or Pap in *Huckleberry Finn*:

> His hair was long and tangled and greasy, and hung down, and
> you could see his eyes shining through like he was behind vines....
> There warn't no color in his face, where his face showed; it was
> white; not like another man's white, but a white to make a body

sick, a white to make a body's flesh crawl—a tree-toad white, a
fish-belly white.

But sharing the same sub-world which Pap inhabits, the world of those who
will not accept or are not permitted to assume social responsibility, is Nigger
Jim, whose good blackness is ironically contrasted with Pap's evil whiteness.
Once Jim has run away, he no longer really belongs to Hannibal at all, but to
the river: symbol of flight and the moral indifference of Nature. It is to the
river that Pap comes at the moment of his sordid death; on the river that the
crooks trapped aboard the *Walter Scott* die, too; the river that the Duke and
Dauphin seek in their eternal flight from the vengeance of the towns. And
beyond the river is Indian territory, the ultimate reach of alienation and anti-
civilization.

   This is the moral geography of the world in which Huck stands poised
just before the moment of adolescence, and his choices are limited by the
narrow possibilities of that world. Either he can accommodate like Tom or
Sid, become the mothers' boy, after all; or he can turn back into his father's
sub-world, the tanyard, the hogs-head, the wharves—accept a perpetual
outsidedness. He cannot, of course, stay where he is in the no-man's-land of
boyhood, where the two adult worlds meet, because the simple passage of
time will drive him out. For all his illusion of choice, he is not really free, but
imprisoned in his "independence"; for he is incapable of remaining inside the
respectable community. There is, on the one hand, too much of his father in
him; and he is actually happy when Pap carries him off: "It was pretty good
times up in the woods there, take it all around." On the other hand, there is
too much Miss Watson in all mothers: "a poor chap would stand
considerable show with the widow's Providence, but if Miss Watson's got
him there warn't no help for him any more."

   Huck's problem is, therefore, not to find his fate but to accept it; and
Huckleberry Finn is the history of his vain attempts to escape that fate. He
believes at first that he is running not from himself but from his father and
Miss Watson, from both limits of the only society he knows. But he does not
know to what he is escaping, except into nothing: a mere anti-society, in
which he is a cipher, a ghost without a real name. "All I wanted was to go
somewheres," he tells Miss Watson, "all I wanted was a change, I warn't
particular." Huck is heading for no utopia, since he has heard of none; and
so he ends up making flight itself his goal. He flees from the impermanence
of boyhood to that of continual change; and, of course, it is a vain evasion
except as it leads him to understand that *no* society can fulfill his destiny.

   It is to the river that he turns, since the river is the only avenue of
escape he knows; but the river betrays him, even as it betrays Jim in his

complementary search for freedom. Bearing Huck toward the South, the river carries him from a matriarchal world to a patriarchal one, from one which believes in Providence to one which believes in honor ("Colonel Grangerford was a gentleman, you see. He was a gentleman all over ..."); but for Huck, honor is a concept as unviable as good works or prayer. The chivalric world of the Grangerfords offers to take him in, to make him a little gentleman just as the Widow had wanted to make him a small Christian. There is even a patriarchal version of Tom Sawyer, young Buck, to be his companion and link to that world; but the end of chivalry is violence, for which Huck has even less taste than he has for telling the truth. And he stands at last, after the feud with the Shepherdsons has erupted into furious and wholesale slaughter, looking down at the dead bodies of two boys, who, unlike him, had been brought up to fight rather than run. "I covered up their faces, and got away as quick as I could. I cried a little when I was covering up Buck's face."

In the end, Huck has got out of the whole experience only a vague sense of guilt (he did carry the message which touched off the final combat), and another nightmare to add to his already full store. "I wished I hadn't ever come ashore that night to see such things, I ain't ever going to get shut of them—lots of times I dream about them." The episode of Colonel Sherburn does little to change his picture of life in the South, only adding a brutal murder (the shooting down for honor's sake of an unarmed, drunken lout, not very different from Huck's Pap) and a failed lynching, from which Huck turns away to go to a circus. The final condemnation of the South is spoken by Colonel Sherburn himself, who is the victim of its mad code of honor, but not its hypocrisy: "If any real lynching's going to be done, it will be done in the dark, Southern fashion; and when they come they'll bring their masks...."

The Wilks episode is transitional, still set in the patriarchal world of the South, but centered, for Huck, around the figure of Mary Jane, "most awful beautiful ... her eyes ... all lit up like glory," on whom he develops a hopeless small-boy crush, seeming suddenly five years younger. The whole section is unforgivably sentimental and melodramatic—a compound of sticky nobility and stage gothicism, in the midst of which Huck's pure love is contrasted with the slobbering lustfulness of the Dauphin. At no point in *Huckleberry Finn* is its protagonist so untrue to himself, or Twain so near to yielding up the truth of his book to sentiment. Yet finally Huck moves on past the temptation of puppy love, as he has already passed through those of chivalry and courage. There is no mock marriage, or even a dream of a future one, as in *Tom Sawyer*, only a somewhat unconvincing touch of pathos, when the only girl is left behind:

I hain't ever seen her since that time that I see her go out of that door, no, I hain't ever seen her since, but I reckon I've thought of her many and many a million times, and her saying she would pray for me; and if ever I'd 'a'thought it would do any good for me to pray for *her*, blamed if I wouldn't 'a' done it or bust.

Beyond this, there is Aunt Sally's farm, which looks at first glance very like the Grangerfords'. There is the same double log cabin, the same howling dogs to greet Huck; but his reception committee is quite different from the "three big men with guns pointed at me," who welcomed "George Jackson" into the world of feuding gentlemen. At the Phelpses', it is a Negro woman with a rolling pin in her hand, then Aunt Sally herself, "her spinning stick in her hand." We have moved from the world of gun-bearing fathers into that of mothers, armed only with the symbols of domesticity. The man of the house is the doddering, ineffective Hiram, scarcely real beside his vivid wife. We are, in effect, back in Hannibal (Twain in *The Autobiography* tells us that the original of the Phelps place was in Missouri, but "I moved it down to Arkansas. It was all of six hundred miles but it was no trouble"), and Huck is not George Jackson, Sarah Williams, George Peters, or Adolphus; he is, disconcertingly, Tom Sawyer! For a little while, he even thinks like Tom, forgets the prescience of death that came over him with the first sound of Aunt Sally's spinning wheel, and accepts her house as if it were his Great Good Place, too. "It was a heavenly place for a boy," Twain writes years later; but it was not a "heavenly place" for Huck, who realizes, when Aunt Sally moves to adopt him, that Tom's Eden is his trap: "... and I can't stand it. I been there before."

To be himself Huck must never cease moving, never learn to belong. Yet he has been for a little while a member of a kind of society, different from all those on the shore, a temporary alliance with that other fugitive from Miss Watson, Nigger Jim; and in this society, he has been called upon to sacrifice nothing of himself. In Jim, Huck finds, that is to say, the pure affection offered by Mary Jane without the threat of marriage; the escape from social obligations offered by Pap without the threat of beatings; the protection and petting offered by his volunteer foster-mothers without the threat of pious conformity; the male companionship offered by the Grangerfords without the threat of the combat of honor; the friendship offered by Tom without the everlasting rhetoric and make-believe. Jim is all things to him: father and mother and playmate and beloved, appearing naked and begowned and bewhiskered and painted blue, and calling Huck by the names appropriate to their multiform relationship: "Huck" or "honey" or "Chile" or "boss," and just once "white genlman."

It is an impossible society which they constitute, the outcast boy and the Negro, who, even for Huck, does not really exist as a person: a society in which, momentarily, the irreparable breach between black and white seems healed by love. Huck, who offends no one else, begins by playing in Tom's company a stupid joke on the sleeping Jim; then almost kills him as the result of another heartless stunt; teases him to the point of tears about the reality of their perils on the river; and finally joins with Tom once more to inflict on Jim a hundred pointless torments, even putting his life in unnecessary danger. And through it all, Jim plays the role of Uncle Tom, enduring everything, suffering everything, forgiving everything—finally risking a lynching to save "Marse Tom's" life. It is the Southerner's dream, the American dream of guilt remitted by the abused Negro, who, like the abused mother, opens his arms crying, "Lawsy, I's mighty glad to git you back agin, honey." It is a reconciliation easier to dream than believe. "It's too good for true, honey," Jim says, "it's too good for true." Even more dream-like and hard to believe is Huck's apology to Jim (not Tom's, alas!), Huck's risking hell for his sake.

Only on the unstable surface of the river and in the dark of night, can such a relationship exist, and its proper home is the raft, which floats on the surge of flood-time into the story, a gift from the non-Christian powers of Nature. "There warn't no home like a raft, after all ...," Huck reflects. "You feel mighty free and easy and comfortable on a raft." But the very essence of life on a raft is unreality. "The motion of the raft is gentle, and gliding, and smooth, and noiseless ...," Twain writes in *A Tramp Abroad*; "under its restful influence ... existence becomes a dream ... a deep and tranquil ecstasy." Yet the dream of life on the river always threatens to turn for Twain into a nightmare. In 1906, he observes, for instance, of a recurring dream in which he was once more piloting a boat down the Mississippi:

> It is never a pleasant dream, either. I love to think about those days, but there's always something sickening about the thought ... and usually in my dream I am just about to start into a black shadow without being able to tell whether it is Selma Bluff, or Hat Island, or just a black wall of night.

The idyll of Huck and Jim is a dream at whose heart lurks a nightmare. All about them on the lawless river, crime is plotted and violence done, while the river itself is ever ready to mislead and destroy with fog or storm or snag. Thieves and murderers seek the same avenue of escape which Huck and Jim follow in domestic peace. And at last, in the persons of the Duke and Dauphin, the evil of river life invades the raft itself. The floating island paradise becomes an occupied country, a place where absurd and sodden scoundrels hatch deceit and seek to avoid retribution. There is no way to escape evil forever, no absolute raft; and once the home of Huck and Jim has been invaded, they cannot manage to establish their little Eden again. For a moment after the fiasco at the Wilks', it seems as if Huck and Jim are about to recapture their first freedom: "it *did* seem so good to be free again and all by ourselves on the big river, and nobody to bother us." But the King and Duke appear at the last minute, and Huck collapses into despair: "it was all I could do to keep from crying."

There is no way out. When after a bit, the two fraudulent tormentors are tarred and feathered, driven out of his life forever, Huck feels only pity at the spectacle of evil driving out evil, violence violence—and strangely enough, guilt, too. "I warn't feeling so brash as I were before, but kind of ornery, and humble, and to blame somehow—though *I* hadn't done nothing." What immediately troubles Huck is the fact that he had not been able to warn his old companions and oppressors in time; but actually he has begun to compound a deeper guilt, of which he never becomes quite conscious. Especially after his reunion with Tom and his assumption of Tom's identity, Huck begins, for the first time in his life, to totter on the verge of pride. It is his utopian relationship with Jim which ironically brings him to the point of betraying his own nature. From the boy on the run, he has been temporarily transformed by his rebirth into the deliverer!

Under the superficial moral issue of the book, which involves the right of an ignorant boy to steal a Negro out of slavery; and even beneath the deeper Faustian question of whether doing so he is damned—lurks what is for Huck the ultimate problem: can he, whose role is to suffer and evade, take a hand in the affairs of the world, make something *happen*? One of the functions of the burlesque delivery of Jim is to show up the vanity of this illusion. Not only Tom's artist's contempt for reality, but Huck's loss of the sense of his own identity are travestied in the long concluding farce. Both lead to an appalling cruelty, whose absurd pathos finally makes it clear that Huck (thank God!) is no hero, and that Tom (alas!) is. In the Wilks episode, where so much else is sentimentally blurred, Huck is permitted to steal the gold from the Duke and Dauphin, to seem for a brief instant the savior of Mary Jane; but he gets neither glory nor public acclaim, and is soon on the run again. In Jim's case, he is granted nothing: all of his first efforts merely bring Jim deeper and deeper into the South, and his second try comes close to getting Jim hanged.

Either Jim is free or he is a slave; but in either case, it is not for Huck to meddle. He can love Jim and be loved by him, offend him and ask his forgiveness; he cannot *free* him! He is not one of the masters of the world;

not even a self-declared king or duke or story-book robber chief; and at the end of the Phelps episode, he is about to take up his long flight again, about to become himself once more. Huck ends with a total renunciation, not only of Aunt Sally but implicitly of Tom, too; for he learns at last that the world of boys sustains the world of mothers, privileged make-believe understraps "sivilization." His decision to light out at the end must be understood not as just one more evasion, but as the acceptance of his fate, which means to be without regrets what he was from the start: neither hero nor citizen, neither son nor brother—but a stranger and outcast, a boy-Ishmael. He rejects not only the claims which sanctify slavery (that was easy enough in 1884), but also those which sanctify work, duty, home, cleanliness, marriage, Chivalry-even motherhood!

IV

In one sense, *Huckleberry Finn* seems a circular book, ending as it began with a refused adoption and a flight; and certainly it has the effect of refusing the reader's imagination passage into the future. But there is a breakthrough in the last pages, especially in the terrible sentence which begins, "But I reckon I got to light out for the territory ahead of the rest...." In these words, the end of childhood is clearly signaled; and we are forced to ask the question, which, duplicitously, the book refuses to answer: what will become of Huck if he persists in his refusal to return to the place where he has been before? It is easier to project Tom's future, and perhaps this is the best way to begin. Huck has been *forced*, in the course of the action, to become Tom; but Tom has eagerly taken on the role of Sid, and in doing so has given away the secret so well kept in *Tom Sawyer*: the Good Bad Boy and the Good Good Boy are not so different after all—mother's boys, both of them. Tom will become a lawyer, a banker, a senator, at best—maintaining even into adulthood his permitted good-badness—a writer, which is to say, Mark Twain! Clemens did not deceive himself about the meaning of this, confessing to William Dean Howells: "If I went on now, and took him into manhood, he would just lie, like all the one-horse men in literature...."

But what if Twain had taken "on into manhood" Huck Finn, who lies, to be sure, but never in any "one-horse" literary way? Having rejected the world of the mothers, Huck is condemned really to "go to Hell," to be lost in a sub-world of violence, a violence so universal that it is not judged but breathed like an atmosphere. It is a world in which one survives by his own wits and the stupidity of others: a world bounded on the one side by Pap, the corrupt victim; and on the other, by the Duke and the King, the feckless victimizers. When Huck catches his last glimpse of those two charming and vicious operators "astraddle of a rail," he expresses for them more pity than he finds to spare for anyone else in the book: "and I was sorry for them poor pitiful rascals, it seemed like I couldn't ever feel any hardness against them any more in the world."

One cannot help feeling that it is his own fate which Huck foresees in their plight, and that it is himself he weeps for. Even so he must end up, too, tarred and feathered, unless he dies like his father, stabbed in the back and set adrift on the river. When his father's fate is revealed to him by Jim at the novel's conclusion, Huck can find nothing to say. A happy ending is going on that Twain does not want to imperil; but had Huck been permitted to speak, one suspects that he might have paraphrased his own comment on the doomed crooks aboard the *Walter Scott*: "I felt a little bit heavy-hearted about Pap, but not much, for I reckoned if he could stand it I could." It is the only reaction really proper to the most lost of all American anti-heroes.

In his relationship to his lot, his final resolve to accept what is called these days his "terrible freedom," Huck seems the first Existentialist hero, the improbable ancestor of Camus's "stranger," or the protagonists of Jean-Paul Sartre, or the negative characters of the early Hemingway. But how contrived, literary, and abstract the others seem beside Huck! He is the product of no metaphysics, but of a terrible breakthrough of the undermind of America itself. In him, the obsessive American theme of loneliness reaches an ultimate level of expression, being accepted at last not as a blessing to be sought or a curse to be flaunted or fled, but quite simply a man's fate. There are mythic qualities in Ahab and even Dimmesdale; but Huck is a myth: not invented but discovered by one close enough to the popular mind to let it, this once at least, speak through him. Twain sometimes merely pandered to that popular mind, played the buffoon for it, but he was unalienated from it; and when he let it possess him, instead of pretending to condescend to it, he and the American people dreamed Huck—dreamed, that is to say, the anti-American American dream.

Yet this thoroughly horrifying book, whose morality is rejection and whose ambiance is terror, is a funny book, at last somehow a child's book after all; and the desperate story it tells is felt as joyous, an innocent experience. This ambiguity, this deep doubleness of *Huckleberry Finn* is its essential riddle. How can it be at once so terrible and so comfortable to read? It is, of course, a book which arises out of the part of the mind for which there are no problems, only experiences; and its terrors are those we know best how to live with, since our memories do not go back beyond the point where they had begun to haunt us. There is, moreover, the lyrical quality of much of the book, the colloquial poetry which celebrates the natural world and childhood as two aspects of a single thing. The historical moment to which Twain's child-centered imagination returned was the moment when America was passing out of a rural childhood into urban maturity; and the pattern of his own life seemed, therefore, the prototype of the national experience. As time has gone on, and for more and more Americans the world of nature has shrunk to the memory of far-away vacations and an occasional visit to the old folks; as even the river has been spanned and harnessed to industry, Twain's vanishing rural community has come to seem more and more mythic, strange and beautiful. One of the troubling mysteries of our life is that we can only know as adults what we can only feel as children; and *Huckleberry Finn* manages to evoke the lost world of boyhood with all the horror and loveliness it once possessed for the child who lived it.

Besides, the book *is* funny; the Duke and the Dauphin as comical as they are unspeakable; the occasional quips riotous; the medley of burlesque and parody and understatement, the performance of an old pro, a practiced and talented clown. Even the long ending, taken by itself, is a masterpiece of sustained farce hard to match in any literature. To deplore the ending has become one of the clichés of criticism; and it is true that it is worked out at so great length that it imperils the structure of the book; it is even apparently true that the gratuitous torturing of Jim is too brutal and painful a joke to seem really funny to the sensitive or enlightened or genteel. Regarded closely enough, Tom's scheme for stealing away a Negro whom he knows to be free is not only sadistic but thoroughly immoral, a confusion of literature and life, which leads to the infliction of artistic tortures upon a real human being!

And why do Jim and Huck, too simple and marginal to be taken in by Tom's affections, play along with his absurd plan? To them, the need to escape is urgent and every delay a threat, for they do not possess Tom's inside knowledge. In a way, of course, the horseplay is intended precisely to keep us from asking such questions, to confuse our sense of what is illusory, what real. But we have a right to demand answers all the same to questions which Twain has himself, however ambiguously, posed; and the answers are not hard to find. In the first place, the essential virtue of Huck and Jim is to endure whatever befalls them; and to them, moreover, there is nothing any more ridiculous about what Tom does than there is about what society inflicts on them every day. After all, what can a man, who all his life has known *he can be sold*, find more absurd than that. To Huck as well as Jim, all heroism and all suffering are equally "unreal," equally asinine; and the tomfoolery of "Marse Tom" seems to them no stranger than the vagaries of Judge Thatcher. Similarly, the pretended royalty of the two scoundrels strikes them as no more or less just and rational than that of the legitimate rulers of Europe. The seediness of the Duke and Dauphin undercuts the pretensions of all aristocrats, even those who smell much sweeter, just as Tom's absurdities (for which, after all, he is wounded!) show up the chivalry of the quite serious Grangerfords and Colonel Sherburn, mock even Huck's self-dramatization.

The burlesque tone of the finale manages to suggest such ideas, but at the same time keeps them in the realm of slapstick, where they do not appear either problematical or horrifying. The essential point of the ending is to reassert the duplicity of the book, to play out its moral issues as *jokes*; for if we were once to stop laughing, we would be betrayed out of the Neverland of childhood back into an actual world of maturity. The book must end just short of Huck's growing up, thus leaving us with the conviction that his gesture of total rejection and the brief, harried honeymoon which preceded it, are as endless as childhood's summers, really eternal. Believing this, we can believe, too, that whatever Huck's final decision may foreshadow or imply, his ending is, indeed, happy—the book which describes it a book about happiness.

If *Huckleberry Finn* is, finally, the greatest of all books about childhood, this is because it renders with a child's tough-mindedness and a child's desperate hilarity a double truth fumbled by most other books on the subject: how truly wonderful it is to remember our childhood; and yet how we cannot recall it without revealing to ourselves the roots of the very terror, which in adulthood has driven us nostalgically to evoke that past.

RICHARD POIRIER

Transatlantic Configurations: Mark Twain and Jane Austen

Mark Twain cannot imagine a society in which his hero has any choice, if he is to remain in society at all, but to be "of Tom Sawyer's party." The evidence for such a comparative limitation on the hero—and, indeed, a justification for making a comparison to the greater freedom allowed Emma—is in the similarity between the situations of the two characters at the central crisis in each book. Beside the famous picnic scene at Box Hill, when the heroine insults Miss Bates, can be placed the corresponding scene in *Huckleberry Finn* when, in Chapter XV, Huck also insults a social inferior who is at the same time a trusting friend. The process by which each of these insults comes about is roughly the same. Emma at Box Hill gradually surrenders what is called her "self-command" to the theatrical urgings and flatteries of Frank Churchill, while Huck often acts in imitation of the "style" of Tom Sawyer even when it doesn't suit him. Emma literally forgets who she is and therefore the identity of Miss Bates in relation to her, and her witty retort to one of the older lady's simplicities expresses not her true relationship to Miss Bates so much as the theatrical and self-aggrandizing role which Churchill has encouraged her to play to the whole group. Her social and psychological situation—and the literary problem thus created— is much like Huck's at the similar moment when imitation of Tom's role has led to his violation of the bond between him and Jim. The central character

From *A World Elsewhere: The Place of Style in American Literature.* © 1966 by Richard Poirier.

in each novel has violated a social contract by being artificial. Both recognize what has happened and both make amends. But at this point there appears an important and essential difference between the situations of these two, and the difference is indicative of the problem in American nineteenth-century fiction of imagining personal relationships within the context of existent social environments. Huck's recognition cannot involve a choice, as can Emma's, against some forms of social expression in favor of others: against the Frank Churchills, Mrs. Eltons (and Tom Sawyers) of this world, and for the Mr. Knightleys. Mark Twain simply cannot provide Huck with an alternative to "games" that has any viability within the social organization which the novel provides. Huck's promise to do Jim "no more mean tricks" is, in effect, a rejection of the only modes of expression understood by his society. At a similar point Emma recognizes and rejects social artifice and is then in a position to accept her natural place in society as Knightley's wife.

Huck chooses at the end "to light out for the Territory ahead of the rest," while Emma, joined to Knightley in "the perfect happiness of the union," is both firmly within a social group and yet saved from all the false kinds of undiscriminating "amiability" practiced at Box Hill. The ceremony is witnessed, significantly, not by the whole community but by a "small band of true friends." "Marriageableness," as Emerson scornfully puts it, emphatically is Jane Austen's subject. Marriage represents for her what he chooses to slight—not merely the act of choice within society but, more importantly, the union of social and natural inclinations. Naturalness and social form are fused in her work in a way that I do not think Emerson, Mark Twain of *Huckleberry Finn*, or even Henry James were able sufficiently to value. It is no wonder that Mark Twain's difficulties begin at a comparable point where Jane Austen most brilliantly succeeds. *Huckleberry Finn* cannot dramatize the meanings accumulated at the moment of social crisis because the crisis itself reveals the inadequacy of the terms by which understandings can be expressed between the hero and other members of his society. There is no publicly accredited vocabulary which allows Huck to reveal his inner self to others.

The comparison between Huck and Emma offers at least a tentative answer to a question of some significance, not merely for *Huckleberry Finn*, but for other American novels of the century in which there is a limited view of the inclusiveness of social environments and of the language that holds them together. The question again is why, precisely at Box Hill, Jane Austen is able to see her way clear to a dramatic resolution of the meaning of her novel, while Mark Twain is stalled at a similar point to a degree that makes him observe, in a letter to Howells, that he liked his novel "only tolerably well, as far as I have got, and may possibly pigeonhole or burn the MS when it is done"? The threat, only partly in jest, was made in August 1876. In barely a month almost a third of the novel had been written. It was not to be finished for seven years. It had reached a point where Huck, having tricked and then apologized to Jim, decides that he can no longer exploit his Negro friend with tricks but will instead try to save him by tricking society. By his decision not to use the "style" of Tom on a runaway slave (Chapter XV), Huck gives up conformist for rebellious trickery. In Chapter XVI, at the point where the novel came to a halt in 1876, Huck, halfway between the raft and the shore, intends to betray his companion. Instead he saves him from capture by inventing an elaborate lie, persuading the two men in the skiff that the raft is occupied by the boy's contagiously sick father. Chapters XV and XVI constitute what I shall be calling the "reversal scenes": they bring about the dramatic crisis by which Huck decisively reverses, for a time, the Tom Sawyerish trend in his relationship to Jim; and they also reverse his efforts to belong imaginatively to society, as most attractively represented by that "respectable" boy Tom Sawyer.

My explanation of Mark Twain's difficulty at this point and of why, after it, his greatest novel goes to pieces will not, I hope, suggest that *Huckleberry Finn* is inferior to *Emma*, whatever that would mean. For one thing, I cannot imagine how *Huckleberry Finn* could have succeeded in resolving the issues that it creates. It makes nothing less than an absolute disavowal, after Huck lies to protect Jim, of any significant dramatic relationship between the hero and all the other characters, whose habitual forms of expression define what I mean by "society" in this novel. The failure is predictable and inescapable in view of the accomplishment, never adequately described by commentaries on the novel, of the first sixteen chapters. These chapters reveal an experimental mastery beyond anything that the author's other works would allow us to expect. Henry Nash Smith points out, perhaps forgetting *The Blithedale Romance*, that not even Henry James had ever dared, by 1885, when *Huckleberry Finn* was published as a book, to entrust the point of view so fully to a character of such evident individuality. My reservations about this judgment are mostly in the interest of pointing to accomplishments and complexities in excess merely of manipulating point of view. For one thing, it cannot be demonstrated that Huck's point of view is maintained with any success throughout the book. The novel is remarkable for the degree to which the heroes voice—from which his point of view is deduced—becomes increasingly inaudible. Even at the beginning, the author uses his narrator to create, all unknown to him and through what are made to seem the most natural habits of his mind—its tendency to verbal repetition—a metaphorical definition of society as no more than a fabrication of art and artifice. Thus, even while we are hearing in Huck's voice a desire for accommodation to this society, as exemplified in Tom, we are seeing in these repeated metaphors Mark Twain's own alienation from that society.

The Shakespearean use of language in the opening chapters allows Mark Twain to blend immediacy and significance, pictorial entertainment and metaphoric implication, in a way that imperceptibly ties the destiny of the narrator to the destiny of the culture defined by Mark Twain's images. In a style that has the easy movement of a boy's story and a compactness usually found only in poetry of considerable density, these early pages reveal a society shaped entirely by fantasy and illusion and that depends for sanction primarily on literary authority. Unlike Emma, who is offered many ways of speaking and may choose even from among competitive definitions of words, Huck's language is rigidly controlled by people who are essentially alien to him. To both adults and companions he sounds like a "numb-skull" because he takes them at their word and finds that he is thereby taken in. By assuming that their statements have at least some literal meaning, he unintentionally discovers the actual self-interest or self-delusion behind their language. These are rather grim suggestions, when in fact the experience of reading the opening chapters is not grim at all and answers the objection, best phrased by Poe, that if allegory "ever established a fact, it is by dint of overturning a fiction." Poe's attack on Hawthorne includes a description of an alternative to allegorical simplicities that might be applied to the metaphoric structure I am about to examine:

> Where the suggested meaning runs through the obvious one in a very profound undercurrent, so as never to interfere with the upper one without our volition, so as never to show itself unless *called* to the surface, there only, for the proper uses of fictitious narrative, is it available at all.

The undercurrent has been indeed so "very profound" that it has never been clearly exposed beneath the surface of the first three chapters, which even some recent commentators have described as belonging to the tradition of *Tom Sawyer*. Such a reaction should not too quickly be dismissed, however. The narrative voice at the beginning does in fact lull our attention to implications lurking in it. The implications are contemptuous of the tradition of *Tom Sawyer*, even while the voice is not nearly so anxious to be separated from it. As early as the second paragraph there is a metaphoric equation which effectively condemns society as embodied in Tom Sawyer; yet the condemnation is so clearly the unintentional revelation of Huck's mind that it is as if Mark Twain himself is trying to exorcise it. Huck's voice is like a screen protecting the author from the abstractions implicit in his own metaphors:

The Widow Douglas she took me for her son, and allowed she would sivilize me; but it was rough living in the house all the time, considering how dismal regular and decent the widow was in all her ways; and so when I couldn't stand it no longer, I lit out. I got into my old rags, and my sugar-hogshead again, and was free and satisfied. But Tom Sawyer, he hunted me up and said he was going to start a band of robbers, and I might join if I would go back to the widow and be respectable. So I went back.

Tom Sawyer's games are intimately related, it is implied, to the "respectable" aspects of adult society. The alternative to both is "freedom," with Huck caught between his impulsive need for it and his equally strong need for company: "so I went back." It is metaphorically suggested that Tom Sawyer and Widow Douglas are in tacit alliance, and both are indicted by the further suggestion that to be "respectable" in her terms is the necessary condition for membership in his gang. "Respectable" society as represented by the Widow is equivalent to a "band of robbers." The parallel is then advanced, with relevance to social artificiality of a specifically literary sort, by the account of Huck's training with the Widow. Evocations of "her book," her Biblical authority for believing things that are not true for Huck, anticipate the even more frequent references in the next and later chapters to Tom's "books," the romances which are also "authorities" for illusion. Before this equation is developed, however, Huck turns for the first time in the novel away from society, not by "lighting out" but by entering into a soliloquy which is in part a communion with nature and spirits. He turns, like Emerson at the opening of Nature, not only away from people but also away from "books," from the "study" which Emerson, in the first paragraph of his essay, also rejects for the "stars":

Miss Watson she kept pecking at me, and it got tiresome and lonesome. By-and-by they fetched the niggers in and had prayers, and then everybody was off to bed. I went up to my room with a piece of candle and put it on the table. Then I set down in a chair by the window and tried to think of something cheerful, but it warn't no use. I felt so lonesome I most wished I was dead. The stars were shining, and the leaves rustled in the woods ever so mournful; and I heard an owl, away off, who-whooing about somebody that was dead, and a whippowill and a dog crying about somebody that was going to die; and the wind was trying to whisper something to me and I couldn't make out what it was, and so it made the cold shivers run over me. Then away out in the woods I heard that kind of a sound that a ghost makes when it wants to tell about something that's on its mind and can't make itself understood, and so can't rest easy in its grave and has to go about that way everynight grieving. I got so downhearted and scared I did wish I had some company.

At the outset the reader might be so beguiled by Huck's narrative voice as to forget not only the metaphoric implications in his language but also that, except for his address to the reader, he is remarkably quiet. He speaks infrequently to anyone else; he is seldom heard in conversation, and he is always inconspicuous in company, even in the "gang." His loneliness, we might say, is a want of conversation, a lack, in terms of the literary problem raised by the book, of dramatic relationships. He listens for sounds from nature and interprets them more confidently than language, which tends to confuse or disturb him. "But I never said so," is one of his characteristic comments. The form of the book itself, an autobiography that is also a kind of interior monologue, testifies to the internalization of his feelings and reactions.

And yet, it is necessary to stress that any Emersonian detachment from society for the companionship of the "stars" would never satisfy Huck (or Mark Twain) for very long. His soliloquies are punctuated with the words "lonesome" and "lonely," ending in the present instance with the direct admission that "I did wish I had some company." Company is announced from below the window in the animal noises of *Tom Sawyer*, and the first chapter ends with tones of deep companionable satisfaction: "Then I slipped down to the ground and crawled among the trees, and, sure enough, there was Tom Sawyer waiting for me."

The organization of the chapter suggests, with pleasure and excitement, that by joining Tom Huck has escaped social entrapment and achieved a Laurentian kind of "freedom"—"freedom together." But Chapter II, with Tom's incessant talk about rules, gangs, and especially books and authority, only confirms the early hint of an essential solidarity between Tom's world and the Widow's, despite her amused assurance that Tom will not qualify for her heaven. Tom's world is dominated by games and fantasies imitated from literature, just as hers is based on illusions derived from religion and the Bible. His tricks, the first of which is an exploitation of Jim in Chapter II, are justified by the "authorities" of boys' games and, by extension, of religion and social respectability, which sanction Miss Watson's exploitation of Jim at still another level. Tom's question in Chapter II when they are discussing the conduct of a game—"Do you want to go to doing different from what's in the books, and get things all muddled up?"—implies even at this point that an argument with the "authority" of boys' games is a disruption of accredited social procedures.

The alternatives promised in Chapter II by Tom's gang and its games to the "civilized" confinements of Chapter I turn out, then, to be no alternatives at all. Offering confirmation of such a reading, Chapter III puts into direct juxtaposition the activities of religious, conservative, respectable society, as embodied in Widow Douglas and Miss Watson, and the activities of children, based on the authorities of romantic literature as interpreted by Tom Sawyer. We have before us the creation in words of a whole society built on games, tricks, and illusions, and the adult version is only superficially different from the children's. You play the game without asking literal-minded questions, play as if it were "for real," or you're a "numb-skull."

The metaphorical equation of the world of adults and of children indicates the relative eccentricity of Huck. Thus while his treatment of Jim during the reversal scenes is a matter of playing one of Tom's tricks, of "playing the game" in the larger sense, his subsequent apology violates the rules of the game as observed both by children and adults. Implicit here, in the most placidly comic part of the book, is what Huck will most painfully discover later: that to give up "tricking" Jim means more than giving up Tom's games. It means, so closely are they imaginatively connected with adult forms of exploitation, that he must also believe himself damned to social ostracism and to Hell.

These significances are not declared nor are they derived merely from images. They are instead the result very often of the similarity of phrasing applied first to the Widow and Miss Watson and then to Tom. The unobtrusiveness by which a parallel is thus established results from the use of phrases having the sound merely of idiomatic repetitiousness, not uncommon in vernacular literature. For example, in the first half of Chapter III, in which Huck is advised by Miss Watson about the advantages of prayer and the Bible, there is a sequence of phrases applied to religion and its promises ("it warn't so," "spiritual gifts," "I couldn't see no advantage to it") that in slightly varied form are applied in the second half to Tom's games and the romantic books which authorize them ("but only just pretended," "done by enchantment," "I couldn't see no profit in it"). In the first half, Huck's literalness, inseparable from a concern for human profit and loss, makes Miss Watson call him a "fool," just as in the second it leads Tom Sawyer to call him a "numb-skull." The list can be extended by anyone who turns to Chapter III, and the implications are in fact summarized in the final sentence of the chapter by Huck himself: "So then I judged that all that stuff was only just one of Tom Sawyer's lies. I reckoned he believed in the A-rabs and the elephants, but as for me I think different. It had all the marks of a Sunday-school." These concluding remarks make the metaphoric intention of the opening chapters unmistakable. Each side of the comparison is modified by the other. Boys' games as Tom plays them are finally, so the comparisons seem to indicate, as genteel and proper as Miss Watson's religion (he always leaves payment for anything he "steals"), and the social respectability and religion which she represents are, like Tom's games, remote from the requirements of natural, literal, daily experience, from a concern for elementary human feelings that are revealed in Huck's "numb-skull" skepticism both about games and religion.

But it is time to remind ourselves again that as we read we are listening to a voice, not drawing metaphoric diagrams. The voice makes the reading of the metaphors and any effort to determine their weight within the total experience of these chapters extremely difficult. Even at this early point we are uncomfortably aware of a gap between Mark Twain's position, his view, expressed through these metaphors, of society merely as system, and the more socially engaged and eager position of the hero. The gap will ultimately mean that the novel becomes simpler later on than it is here. After the reversal scenes, personal drama is not allowed to intrude into a massive parade of social games and disguises. The sound of Huck's socially involved voice first wavers, then nearly disappears, then returns as a sickly version of what we find in these opening scenes. Here, though, it is heard distinctly enough to make the metaphors amusing and affectionate, however damaging they become if one isolates their implications.

The great difficulty for the reader in the opening chapters is that we feel no confidence in balancing the implications of style, its tendency to repudiate what is at the same time being affectionately rendered. It is no wonder that there are many differences of opinion about the structure of the book and about whether or not it expresses an ultimate surrender to the so-called genteel tradition or a final repudiation of it, and of Hannibal, the so-called Happy Valley of Mark Twain's youth. Those critics who respond weakly, or not at all, to the metaphoric implications of the early chapters ignore as a consequence the extent to which Mark Twain has begun even here to isolate the consciousness he values from the society in which it seeks to express itself. Put simply, it is predictable from the outset that the book must elect to give its attention either to the development of the hero or to a review of the environment which forestalls that development. The two cannot be synchronized. This literary difficulty is what plagued the author in the summer of 1876, not any discovered contempt of his own, presumably released only by his trip to the Mississippi in 1882, for the environments of his youth. His criticisms are already evident enough in 1876. On the other hand, those who do stress the evidences of repudiation in the early chapters are apt to miss the complications brought about by the freedom Mark Twain allows to the more loving, socially agreeable expressions of his hero. The latter reading is best represented by Leo Marx, whose criticisms of T. S. Eliot and Lionel Trilling for approving of the later portions of the novel have been much admired. But I think the reading he himself offers in his essay confuses Huck Finn with Mark Twain in the opening chapters, not letting us see how much Huck's voice modifies the social criticism, and it then confuses Mark Twain with Huck in the concluding chapters, missing, it seems to me, the degree to which we can only respond to Huck within what has become by then the author's rigidly bitter and impersonal metaphoric design.

What happens to this novel is what happens to Huck at the hands of his creator. The problem for the author after the crucial scenes in Chapters XV and XVI is that the novel can no longer be the autobiography of Huck Finn. It must instead become a kind of documentation of why the consciousness of the hero cannot be developed in dramatic relations to any element of this society. Kenneth Lynn's version of the problem—that after Chapter XVI Mark Twain discovered he must damn the Happy Valley and was loath to do so—has already been paraphrased and questioned in the preceding paragraph. But his reading of this part of the novel can, with some important modifications, take us close to the difficulties that the novelist himself must have felt at this point in the writing. Mark Twain has written himself into a position where he can no longer sustain a double relationship to the social environment of his novel—on the remote contemptuous critic, on the one hand, and, on the other, of the man with illusions that some closer relationship, such as Huck himself seems to want with Tom, can be maintained.

Were we to read the last sentences of Chapter III as Mr. Marx suggests—"With this statement which ends the third chapter, Huck parts company with Tom"—there would of course be no such problem as I describe. Without Huck's continued longing for some kind of tie with Tom ("respectable" society at its most palatable), the novel would be a relatively unmodified criticism of society carried out by Huck himself, until the author, so Mr. Marx's argument runs, in his essay and in *The Machine in the Garden*, forces a surrender to society at the conclusion. Some such development does occur but it is blurred by the fact that Huck is cultivating an imaginative association with Tom (and therefore society) all the way from Chapter III to Chapter XV. He consistently imitates him, and to that extent is, like the rest of this society, imitating "books" and "authorities." He repeatedly cites Tom as his own authority for tricks and adventures that are conspicuously at odds with both his feelings and self-interest. The attractions of social life for Huck, his persistent wish that "I had some company," are never wholly satisfied by the companionship of Jim, which explains why, when they are separated, Huck can so easily put him out of mind. Tom is evoked, however, no matter how lengthy the separation. When he frees himself from Pap, with elaborate trickery in Chapter VII, Huck "did wish Tom Sawyer was there; I knowed he would take an interest in this kind of business, and throw in the fancy touches. Nobody could spread himself like Tom Sawyer in such a thing as that." In Chapter XII, his escapade on the *Walter Scott* is justified to Jim by asking, "Do you reckon Tom Sawyer would ever go by this thing?" and it could be inferred at this point that Jim, as a companion on adventures, is implicitly dismissed by the added remark that "I wish Tom Sawyer *was* here."

The evocation of Walter Scott as a ruined steamboat, in the context of the metaphors already discussed here, is itself an image of a romantic, conservative, and religious society in a state of wreckage. What we infer from the novel alone is confirmed and extended by Mark Twain's excessive charge (quoted in *Mark Twain in Eruption*) that Scott was in "great measure responsible for the Civil War." It was he who made the South fall in love with "the jejeune romanticism of an absurd past" and who created "a reverence for rank and cast, and pride and pleasure in them." Though expressed in 1882 after his visit to the "New South," the attitudes are apparent enough in the early parts of *Huckleberry Finn*, and the term used to characterize Scott's romanticism, "jejeune," has a popular meaning that was dramatized in 1876 in the adventures of boys acting out the romantic predilections of adults. Huck's imitations of Tom indicate the degree to which he must become an artificial man, an imitator of literary models, if he is to be a part of society at all or be accepted by it as a "real" boy, like Tom.

As the novel moves to the crisis of insult and apology in Chapter XV, "imitation" is shown, just as at Box Hill, to result in the loss of "self-command" and an enslavement to alien forms of expression that distort genuine feelings. Chapter XIV, "Was Solomon Wise?" is a preparatory and comic version of Chapter XV, "Fooling Poor Old Jim." In the first, the imitative tendencies of Huck are developed to a point where, with brilliant comic significance, he has stylistically become Tom Sawyer, while transferring his own identity as a "numb-skull" to Jim ("I said these things are adventures; but he said he didn't want no more adventures"), and he tries to win the argument by citing the Widow ("the Widow told me all about it"). He thus adopts for his "authorities" the two figures who together represent aspects of the artifice which, in this novel, are equivalent to society. Huck, trying to be Tom, bases his arguments on a faith in symbolic actions, regardless of the practical consequences, while Jim, like Huck himself in earlier arguments with the real Tom, insists on them: "En what use is half a chile? I wouldn' give a dern for a million of um." To which Huck replies, much as Tom does to him, "Hang it, Jim, you've clean missed the point."

Huck's imitation and assumption of Tom's role at this point prepares us for the crucial scene about to take place. In the next chapter, after the separation in the fog, Huck continues the tricks begun by Tom in Chapter II. He tries to convince Jim that he has merely been dreaming, that what he believed were naturally stimulated feelings of loss and love were the result rather of fantasy. When Jim realizes that he is being tricked, he responds with a speech that evokes all the affectionate trust that has been evident as the unspoken reality of their relationship. It is only at this point, not at any earlier one, that Huck does separate himself from Tom:

> It was fifteen minutes before I could work myself up to go and humble myself to a nigger—but I done it, and I warn't ever sorry for it afterwards, neither. I didn't do him no more mean tricks, and I wouldn't done that one if I'd 'a knowed it—would make him feel that way.

The nature of Huck's regret here makes his later adoption of Tom's name and his later acceptance of Tom's leadership in the mock freeing of Jim much more than a sacrifice of the emotional growth registered in this passage, much more even than a nearly total collapse of Mark Twain's characterization of the hero. These later developments show the extent to which Mark Twain, no less than his hero, has fallen victim to the world structured by this novel. That the circumstances of Huck's characterization, his environmental placement, make it impossible to sustain the identity he momentarily achieves in the reversal scenes is apparently recognized by Mark Twain himself in the chapter immediately following. The very title of it, "The Rattlesnakeskin Does its Work," again suggests how Huck's tricks on Jim always do have painfully real consequences. In this chapter we find Huck trapped in verbal conventions that prevent the release of his feelings in words. The terminology he has been taught to use and that binds him to Tom Sawyer and the others cannot let him express the nature of his relationship to Jim. He feels the "pinch of conscience," which is to, say the "pinch" of training, of system, of education. ("It [conscience] is merely a *thing*," according to an entry in Mark Twain's notebooks, "the creature of *training*; it is whatever one's mother and Bible and comrades and laws and systems of government and habitat and heredities have made it.") In the novel, conscience is the product of the "games" of comrades and of the "authorities" of books, including the Bible. The meanings which these impart to Huck's language are inadequate to his feelings. Having been defined most significantly for the reader in scenes of flight with a runaway slave, Huck is still enslaved himself to the language of Tom's settled world, still inescapably attached to it: "Here was this nigger, which I had as good as helped to run away, coming right out flat-footed and saying he would steal his children—children that belonged to a man I didn't even know; a man that hadn't ever done me no harm."

Huckleberry Finn is an instance of what happens to a novel when society, as the author conceives it, provides no opportunity, no language, for the transformation of individual consciousness into social drama. The provision is lacking because Mark Twain cannot imagine a society that offers alternatives to artificiality or that has in it, like Joyce's Dublin, evidences of an official culture that has historical dignity and value. Huck's problem here represents the crisis in the novel itself. This last quotation, and Huck's use nearby of "right" for what Mark Twain has made us see is "wrong," of "wrong" for "right," involves a recognition by the author, more perplexed than any it anticipates in Joyce, of what happens when the hero of a novel must define his alienations from society in terms that take their meanings for him, as much as for anyone, from the very "authorities" he has come to reject. Joyce's theme by choice is Mark Twain's dilemma. By 1916 Joyce would be so aware of the problem as a literary and linguistic one that he would make his hero veritably an artist of words. Stephen Dedalus is a kind of Pateresque Huck Finn. He tries vainly to dissociate himself from the sources that give validation to his language—home, church, country—and he declares his freedom to "change the laws of nature" in words that reveal, by their associative connections with earlier experiences, his inescapable obligations to the past.

No wonder Mark Twain could not recognize in the novels of Jane Austen the existence of a society of alternatives. The existence of such a society in her work explains the necessary difference between *Emma* and *Huckleberry Finn* revealed at the point in each where the social order is disrupted by an insult. In *Emma*, the crisis results in a restoration to social intercourse of a naturalness temporarily lost through artifice; in *Huckleberry Finn* it can lead only to the hero's painful and confused recognition of what his creator has been showing all along—that what is natural for society is in fact nothing but artifice, tricks, games, and disguise. When Huck enters society again in Chapter XVII by going ashore, it is in disguise as George Jackson and among a group, the Grangerfords, who are given to extravagant forms of genteel and sentimental literary expression and to the romantic waste of a family feud.

To enter society at all as it exists on the shore, to deal with it without disastrous exposure of the sort of person we know him to be, means that throughout the rest of the book Huck must move about in various disguises, tell lies, play roles even more than he has before. And he will at last become

"Tom Sawyer" all over again in Chapter XXXII. Still more important, the Huck Finn shown to us at what is obviously the dramatic crisis of the book is disguised thereafter even from the reader. The style of the book after that carries his voice only sporadically: in some lyrical descriptions of life on the raft, and with significant moral complication only once more—for a moment in Chapter XXXI. The implications are historically important: this novel discovers that the consciousness it values most cannot expand within the environment it provides, that the self cannot come to fuller life through social drama, upon which the vitality of this and of most other novels of the last century at some necessary point depend.

There is evidence that Mark Twain himself came to this realization, that he saw his problem in the literary terms in which I am describing it, and that he recognized that his literary dilemma was historically revelatory. The evidence, in addition to his prolonged difficulties in finishing the novel, derives from what the book expresses after the reversal scenes. It never again, except in bits and pieces, expresses the person whose voice there fully answers for almost the last time to the name "Huck Finn." Thereafter, the chapters can be taken as images of justification for Mark Twain's failure to resolve the meanings accumulated at that point. Through a series of burlesque incidents, in some of which Huck plays no part at all—the Grangerfords (XVII–XVIII), the introduction of the King and the Duke (XIX–XX), the Arkansas episodes (XXI–XIII), the Wilks sequence (XXIV–XXIX), and, finally, the staged version of the "freeing" of Jim (XXXIV–XLII)—through these only tenuously linked incidents Mark Twain pictorializes the literary and social conditions which confront the American novelist writing such a book as this. The general implication is that to be born into the world of Huckleberry Finn is to be born, as Hawthorne earlier remarked of all of us, "into a world of artificial system." Between Huck and reality there is always a curtain of "style"—a term sacred to Tom Sawyer. The dominant social style, as these episodes reveal it, is imported and literary, not only from Scott, but also from Don Quixote, Casanova, Benvenuto Cellini, and Shakespeare, all mixed with domestic melodrama, the poetry of gift books, and, as in scenes at the Grangerfords, those "novels of costume" that Emerson said had "filled the heads of the most imitative classes" in America.

Mark Twain's arrangement of the scenes involving the Grangerfords and the King and the Duke are especially relevant to the allegorical implications of these later chapters. Having escaped the family feud, a violent expression of the sentimental romanticism that belongs to the painting and poetry of the Grangerfords, Huck is almost immediately trapped by fake royalty, whose imitations have debased Shakespeare into sentimental twaddle. But for a moment in between we are given the beautiful renewal of the idyll of Jim and Huck, so memorable that, though it runs for barely two pages, it has for some readers become equivalent to the "raft" itself and led to inaccurate schemes that too sharply separate the "raft" from the "shore," elements of which will very soon possess the raft and the life on it:

> Soon as it was night, out we shoved; when we got her out to about the middle, we let her alone, and let her float wherever the current wanted her to; then we lit the pipes, and dangled our legs in the water and talked about all kinds of things—we was always naked, day and night, whenever the mosquitoes would let us—the new clothes Buck's folks made for me was too good to be comfortable, and besides I didn't go much on clothes, no how.

The appearance of the King and the Duke does not, as sometimes claimed, bring a new element into the book. They are merely an outrageous example of the theatricality so persistent from the beginning. They come to destroy the natural and spontaneous life that in this very brief interval of time has released its direction not to current styles but to the current of the river, not to clothes supplied by others but to personal nakedness. We are not allowed simply to equate the "raft" with "freedom," except as it reminds us of what is to be lost when the control of it falls almost at once to the powers of fakery and theatrical enterprise. Huck and Jim are made literally the prisoners of these things. They are in the grip of artifice, and their nakedness will henceforth give way to traveling in costume.

The stylistic organization of the novel, as we have been observing it, allows us to see the destiny of the "raft" in still larger terms. The raft is like America itself, as viewed regionally here by Mark Twain and more generally elsewhere by Cooper, Emerson, and Whitman, all of whom at various times complained not that America was "artless" or "bare," to recall Henry James's description, but that it had surrendered to imitation and a dependence upon foreign models in social conduct and in literature. It had been transformed almost immediately from a place of "nakedness" and "freedom" into what Whitman claimed in 1870, and John Jay Chapman somewhat later, was a "thoroughly upholstered exterior appearance" in excess even of the Old World.

The "Arkansas Difficulty," in Chapters XXI to XXII, contributes to the novel's developing indictment by suggesting how even forms of violence, melodramatic in their own right, effectively touch the feelings of the community only after they have been further stylized and made into a form of entertainment. When Sherburn kills Boggs, the most conspicuous initial reaction is from the "long, lanky man" who does an imitation for the townspeople of what has only just occurred. As the novel describes it, his rendition is in fact a performance for which he is paid by his fellow citizens, who "got out their bottles and treated him." Only then do they join in the unsuccessful lynching bee, as a kind of afterthought: "Well, by and by," the last sentence of the chapter casually begins, "somebody said Sherburn ought to be lynched." The implication that the society of this novel can only feel things that are expressed in ways belonging not to life but to art is apparent still later in the melodrama of "tears and flapdoodle" during the episodes at the Wilks's in Chapters XXIV to XXIX. Here again, the governing style of the community, despite some efforts at good sense, is one of costume drama in which two of the principals are, significantly, pretending to have arrived recently from England. "'*Here* is my answer,'" says Mary Jane when asked to put her English "relatives" to the test: "She hove up the bag of money and put it in the king's hands, and says, 'Take this six thousand dollars, and invest it for me and my sisters any way you want to, and don't give us no receipt for it.'" We are permitted to think, in summary, that the "fine looking man," the social leader who jumps up at the performance of the Royal Nonesuch and admits that "we are sold," is substantially describing the formative processes of society as a whole: the audience should promote the fraudulent theatricals around town, he advises, so that "Then we'll all be in the same boat."

During these episodes, from Chapter XVIII to XXIX, the freeing of Jim is obviously not the subject of the novel. These chapters are indicative of the fact that the book is concerned with Negro slavery only as one aspect of a more general enslavement—of feeling and intelligence within inadequate and restrictively artificial modes of expression. Dramatically, the book is victim of the conditions illustrated in these chapters, during which Huck is allowed only an attenuated contact with what is going on. His oppositions provide no meaningful dramatic interest. He does not like what is happening—that about sums it up. We witness an intensification of social criticism carried out by episodic illustration and a further development of the metaphors of artifice, but there is no corresponding intensification of drama within the social life that involves Huck. He does help Mary Jane and he does not laugh at the circus performer who he thinks is endangered by the horses, again revealing his lovable seriousness about the human consequences of tricks. But such incidents are themselves flatly representative of relatively static attitudes; they catch none of the complications of response that have been developing up to the reversal scenes. Neither does the remark, by this point tiresomely indicative of a trapped mind slowing down, that "I do believe he [Jim] cared just as much for his people as white folks does for their'n. It don't seem natural but I reckon it's so."

More is lost in that sentence, especially feeble in contrast to Jim's heartbreaking story about his deaf daughter, than the vivid eccentricity of voice that was an earlier indication of Huck's personal, self-critical involvement with life around him. There is a loss even of the vitality of reaction that led to the crucial insult and apology, much less the consequent knowledge of what is "natural" for Negroes. The deterioration is made even more apparent by the degree of explicitness with which Huck is allowed at a few points to condemn the activities he witnesses: "It was enough to make a body ashamed of the human race" is a statement with none of the rewarding complications that have been characteristic of Huck's responses to meanness and his expression of them. Even the vividness of description that results from his spontaneous feelings of relationship to sights and sounds is rarely found in the last half or more of the novel. "If I trod on a stick and broke it, it made me feel like a person had cut one of my breaths in two and I only got half, and the short half, too"—we need only remember such a line as this to recognize how much of Huck has disappeared from the novel when we get to the Arkansas episode and hear what purports to be Huck's description of a town:

> On the river front some of the houses was sticking out over the bank, and they was bowed and bent, and about ready to tumble in. The people had moved out of them. The bank was caved away under one corner of some others, and that corner was hanging over. People lived in them yet, but it was dangersome, because sometimes a strip of land as wide as a house caves in at a time. Sometimes a belt of land a quarter of a mile deep will start in and cave along and cave along till it all caves into the river in one summer. Such a town as that has to be always moving back, and back, and back, because the river is always gnawing at it.

Huck is barely present in the language here, the virtues of which do not include the sound of the identifying narrative voice heard earlier. "People live in them yet," or "such a town as that," belong to the narrator of *Life on the Mississippi*, to Mark Twain himself. It is not surprising that having put the manuscript of the novel aside in 1876, near the end of Chapter XVI, he could feel free to borrow a section of that chapter for *Life on the Mississippi* in 1882, the famous "raftsmen passage." And it is of course not irrelevant to my argument that the borrowing should have come from precisely the spot where Mark Twain began to feel the difficulty of maintaining Huck as the dramatic center and narrative voice of his novel.

After the reversal scenes, the novel does not again, for any considerable stretch, sound like the "autobiography" of Huckleberry Finn until "You

Can't Pray a Lie," Chapter XXXI. There, the language once more expresses some of the musing, characteristically painful effort of Huck to liberate and reveal his complicated feelings. Significantly, there is also a resurgence of the lyricism of description which gives evidence of his affectionate liveliness of response to people and scenery: "and I see Jim before me, all the time, in the day and in the night-time, sometimes moonlight, sometimes storms, and we a-floating along, talking, and singing, and laughing." It seems as if the book is at last reassembling the hero in a style and situation that will reveal again how dangerously unique he is.

But even here there is a conspicuous repetitiousness, a failure to advance the novel dramatically beyond Chapter XVI. Chapter XXXI is in many ways only a redoing of the earlier crisis, with a "pinch of conscience," a decision, not more or less intense, to do "wrong" and help Jim to freedom. And immediately thereafter, Huck disappears again into the artifices of society. He assumes the identity of Tom Sawyer in Chapter XXXII, "I Have a New Name," and he does so in a phrase ("I was so glad to find out who I was") that pointedly and it seems to me intentionally reminds us of how the movement of the book in its best and most "autobiographical" parts was committed to exactly the opposite development: of Huck's freedom from the imitative artificiality of Tom Sawyer. On the subject of "authorities" and "tricks" by which Tom would "free" the already free Jim, the narrative voice hereafter becomes sickly and accommodating, when it is not timidly pouting: "I ain't going to make no complaint. Any way that suits you suits me." Such a blatant, even contemptuous denial of any dramatic development for which the novel has prepared us, such an articulated destruction of the growth of the hero, seems to me a pathetic admission to the reader of the only grounds on which Huck and his society can be brought into a dramatic relationship that will allow the book to end. Huck's illusion—that Tom has now, shockingly, become revolutionary in his use of tricks—does not modify for the reader the inherently distasteful "literary" quality of Tom's procedures. They would reveal a self-indulgent lack of feeling for the effect of tricks on Jim even if they were intended actually to free him.

It is necessary to repeat that this development cannot in any sense represent a surrender by Mark Twain to the genteel tradition. The split implicit in the opening chapters between Huck's narrative and the author's surreptitious metaphorical ordering of it has now become a chasm between worlds. From the remoteness of a confused repudiation, Mark Twain witnesses with as much exasperation as we do the evidence that to remain in the society of the novel at all requires the capitulation that Huck has made to Tom. The author's judgment of Tom at the end is implied in a number of ways that belong to the impersonal metaphoric structure he has created, even while dramatically the novel can only show Huck in his acts of sulking agreement. The metaphoric pattern implies an important degree of similarity between Tom, and the King and the Duke. His tricks, like theirs, are designed to exploit human feeling, while their own feelings are called forth only by artificial stimulation. The King and the Duke can slobber over Shakespeare and their own fabricated melodrama, knowing that their audience will do the same, and Tom can make up epitaphs for Jim ("here a captive heart busted") and be so carried away by his own versions of phrases scrawled on prison walls by such heroes as the Count of Monte Cristo that his "voice trembled, whilst he was reading them, and he most broke down." The three are related even more specifically, however, in their treatment of Jim. In a book so given to parallels, much is implied by the fact that at the end Tom gives Jim forty dollars for playing games with his freedom and that this is precisely the sum paid the King for selling Jim as a runaway. While the parallel is not exact, it is sufficiently indicative of the value to either party of Jim's remaining in bondage, even if in Tom's case the prolonging of his enslavement is in the interest not of economics but of games and adventures.

The style and design of any book trains us as we read to respond in some ways and not others to certain uses of language, to find some kinds of conversation artificial and others natural. It matters very little, therefore, that in some other book the author approves of certain kinds of behavior if in the one we are reading he has managed to make them ambiguously attractive or even reprehensible. *Huckleberry Finn* so insistently educates us to feelings of exasperation about tricks, games, and theatricality that we cannot have learned our lessons and want when we reach the last chapters still to be entertained by Tom's prolonged antics. The uncertainty that one feels, nevertheless, about the intended effect of the concluding scenes results from the fact that the weight of prejudice urged upon us by what precedes so brutally outbalances Tom's innocuous behavior.

Mark Twain's metaphoric rejection of society in this book saps the potential energy of any of the dramatic relationships within it. The effect is apparent in his lassitude and indifference at the end when he shows Huck Finn confronted by the representative members of this society, young or old. Mark Twain's distaste for Tom and Aunt Polly in their final conversation is directed at their characteristically seeing even one another as embodiments of style and as acting out stereotyped roles. What Aunt Polly really wants in Tom is a literary "good-bad boy," so long as his actions are "bad" only as a "good" boy's should be:

> "Then what on earth did you want to set him free for, seeing he was already free?"

"Well, that is a question, I must say; and *just* like women! Why, I wanted the *adventure* of it; and I'd 'a'waded neck-deep in blood to—goodness alive, *Aunt Polly!*"

If she warn't standing right there, just inside the door, looking as sweet and contented as an angel half-full of pie, I wish I may never!

The cloying effect of this passage is obvious. And yet the reaction of the reader to it is strangely muffled by Huck's presentation. It is apparent that he does not respond in the way the book has prepared the reader to respond, and that he is here glaringly unlike the character we have loved and respected earlier in the book. What is most significant, however, is that Mark Twain does not seem to think it matters much that Huck be given any place in the scene at all. His unctuous "angel half-full of pie" and the effeminate exclamation "I wish I may never!" merely scan the scene in terms too abundantly provided by it already. He is merely of the scene, uncritically absorbed into it.

Huck is given back to us at the very end in his declaration of independence, but it is significant that he is re-created primarily in the image of flight, of "lighting out for the Territory ahead of the rest." He is a character who can exist at all only outside the society that the novel allows us to imagine, who can exist in our imagination, finally, only outside the novel itself. Understandably, Huckleberry Finn became for Mark Twain a kind of obsession, appearing in the years that followed in various sketches for stories and sequels to the novel. It is as if his creator wanted yet another chance to find a home, to build a world, to make a place for him. And yet each version only further disfigures the wondrous boy created in the first sixteen chapters of *Huckleberry Finn*.

The career of this character reveals a great deal about the career of Mark Twain and of American literature just before the turn of the century. As Huck Finn gradually disappears from the novel, Mark Twain himself becomes absorbed in social panorama. Santayana's familiar comment about American humorists helps us understand only the preliminary stages of the process: they "only half escape the genteel tradition," he writes, and they cannot abandon it because "they have nothing to put in its place." What interests me in this, as in other instances of uncompleted rebellion in American writing, are the initial struggles in language, struggles which provide in *Huckleberry Finn*, as in other works we've considered, most of their exotic and unforgettable life. And what is still more interesting is that once Mark Twain gives up the struggle to bring Huck to verbal consciousness within his social environment, once he surrenders Huck's consciousness to that environment, he then shows a zestful appetite for environmental delineation. It does not matter that he increasingly came to see the world as the "mysterious stranger" was to see it—as only "the silly creations of an imagination that is not conscious of its freaks." From a literary point of view it is important only that as this attitude took hold of him he became fascinated in the detailed lineaments of what he claimed to find oppressive. In this he predicts and helps define the essential quality of an emerging naturalistic strain in American fiction. His distaste for Jane Austen is an example of the theoretical quality of his distaste for "society"; he was incapable of knowing what the concept could have meant to her. Nonetheless, and despite the condemnation of authorized environments in *Huckleberry Finn*, the novel lavishes energy and attention on the artificial worlds of force, on a spectacular review of them. Huck Finn and his introverted voice are sacrificed to social panorama, the dominant aspect of the last half of the novel and the determining mode of the two novels with which this present study concludes: *Sister Carrie*, published only fifteen years later, and *The House of Mirth*.

MILLICENT BELL

Huckleberry Finn *and the*
Sleights of the Imagination

Like the second half of *Don Quixote*, *Huckleberry Finn* begins with a reference by the hero to his previous existence as a literary character: "You don't know about me, without you have read a book by the name of *The Adventures of Tom Sawyer*, but that ain't no matter. That book was made by Mr. Mark Twain, and he told the truth, mainly. There was things which he stretched, but mainly he told the truth" (p. [17]). It is sometimes thought that this opening is a remnant, merely, of Twain's intention to write a sequel to his earlier success made up out of discarded portions of it, parts he might have eliminated as the book grew into an independent and very different act of the imagination.[1] But the literary self-consciousness introduced by Huck's awareness of his status as fiction is perhaps quite significant. Borges remarks that it disquiets us to know that Don Quixote is a reader of the *Quixote* because "if the characters in a story can be readers or spectators, then we, their readers or spectators, can be fictitious."[2] Making allowance for Borges's particular readiness to see fictionality in existence, we still can take note of the way in which fiction and "life" are mixed as the result of the promotion of character to reader. And as the author, the maker of fictions, becomes the author of what is also "real," we are also reminded of reality's fictionality.

Huckleberry Finn seems to eliminate the author by the superior authority of its hero's first-person narrative. Yet it admits, indeed

From *One Hundred Years of Huckleberry Finn: The Boy, His Book, and American Culture*, eds. Robert Sattelmeyer and J. Donald Crowley. © 1985 by the Curators of the University of Missouri.

incorporates into that pretended reality, a profounder awareness than its predecessor of the role of the imagination in all human gestures. The three opening chapters are, in fact, highly relevant to this awareness, as are the last ten chapters, so often considered a regrettable superfluity that Twain would have done better to eliminate.[3] John C. Gerber has properly identified *Huckleberry Finn* as a "modified frame story" because Tom Sawyer, instead of Huck, is the major character in these opening and concluding sections.[4] Technically, of course, the narration is still Huck's, but Tom's mind is omnipresent in these parts since the action is primarily dictated not only by what Tom does but also by his way of thinking, his version of life. And this version is now felt-as it is not so deeply felt in *Tom Sawyer*—decidedly to be a fiction, a viewpoint that consciously constructs reality into certain formal arrangements. The Tom Sawyer frame serves to prepare the reader to regard what it encloses as also structured by imaginative invention.

We say at once that Tom's imagination is "literary." He represents that side of Twain's own mind that was capable of absorbing a multitude of literary models. Twain recognized in himself, indeed, a tendency to "unconscious plagiarism" and approved the statement of Dumas, "The man of genius does not steal; he conquers; and what he conquers, he annexes to his empire."[5] *The Adventures of Tom Sawyer* has been shown to utilize suggestions and details from literature at every level—from the work of native Southwest or Yankee humorists, from dime novels and melodramas, and from the tradition of belles lettres. Among literary respectables from whom it borrows are Dickens, Charles Reade, Wilkie Collins, and Poe—the grave-robbing scene in the book can be related to an episode in *A Tale of Two Cities*, for example, and the digging for buried treasure to "The Gold Bug." The absorption of literary models and suggestions continues in *Huckleberry Finn*, which uses some of these same sources.[6]

Both works, in being openly imitative of known literary and popular models, tend toward parody, making comment not only on life directly but on other versions of life. In its earliest form as "The Boy's Manuscript," *Tom Sawyer* began, probably, as a literary burlesque, suggested by David Copperfield's courtship of Dora.[7] The suggestion of parody reminds us that what we are reading is itself only another text, another fiction without absolute standing as a version of experience. But *Huckleberry Finn* goes further than *Tom Sawyer* in this direction, as I have said, partly because it also replicates and comments upon its own predecessor by the same author. It reproduces certain situations from the earlier novel—such as Huck's discussion with Tom about the lives of pirates and robbers or the behavior of prisoners—that particularly reflect the conventions of literature. In the context of Huck's narration these discussions become self-conscious references to the art of fiction as practiced by Tom himself as well as by his creator. More covertly than by the direct reference of the opening sentence but still significantly to the recognizing reader who knows the earlier book, the text of *Huckleberry Finn* informs one that it is a text and suggests the textuality of experience.

When we say that Tom Sawyer's imagination is "literary" we also remind ourselves that he is one of the great examples, like Quixote, of the mind saturated with literature almost to the point of delirium. This is true not only because Tom wants to make reality conform to literary models and consciously invokes these models as "authorities" but also because his concept of "style" is the governing, principle that directs his actions. *Style*, after all, is a term only restrictedly applied to art; in a more general sense it is a way of describing human behavior as it approximates some ideal pattern. Tom's preoccupation with form, evident throughout *Tom Sawyer* and still more conspicuous in the portions of *Huckleberry Finn* in which he is present, persists in the "interior" parts of the book where Sawyerism is felt as a continuing presence even though Tom is gone, an element internalized sometimes in Huck himself.

Yet Huck's mind is fundamentally opposed to Tom's, as Sancho's is to Quixote's. Huck has only recently become literate, and his speech is still free of the elegancy or obfuscation induced by written models. Huck's moral imagination is also free, despite the "deformed conscience"[8] that seems to overwhelm it from time to time. His "primitive" responses to experience have no available justification or even name; they remain outside the patterns of approved social value and of language as well. Yet his personal speech, the governing voice of the book, is as near a literary equivalence of his existential ethic as it is possible to imagine, a miracle of the emergence of validity out of the unlearned powers of mind and the least refutable aspects of perception.

Huckleberry Finn's colloquial autobiographical mode effected, of course, an alteration in the relation between language and literature in our culture. It converted an oral-comic tradition, previously employable only in sub-literature or journalism, to the highest literary ends. After Twain, in fact, there is no longer any reason to distinguish between low and high styles at all. But the immediate impact of this novel derived from the fact that the distinction, at the time of its writing, was still a powerful one. Colloquial speech, the speech of a half-educated country person, was adapted in this unclassifiable prose to ends that proved serious, even "poetic" in an unprecedented way. Yet, because of its thrust against the traditional mode for such expression, it was felt to be subversive. This historic subversiveness had obvious objects: literary genteelism, to begin with—but literary genteelism was linked in Twain's mind with the social pretensions of aristocracies in general and with the self-justifications of a defunct Southern aristocracy in particular. Twain, connecting styles of life and language he judged equally dishonest, related the false dignity and claims of refinement of the slaveowners to their defensive rhetoric. He thought there were particular sources for both in literature itself, specifically in the novels of Sir Walter Scott, which he accused of poisoning literature with "wordy, windy, flowery 'eloquence,' romanticism, sentimentality" and with bringing on the Civil War.[9]

We only faintly sense this political motive in *Huckleberry Finn*'s stylistic innovation. But, a hundred years later, we can still perceive how the book opposes all aspects of *any* dominant culture with what Henry Nash Smith has called the "vernacular attitude."[10] Twain's skepticism seems wholesale and modernist. His suspicions that all social forms—not merely American Southern aristocratic ones—might be impositions had already begun to surface in this, his greatest work. Eventually they would reach that nihilism visible in the writings of his last years which belong so clearly to our own century. It is this total distrust of received values and meanings that earlier had energized his propensity to satire and burlesque of any and every propriety. Nor do Twain's biographers stress irrelevantly the fiasco of the *Atlantic Monthly* Whittier dinner in 1876,[11] when Twain was working on the early chapters of the novel. On this occasion, to his own chagrin, some inner demon caused him to hold up to ridicule those distinguished fellow guests and cultural idols, Longfellow, Holmes, and Emerson. Twain's mockery knew its own ultimate objects despite his "deformed" inner censor.

Huckleberry Finn expresses this same irreverence filtered through Huck's innocent humorlessness. To every cultural or social pretension, the novel's mode of narration opposes an anti-stylistic style. Scrupulously pruned of rhetoric, reduced in syntax and vocabulary to simple elements of plain statement, Huck's first-person retrospection appears, in the best passages of the book, to be artless. It is nothing of the sort, of course, but it was *designed* to seem so, to convey the effect of spontaneity because the spontaneous, the untutored, was a value to be set against that which surrounded it, the behavior patterns and language dominant in the culture and expressing its bad faiths. Devoid of literary and social preconceptions, this pseudo-oral style was made to seem the direct record of honest sensation and feeling.

This subversion of "style" as such is part of a general antiformal impulse in the work. We should, I think, take with utmost seriousness Twain's notice to the reader: "persons attempting to find a moral in it will be banished; persons attempting to find a plot in it will be shot" (p. [5]). Twain discarded quite deliberately the apocalyptic fictional form long dominant in the novel and drew instead on an early, looser model, the picaresque, with its license to disjunctive, open-ended narrative and to a hero who does not develop as his history progresses. The correspondences of *Huckleberry Finn* with *Don Quixote* are less fundamental than one might suppose, despite the obvious parallels.[12] Cervantes's view of Quixote is more complex than Twain's view of Tom; Huck is very different from the pragmatic Sancho. But the "open form" resulting from what Robert M. Adams calls an "unresolved tension" between Cervantes's pair[13] may have provided a suggestive design along with adapted details. Twain himself, we know, greatly approved the Spanish classic and contrasted it, in the passage in *Life on the Mississippi* already referred to, with Scott's *Ivanhoe*, because it "swept the world's admiration, for medieval chivalry-silliness out of existence,"[14] while *Ivanhoe* restored it. In his own attack on the same delusions, he may even have identified himself with Cervantes but been influenced more than he was aware by the subtle rejection of resolution that makes the Spanish masterpiece so different from such a work as Scott's.

The title of Twain's book expresses the fact that Huck has "adventures," has, that is, engagements with change, and that the incidents he relates are not caused by him and do not change him. Of course, we are tempted to think that something else is going on, despite the picaresque form, for *Huckleberry Finn* does more with its hero than conduct him, in the picaresque way, through the layers of his society, so revealing them to us. The work does not seem to be a comic journey without goal, for Huck appears to "grow," like the hero of tragedy, as he passes along the stages of his downriver voyage with Jim. We are even likely to see in his experience one of the standard patterns of the novel of character, the penetration of illusion, the coming to maturity through trial, of the youthful protagonist. But reading the book in this way brings us up (with a cry of critical anguish, generally) against the ending. For if Huck *has* changed and grown, if we have really gone somewhere with him, what is the meaning of that return, in the Phelps Farm chapters to the exact conditions of the opening when he is enrolled in Tom Sawyer's band of make-believe robbers and Jim is merely the object of a boyish practical joke?

It is my contention that we must understand *Huckleberry Finn* in some other way than as a novel of development—and that still the book is "serious." It expresses not only Twain's view of his own society but also his understanding of human life in general as a condition of precarious continuity in which identity is maintained only by our willingness to accept definition of ourselves from the norms of society and the expectations of others. Huck's experiments with freedom, the sloughing off of old habits of thought and action, are the experiments of utopia, the utopia of the raft.

That utopia cannot survive on the shore, which finally even invades and destroys the raft itself. Huck's adventures involve him in the greatest risk because of their continued invitation not so much to the discovery of a new self as to the loss of membership altogether in human society, the source of all role and ail selfhood. It is no accident that the narrative is permeated by references to death and by the narrator's own death thoughts, lyric moments in which he seems ready to surrender selfhood altogether, to merge with the flow of natural forces that bear him onward, not to any landing where he and Jim can continue as they are, but toward a sea of silence.[15]

If indeed the plot of *Huckleberry Finn* can thus be described as an antiplot, a frustration of our expectations of development and consequence, it may suggest that life in general may not possess inherent design. Plot, character, formal closure, even "theme" are, after all, ways of saying that life has inherent form. If these can be seen as the inventions of the human imagination, we are reminded that life is not, after all, a coherent story and that we can only pretend that we know who we are. This, of course, is itself a statement, a theme, and perhaps *Huckleberry Finn*, while undermining more obvious themes, leaves this one on our hands.

The mark of such an intention is the obsessive stress in the book on the games literature plays in imposing its designs upon life and the interpretation of social forms as games perfectly analogous to the games of literature. The Phelps Farm coda is distinguished from what has gone before only because the emphasis on language and literature—present earlier too—takes over completely from the social and psychological interests that are finally revealed in all their desolating vacuity as make-believe. It is indeed a pessimistic reduction from the previous richness of Huck's moral effort and hope. His story-telling is over now, subdued to Tom's art-for-art's-sake view of life as an aesthetic opportunity. Huck escapes at the very end with a vow of silence, "If I'd a knowed what a trouble it was to make a book I wouldn't a tackled it and ain't agoing to no more" (p. 366): Tom's art prevails and survives, however; his is the unresting imagination forever generating roles for himself and others out of the conventions of society and the formulas of literature.

As I shall try to show, the literary imagination, chiefly identified with Tom at the start as at the end, comes to stand for all lies imposed by social life. But what forms of social life are not lies? The literary imagination is the enemy of Huck's existential freedom and yet, paradoxically, it is the only means of his survival. His adventures, even when he is separated from Tom—as he is for most of the story—involve him in the play-acting, the charades and deceits of other: an assortment of characters who represent both the respectable and the disreputable in society. Only the private life established between Huck and Jim on the raft is free from such deceits, though Huck can play games that make "trash" out of Jim's feelings in the early stages of their relationship and though he subscribes to society's cruel fiction that a human being can be regarded as a piece of property. But even more benignly Huck is compelled in his contacts with a lying society to resort to life-saving fictions; Huck's own fertility of self-invention produces a succession of impersonations that both express, in a symbolic mode, his orphanhood and peril and combat the destructive designs of society. Thus, the descent in tone, the tedious burlesque of the ending with its emphasis on game-playing pure and simple, is anticipated in the whole of the work more than critics have been willing to admit. The Phelps chapters are not so much an anticlimax as consistent with much that has gone before.

The ending also implies a cyclicity rather than a linearity in experience, for though Huck initially resists the seductions and sleights of Tom's imagination, he submits to the forms of respectability, agrees to go to live with the Widow Douglas, as the price of that same membership in the gang, joining the make-believe of society and of the gang at the same time. It is clear that respectability, membership in societies, is the same in both the larger world of adults and the imaginative world of the boys. The final paragraph tells us that he will be joining Tom for new adventures over in the Territory but will somehow manage to evade Aunt Sally's intention to adopt and "sivilize" him. Yet we cannot help seeing here only the temporary rebellion and self-exile that had preceded his original submission in the first chapter. Tom's price will be the same as before. The whole narrative, indeed, exhibits a continuation of such resistances and returns, and anticipates the end. One may mention, for example, Huck's decision not to oppose the pretenses of the Duke and the Dauphin "'long as it would keep peace in the family" (p. 166), recognizing as he does that lies are somehow the very essence of social cohesion.

There is no real difference, it is plain at the start, between the making-up of reality by the gang and the Bible stories Huck is told by the widow. He loses interest in the latter when he learns that "Moses had been dead a considerable long time ... because I don't take no stock in dead people" (p. 18). He finds that religion asks him to interest himself in either an imagined past or an imagined future, Miss Watson's theology leaves him cold: "All I wanted was to go somewheres: all I wanted was a change, I warn't particular" (p. 19). Tom's preference for art over nature exhibits itself just as promptly and just as bewilderingly to Huck. On the night of their first escapade he wants to tie the sleeping Jim to a tree "for fun" until Huck points out that this would wake him, but still "nothing would do Tom but he must crawl to where Jim was, on his hands and knees, and play something on him" (p. 23).

This "play" is the first of the three practical jokes inflicted on Jim during the course of the story, the first of the three impositions of fancy that become increasingly dangerous until Huck rejects all such games as a way of dealing with his friend. A staple of American humor that Twain himself found detestable, the practical joke is essentially a fiction, a made-up explanation of appearances intended to deceive and when the deception is disclosed to embarrass the victim. Jim's own self-seduction by fantasy collaborates here when he finds his hat hung on a tree to make him think that he has been acted upon by witches and is then tempted himself into extravagances of story-telling as he develops an account of what happened in more and more fanciful versions. Story-telling thus begets more story-telling.

The inspiration for Tom's robber-band is openly literary. Tom's "beautiful oath" to which all must swear comes, he admits, only in part "out of his own head," the rest "out of pirate books, and robber books" (p. 26). Tom—or Twain—draws, in fact, on sources as diverse as Carlyle's *History of the French Revolution*, Dickens's *A Tale of Two Cities*, and Robert Montgomery Bird's *Nick of the Woods* for details here.[16] The fidelity to formula is, indeed, compulsive: Huck is almost excluded because he hasn't a family to be killed if he tells the gang's secrets. The business of the gang is routine, "*only* robbery and murder" (emphasis mine), but it is no mere unimaginative burglary: "We ain't burglars. That ain't no sort of style," says Tom. "We are highwaymen. We stop stages and carriages on the road, with masks on, and kill the people and take their watches and money" (pp. 26–27). "Killing people" is part of the prescription for proper style, except perhaps when the robbers hold their captives for ransom, a variation permitted by some "authorities," which is to say, by some texts. Tom doesn't really know what the word *ransom* means, and when Ben Rogers says, "Why can't a body take a club and ransom them as soon as they get here," he answers, "Because it ain't in the books so—that's why" (p. 67).

After a month of playing robber, Huck and the other boys resign from the gang. Realists, they tire of fancy: "We hadn't robbed nobody, we hadn't killed any people, but only just pretended" (p. 30). Tom alone retains the taste for calling things what they are not—only for him are hogs "ingots," turnips "julery." The attack upon a camp of Spanish merchants and A-rabs "warn't anything but a Sunday-school picnic, and only a primer-class at that" (pp. 31–32). When challenged about wonders the others fail to see, Tom refers Huck to *Don Quixote* and explains that "enchantment" had converted the A-rabs and elephants into picnickers. Tom is thus explicitly identified with Cervantes's hero, and the twist of logic that makes him argue that *appearances* are what is unreal suggests that the consequence of believing in the reality of fantasy is, as Borges (in the remark quoted earlier) observes, that one must suspect the fantasy of reality. So, Huck tries to work the enchantment himself by rubbing an old tin lamp, "calculating to build a palace and sell it," but he gets nowhere: "all that stuff was only just one of Tom Sawyer's lies" (p. 33). It is a famous deflation of the literary imagination at its game of reversing the relation between fancy and fact, a game more serious than it seems at this early point, for though we can laugh easily at the harmless nature of Tom's play-acting, more serious fictions upon which society's very existence bases itself—such as racial inequality—will soon be posing as reality.

Huck himself is getting used to the artifices of society, though various signs tell him that Pap—the demon presence behind the fine appearance of the social world—is around. Then Pap appears, the destroyer, it would seem at first, of all civilized lies, with a particular hatred for literature; Huck is reading about George Washington when the old man whacks the book out of his hand and shouts, "First you know you'll get religion, too" (p. 40), correctly—from Twain's point of view—connecting the fictions of history and religious belief. But, of course, Pap is no real enemy of these things—he is the Master of Lies, expert in his own right in all pretenses and fabrications sanctified by social usage. Gaining the sympathy of the judge by enacting the convention of father-love, he takes him in further by his parody of "reform." Pap is really a subscriber to society's formulas, for all his seeming unregeneracy—as his drunken reproaches to Huck that he has been cheated of the due rewards of fatherhood and his denunciations of the state of Ohio for letting a "nigger" vote both illustrate. He is, in fact, the wicked soul of conventionality, his hypocrisy simply more blatant still than that of respectable society.

Huck makes his escape from both respectable and disreputable versions of constraint, from the Widow and Pap, by a device of make-believe, his own faked murder. On the one hand this is symbolically veracious and life-saving; Huck must "die to" an old life in order to reach for freedom, and this reaching must threaten to extinguish the sense of self by which one survives in society. It can be contrasted with the theatrics of Pap that precipitate it— Pap's drunken delusion that Huck is the "Angel of Death." But Huck is right to recognize, on the other hand that he is engaging himself, out of necessity, in the very mode he is bidding farewell to, the mode of fiction-making. He acknowledges that his is an inferior achievement to what Tom might have devised: "I did wish Tom Sawyer was there, I knowed he would take an interest in this kind of business. and throw in the fancy touches" (p. 57). Yet henceforth such story-telling as Huck engages in will, for the most part, be enforced by the necessity, paradoxically, of keeping himself free from the world of social lies or of protecting Jim from its designs.

Only occasionally is he afterward tempted to regress to idle, mischievous make-believe. The second practical joke on Jim, the snakeskin laid at the foot of his bed, brings the dead snake's mate to bite Jim on the heel. Jim thinks that bad luck has been invoked, but Huck knows that the misfortune has been brought on not by handling the snakeskin as such but by his own undisciplined impulse toward "fun." Then directly, Huck must himself, again, needfully make-believe to find out the state of things in St. Petersburg, and he goes onshore as a girl, with a tale of a sick mother needing help. Detected as a boy, he is quick with another tale—this one of a runaway orphan bound to a mean, old farmer—and is believed, his story-telling thus having served the function of keeping him safe from discovery while truly in this second case, representing his condition of orphanhood and flight.

He is tempted again by the lure of motiveless "adventure," the distractions so often offered him by Tom, who is, in this sense, still present within him when he goes aboard the wrecked steamboat despite Jim's misgivings. He is thinking of Tom, indeed, as he says to himself, "wouldn't [Tom] throw style into it?" (p. 97). His reproof is the harrowing sight of the murderers aboard the wreck and the loss, temporarily, of the raft—admonishment, as after the snakeskin trick, of the consequence of idle fancy. To do what he can for the murderers, now trapped on the sinking vessel, he resorts to another invented story to the ferryboat watchman, trying to rescue them by his tale as he had tried to safeguard himself and Jim by his tales to Mrs. Loftus, for, as he says, "there ain't no telling but I might come to be a murderer myself" (p. 103). But imagination cannot work its life-saving magic this time, and the vessel sinks before help can come.

She is called, of course, the *Walter Scott*, and with her, taking this opportunity to mock once more the novel's antimodel, Twain sinks Huck's appetite for romance. As for Jim, he "didn't want no more adventures," the word now signifying Tom Sawyer-style escapades, and Huck concludes, "he was right; he was most always right; he had an uncommon level head, for a nigger" (p. 109). Part of the "truck" they have carried off from the *Walter Scott* is, not surprisingly, "a lot of books," from which the recently literate Huck reads to Jim—"about kings, and dukes, and earls, and such" (p. 109)—and they discuss the ways of such fabulous beings. They also discuss the ways of the greatest of Old Testament kings, Solomon, who wanted to cut a baby in half, and Jim thinks him plagued by the "dad-fetchedes' ways" (p. 111) he has ever seen. Jim scores, too, over Huck's book-learning by "proving," with irrefutable logic, that although cats and dogs "talk" differently, Frenchmen and Americans must talk alike. All this conversation may seem simply a comic interval between significant action unless we realize its import—Jim, the illiterate and even more alienated refugee from society, must teach Huck the futility of the "truck" of notions he has rescued from the sinking vessel of his social membership.

It is at this point, however, when the raft and the canoe are separated in the fog, that Huck loses Jim, his instructor in pragmatic wisdom. When he finds him again, he has forgotten what he learned about idle story-telling and plays the third of his practical jokes on Jim, pretending never to have been gone at all, even though Jim has worried solely about him. Jim's reproach, his reduction of cruel fantasy to truth, is telling: "Dat truck dah is trash; en trash is what people is dat puts dirt on de head er dey fren's en makes 'em ashamed" (p. 121). Again the word *truck* stands for the useless—and sometimes dangerous—freight of lies that even the raft is carrying, as the *Walter Scott* had, something that is no better than "trash." Huck's apology, as every reader notes, is a giant step in his moral progress. It also represents his resolution to dispense with Tom-Sawyer-foolery. He will tell no more false tales, unless he has to, to save life. So, he immediately lies again, but only for this reason, with a lie that is better than the truth he intended to tell the men with guns who are on the lookout for runaway slaves. Not even Tom could have improved upon his suggestion, by implication, that his family is afflicted with smallpox. That he does not actually say this—but leaves the specification to the imagination of the bounty-hunters, is probably significant; Huck's restraint is more than strategic, for it may represent his disinclination, now, for elaborating even necessary fictions.

Again separated from Jim when the steamboat collides with the raft. Huck must once more reinvent himself as "George Jackson," just fallen off the steamboat, a fiction of orphaning symbolically justifiable. But it is not Huck who is the source of the engulfing and ultimately murderous fiction of the Grangerfords, whose adopted son this orphan becomes. At first he is delighted to find himself in such a fine family, one so completely equipped with all the standard appurtenances and practiced in the appropriate rituals of gentility. Huck has never before seen a house that has "so much style" (p. 136), so many objects too elegant to function, like the mantel clock, with the picture of a town painted on it and a beautiful tick, which would "start in and strike a hundred and fifty before she got tuckered out" (p. 137) after a traveling peddler repaired it, or the crockery basket filled with painted plaster fruit. Indeed, the house is all style without substance, filled with what might be called stage-props rather than realities.

Of course, the Grangerfords possess books. There is *Pilgrim's Progress*, which Huck summarizes, in his ignorance, as "about a man that left his family it didn't say why" (p. 137), a Bible, a gift-book annual full of poetry, a home medical manual, Henry Clay's speeches, and a hymn book. The collection is ironically significant, as Walter Blair has pointed out, enforcing "the evidence of fraudulent pretense"[17] in the Grangerford way of life. Though they subscribe to "Friendship's Offering," though they possess the religious texts that instruct one to love one's neighbor, though they can learn from the medical volume how to treat the injured and save life, the Grangerfords inhabit a house of hatred and death where the most powerful feeling is enmity for one's neighbor and a desire to injure and destroy him. And in this family of fictionizers there has even been one literary creator, the lamented Emmeline, whose grotesquely sentimental verses and drawings not only parody a tradition of false art but also demonstrate the falsifying artifice of Grangerford being.

For in this House of Fiction, the greatest fiction of all is the Grangerford family itself. At the Grangerfords', social behavior is as ritualized as the ceremonies of Tom Sawyer's band, got up from the best authorities. The fine manners and high principles, like the accumulations of artifacts in their house, are as much a fiction as are the practices of the make-believe boy-robbers, as much a structure of the imagination unrelated to reality. But, unlike the boys' games, the Grangerfords' pretenses are not for fun; the feud will become murderous and cost the lives of all the male members of the clan, even down to young Buck. Buck, save for a letter of his name, is Huck himself, who is nearly dead with horror as he witnesses the slaughter of his twin. But Buck, because of his implication in the gang-war of the adults, is also that other brother to Huck, his friend Tom, the young knight of pretenses and the willing collaborator in the social game.

Huck escapes this death of self and the imagination by the narrowest squeak and reaches the eden, once more, of the raft. But it is soon invaded by those final virtuosi of story-telling, the Duke and the Dauphin. They are, even more obviously than the Grangerfords, literary fabricators, conscious tellers of tales, inventors of false identity. These scoundrels perpetrate frauds that are parodies of social roles, dramatic impersonations behind which no definable selfhood or meaningful history exists. When first encountered each has got into trouble for a false tale—one for vending a dentifrice that really melts the enamel off teeth, the other for running a temperance revival while swigging the jug on the sly. The first soon tells his story of his descent from the Duke of Bridgewater, only to have it immediately topped by the other's claim to be Louis the Seventeenth, the lost Dauphin. It doesn't take Huck long to discern that the liars "warn't no kings nor dukes at all, but just low-down humbugs and frauds," but he raises no fuss, understanding by this time that society is sustained, peace is kept in the family, by lying tales. "If I never learnt nothing else out of Pap," Huck observes, "I learnt that the best way to get along with his kind of people is to let them have their own way" (p. 166).

The Duke and the Dauphin, then, are replications of his own terrible father, representatives of the deceitful, pretending, and enslaving parent-culture to which, for the sake of family peace, Huck has learned to accommodate himself.

To protect Jim, whom the scoundrels immediately suspect of being a runaway slave, Huck must still another time subdue himself to the mode of pretense and tell his false identity tale (in which he is again, so truly, the orphan with no one but Jim to cling to). But the Duke soon devises new identities for Jim, supposedly also meant for protection but really bringing him into closer correspondence with the endangering condition of criminal and racial outcast, printing his picture on a "Reward" poster to be used when they want to claim him as their captive or making him up to represent a "sick Arab." None of the Duke and the Dauphin's lies can have any effect, in the end, but destruction—it is they who soon enough will collect a forty-dollar reward for turning Jim in.

The inventions of the Duke and the Dauphin elaborate Twain's ridicule of the formulas of society. Religion, the object of satiric contempt in almost everything Twain wrote from *Innocents Abroad* to *The Mysterious Stranger*, is immediately represented not only by the campmeeting sermon but also by the King's pose as repentant pirate, itself reminiscent of Pap's earlier posturing as repentant sinner. At the Wilks funeral, again, the false piety of society at large is only echoed by the hypocrisy of the King posing as the preacher uncle from Sheffield. The funeral sermon of the Reverend Hobson is less significant to his audience than the racket of the dog who has caught a rat in the cellar of the house, and at the auction of the Wilks property the King is on hand, "looking his level piousest ... chipping in a little Scripture, now and then, or a little goody-goody saying" (p. 249) to the general edification.

But the most significant pretenses of the Duke and the Dauphin are parodic of language itself. The garbled Shakespeare speeches may seem tedious unless we realize that Twain has undercut the dignity of the most profound passages by mixing lines that almost coalesce; all coherence is mocked when one's ear is lulled into accepting the false connectedness of "To be or not to be; that is the bare bodkin / That makes calamity of so long life" (p. 179), and so on. Similarly, the coherence of history is a little later made ridiculous by Huck when he undertakes to explain to Jim that "kings is mostly rapscallions" (p. 199), mixing the Domesday Book and the Arabian Nights, the lives of Henry VIII and the Duke of Wellington, and conflating the mistresses of Henry II, Edward IV, and Charles II.

The question of language as the source of deceits and fictions is crucial, and Twain seems willing to turn even upon the colloquial style he has reserved for Huck's monologue and to show that it, too, can be the container of corruption and conventionality. At Bricksville, that devastating second look at St. Petersburg, the common men who exchange their banalities as they lounge along the filthy main street are quite deserving of the contempt of Colonel Sherburn who, like another Grangerford, has shot down the drunken lout Boggs out of offended dignity. The lecture he delivers to the crowd that thinks it wants to lynch him is couched in a style as formally correct as it is coldly superior in logic and truth to that of his hearers. But the Duke and the Dauphin are capable of parodying all styles, high and low. Their final caper, the attempt to fleece the Wilks family, exhibits them as polite gentlemen from the birthplace of the idea of the gentleman, old England, while constantly revealing, as though through the rents in their shoddy costumes their true coarseness. The speeches of the King—"tears and flapdoodle" (p. 212), as Huck says—are never more deliciously comic versions of the rhetoric of high occasions than when they focus on a malapropism, his use of the word *orgies*. When he even offers a pseudo-etymology to justify it, Huck declares, "He was the worst I ever struck" (p. 217). Yet their imperfect command of their roles proves their undoing, for it is their speech that distinguishes them from the genuine English relatives and gives the cue to Doctor Robinson.

To foil the plotters Huck must rouse himself from his customary passivity and, devising a plot himself, make a confidante of Mary Jane so that she may witness to the truth after he has escaped. He knows that his plot is in the Tom Sawyer mode, but beneath Tom's purity of impracticality and superfluous style. "I judged I had done it pretty neat—I reckoned Tom Sawyer couldn't a done it no neater himself," says Huck, though he admits, "Of course he would a throwed more style into it, but I can't do that very handy, not being brung up to it" (pp. 248–49). His stratagem has rested on truth rather than falsity, an unorthodox procedure indeed As he reflects after his revelation to Mary Jane:

> I reckon a body that ups and tells the truth when he is in a tight place, is taking considerable many risks, though I ain't had no experience, and can't say for certain; but it looks so to me, anyway; and yet here's a case where I'm blest if it don't look to me like the truth is better, and actuly *safer* than a lie. l must lay it by in my mind, and think it over some time or other, it's so kind of strange and unregular. I never see nothing like it. Well, I says to myself at last, I'm agoing to chance it; I'll up and tell the truth this time, though it does seem most like setting down on a kag of powder and touching it off just to see where you'll go to. (p. 240)

To tell the truth—not to "make up a story"—is, of course, to deny the superiority of fiction to fact, to deny the validity of pretense, to deny Tom Sawyer. Huck's resolution to dispense with falsehood this time fills him with misgiving, goes against his sense of what he ought to do, and is a crisis in which his heart triumphs over his conscience, anticipating the more famous crisis that immediately follows. Before this happens he turns, ineptly, to lying again, trying to describe life in the pretended English home of the fake Wilks uncles and himself, and Levi Bell, the lawyer, observes, "I reckon you ain't used to lying, it don't seem to come handy; what you want is practice. You do it pretty awkward" (p. 254).

He makes his most famous repudiation of lying when he discovers that he cannot pretend to himself that he wants to turn Jim in: "You can't pray a lie" (p. 70), he observes, and, though he proceeds to write the letter to Miss Watson, he decides to damn himself and "steal Jim out of slavery again" (p. 272), and so tears up the letter. Paradoxically, he is full of inventive ingenuity on behalf of the truth to which he has committed himself and successfully talks his way out of obstruction by the two knaves as he makes his way to the Phelps Farm—he must still resort to life-saving fiction to combat a world of lies.

When he arrives at the Phelps Farm in Chapter 32, he is once again in one of those moods of melancholy transcendence to which I have referred and even wishes himself dead as the breeze whispering of dead spirits quivers the leaves. And he is ready for his last relapse into the character of Tom Sawyer, ready to accept Tom's name and serve Tom's imagination. His own existential truthfulness, his independence of the lies and the fictions of the social world, must be surrendered. But if what I have been maintaining is true, we should not be surprised. The last ten chapters are no reversal, after all. If Huck is to survive he must reattach himself to his world and to its lies, fabricate the self out of them. At this moment, indeed, Huck is, for once, without a prepared selfhood. He is a ghost without a name, listening to the words of others for a cue to his identity: "I wanted to get them [the children] out to one side, and pump them a little, and find out who I was" (p. 281). When he is at last "recognized" as Tom, he is overjoyed: "if they was joyful, it warn't nothing to what I was; for it was like being born again. I was so glad to find out who I was.... Being Tom Sawyer was easy and comfortable" (pp. 282–83). The exhausting struggle for free formlessness of being is over, and he is easy and comfortable in the role of the inventor of fictional selves and stories, Tom Sawyer.

Tom himself greets Huck as an impersonating ghost and warns him, "Don't you play nothing on me, because I wouldn't on you" (p. [284]), which is a joke, we will realize, for Tom is about to "play" a joke on Huck—one of those practical jokes that hurt—to pretend to be a "nigger-stealer," willing to help him free Jim, It is Tom's deception underlying all the deceptions the boys will now practice together upon others. Meanwhile, he welcomes Huck back, in effect, to the robber-band. He is full of praise when he hears how Huck made his escape from Pap by the faked murder: "I warn't ever murdered at all—I played it on them," says Huck with some pride, suggesting by "them" some vaguely general social audience. Tom calls Huck's story, "a grand adventure, and mysterious" (p. 285). As Huck says, "it hit him where he lived" (p. 285).

So, under the rule of Tom's imagination, made-up history, appearance as costume, and theatrical improvisation all flourish. Tom pretends to be someone else before he assumes the "true" (but really still false) identity of Sid. When the Phelpses see him at their door, says Huck, he has "his store clothes on, and an audience—and that was always nuts for Tom Sawyer. In them circumstances it warn't no trouble to him to throw in an amount of style that was suitable" (p. 286). So, first he claims to be William Thompson, a young traveler from Hicksville. Ohio—which then appears to be one of those practical jokes so relished by the Sawyer imagination when he "reveals" himself to Aunt Sally as Sid. She declares, "I'd be willing to stand a thousand such jokes to have you here Well, to think of that performance" (p. 289), not realizing that "Sid's" disclosure is but another layer of performance. Unlike Huck's disguises, Tom's are prompted not by need but by his insatiable appetite for histrionics.

Sleights and disguises are all, indeed, that we will ever get from Tom, who is not, when finally revealed as himself, ever reduced to a final essence, an unalterable core, since he is always precisely no more than what he appears. Huck is awed as Tom begins to develop schemes for the liberation of Jim, and he yearns to complete his own submergence in the mode of the protean imagination, already signaled by the adoption of Tom's name: "if I had Tom Sawyer's head, I wouldn't trade it off to be a duke, nor mate of a steamboat, nor clown in a circus, nor nothing I can think of" (p. 294). No particular role can offer more delight than the artist's, for his is the capacity to impersonate all roles. For the artist there is, really, no "authenticity."

Huck realizes that his own capacity for creating plot is rudimentary compared to Tom's. His plan for freeing Jim has the defect of mere functionality (as Tom says, "it's too blame' simple; there ain't nothing to it"), whereas Tom's own, Huck says, "was worth fifteen of mine, for style, and would make Jim just as free a man as mine would, and maybe get us all killed besides" (p. 294). The fantasy that entails real danger, even the threat of death, is the best of all, as Tom had long before pointed out to his boy-robber companions when he insisted that they were highwaymen who "killed people" and could get killed themselves, and not mere burglars. The Grangerford fantasy proved its excellence by its murderous—and suicidal— consequences. And this elegant plan of Tom's will nearly get Jim and themselves killed, as it turns out.

When Huck suggests with plain practicality that Jim escape through the cabin window, Tom reproaches him, "I should *hope* we can find a way that's a little more complicated than *that*, Huck Finn," and proposes that they dig the prisoner out. At the house, the back-door fastened by a latch-string "warn't romantic enough for Tom Sawyer: no way would do him but he must climb up the lightning-rod" (p. 297). Tom is actually distressed by the altogether too "easy and awkward" conditions they confront—"It makes it so rotten difficult to get up a difficult plan. There ain't no watchman to be drugged—now there *ought* to be a watchman. There ain't even a dog to give a sleeping-mixture to. And there's Jim chained by one leg, with a ten-foot chain, to the leg of his bed: why, all you got to do is lift up the bedstead and slip off the chain" (p. [300]).

The absence of the conventional plot ingredients enforces artistic creation: "You got to invent *all* the difficulties." But the more to be invented the more honor to the artistic imagination: "there's more honor in getting him out through a lot of difficulties and dangers, where there warn't one of them furnished you by the people who it was their duty to furnish them, and you had to contrive them all out of your own head" (p. 301). Of course, getting them out of one's own literary head means getting them from the "best authorities" and examples—among whom Tom names Baron Trenck, Casanova, Cellini, King Henry IV of France, and Dumas's *The Man in the Iron Mask* and *The Count of Monte Cristo*, getting the idea for titling his escapade on "evasion" from Dumas's *L'Évasion du Duc de Beaufort*. Tom is proud to claim an authority for everything—the rope ladder that Jim has to hide in his bed, the "journal" that Jim must write on his shirt, though he can't write, and so on.

When Tom finally agrees to use pick and shovel instead of case knives to dig Jim out, he admits it isn't moral, reversing the sense of *morality* to make it mean aesthetic impracticality, inefficacy. Huck's stubborn anti-aesthetic immorality (as Tom would judge it) makes him insist, "Picks is the thing, moral or no moral; and as for me, I don't care shucks for the morality of it, nohow. When I start in to steal a nigger, or a watermelon, or a Sunday-school book, I ain't no ways particular how it's done so it's done. What I want is my nigger; or what I want is my watermelon; or what I want is my Sunday-school book; and if a pick's the handiest thing, that's the thing I'm agoing to dig that nigger or that watermelon or that Sunday-school book out with; and I don't give a dead rat what the authorities thinks about it nuther" (p. 310).

Morality here is absolutely synonymous with *conscience* as Huck has used the latter word, the "deformed" conscience of social modes that reproves the instinctive promptings of his heart.

Even Tom must yield, somewhat, to the practical, though in that case the pretense of impracticality must be maintained. Picks must be thought of as case knives and stairs as the lightning rod it is really too difficult to climb. But wherever possible the complications of imagination are to be preferred to the merely efficacious, especially if the former are *less* efficacious. Jim, who could be freed by the quick application of a cold chisel to his shackles, must be subjected to the tedious, the distressing, even the dangerous devices of Sawyerism. "Tom was in high spirits. He said it was the best fun he ever had in his life, and the most intellectural; and said if he only could see his way to it we would keep it up all the rest of our lives and leave Jim to our children to get out" (p. 313). Jim must be a proper literary prisoner, with tools or rope ladders smuggled to him in a pie, must scratch inscriptions and a coat of arms on the wall, and must adopt a pet rat and plant a garden, however incomprehensible these things are to him. And the Phelps household must be thrown into confusion by the disappearance of sheets and shirts and spoons and the escape of the rats and snakes the boys have collected. It is all almost as tiresome to the reader as it is to Jim himself, and even to Huck.

The warnings and anonymous letters that Tom now insists upon prove, however, the source not merely of "style" but of near disaster, though perhaps one should say that high style requires a flouting of the utilitarian to the point of a deadly indifference. Jim and his two liberators make it to the raft despite the real pursuit they have generated, and even Jim must admit, "It 'uz planned beautiful, en it 'uz *done* beautiful; en dey ain't *nobody* kin git up a plan dat's mo' mixed-up en splendid den what dat one wuz." Tom himself is positively delighted that make-believe has almost had fatal consequences: "Tom was the gladdest of all, because he had a bullet in the calf of his leg" (p. 344). "Boys," he says, "we done it elegant!" (p. 344) Tom is consistent enough to instruct that the doctor now needed must be kidnapped and brought blindfolded, but Huck is practical enough to employ his own lower kind of make-believe in a story about a brother hurt in a hunting accident. This tale, though not very convincing, is a correct and consistent summary of what actually happened: "He had a dream," Huck tells the doctor, "and it shot him." And the doctor comments, "Singular dream" (p. [347]). Indeed, dreams or fictions play real and sometimes dire roles in our lives, as the dreams of the Grangerfords and Shepherdsons have already done in the novel, or, as Twain probably thought, the dreams of North and South had done in the country's recent history.

Yet, now that the Evasion is ending, Huck is ready to be reconciled to the dreams by which life sustains itself. Aunt Sally, it seems, is much nicer than the widow, though the cyclicity of the plot tells us that she is really a duplication of that matriarchal authority from which he has been in flight. Huck cannot stand any longer the deception he has practiced on her and swears to himself that he "wouldn't never do nothing to grieve her any more" (p. 354). Society now offers him its most self-flattering versions of itself. Though Jim is put back into chains, he is acknowledged, after the doctor's report, to be "a nigger ... worth a thousand dollars—and kind treatment, too," and the Phelpses take one or two of his chains off and let him have meat and greens with his bread and water. Huck no longer thinks of Jim's freedom—or of his own.

So it is time for Tom's revelation that Jim has been free all along because of Miss Watson's will. It does not matter that her death-bed repentance for her resolution to sell him downriver is blatantly improbable, a formula of cheap romance. As for Tom's commitment, even temporarily, to the project of setting a free nigger free, it is clear, now, that this has been only another of his make-believe adventures, a fiction. If it had succeeded it would only have been the start of further adventures; the three would have continued downriver on the raft and had "adventures plumb to the mouth of the river," and only then, perhaps, would Tom and Huck tell Jim that he was a free man and take him "back up home on a steamboat, in style, and pay him [forty dollars] for his lost time" (p. [364]). Tom does give Jim forty dollars for being a patient prisoner. Is it only an accident that this is the same sum for which the Duke and the Dauphin had sold him back into slavery? Huck, at any rate, is ready for "more howling adventures," and he will even be member enough of respectable society to be able to purchase the necessary outfit, his six thousand dollars having been kept safe for him all this while by Judge Thatcher.

With deliberate irony the last chapters overturn any expectations we have cherished, despite Twain's numerous hints and warnings, that the search for a meaningful design in experience is anything but a game. That Jim was free all along makes Tom's Evasion properly titled. His plan had been, as he would claim, "beautifully" purposeless, an evasion of the whole issue of personal freedom. And all Huck's efforts, earlier, to help Jim gain freedom, those struggles, even against conscience, to stand by his friend, to protect him from those who would keep him a slave—these too, in retrospect, become plot without motive, pure art or adventure in the Tom Sawyer sense. Huck has risked social selfhood, the only identity society allows, in his passage down the river, but now he accepts once more his role as Tom Sawyer's lieutenant, becomes the willing accomplice in the sleights of the imagination.

NOTES

All citations to *Adventures of Huckleberry Finn* are taken here from the reproduction of the first American edition of 1885 included in *The Art of Huckleberry Finn: Text, Sources, Criticism*, edited by Walter Blair and Hamlin Hill (San Francisco: Chandler Publishing Co., 1962).

1. Compare *Adventures of Huckleberry Finn*, ed. Sculley Bradley et al. (New York: W. W. Norton & Co., 1977), n. 1, p. 7.

2. *Other Inquisitions: 1937–1951* (New York: Simon & Schuster, 1968), p. 46.

3. A considerable literature has accumulated on this point, but the most famous expression of dissatisfaction with Twain's ending of the novel may be the comment of Ernest Hemingway (in *Green Hills of Africa* [New York: Charles Scribner's Sons, 1935], p. 22): "If you read it you must stop where the Nigger Jim is stolen from the boys. That is the real end. The rest is cheating." Bernard DeVoto wrote of the ending, "Mark was once more betrayed. He intended a further chapter in his tireless attack on romanticism, especially Southern romanticism, and nothing in his mind or training enabled him to understand that this extemporized burlesque was a defacement of his pure work" (*Mark Twain's America* [1932], excerpted in *Huckleberry Finn*, ed. Bradley et al., pp. 302–3). Twain's denouement was defended, though only casually, by Lionel Trilling, who remarked in 1948 that it permitted Huck to "return to his anonymity, to give up his role of hero which he prefers, for he is modest in all things," and by T. S. Eliot in 1950: "Huck Finn must come from nowhere and be bound for nowhere ... he is in a state of nature as detached as the state of the saint." In 1953 Leo Marx responded to both in an essay maintaining that Twain had "jeopardized the significance of the entire novel" by an ending in which Huck's search for freedom is surrendered and his growth of character denied (all three essays reproduced in *Huckleberry Finn*, ed. Bradley et al., pp. 318–49). To Marx there have been a number of important replies, among them those of Frank Baldanza ("The Structure of *Huckleberry Finn*," *American Literature* 27 [1955]: 347–55) and Richard P. Adams ("The Unity and Coherence of *Huckleberry Finn*," *Tulane Studies in English* 6 [1956]: 87–103), who argue for the coherence of the whole book including the ending as a result of rhythms of repetition and variation and patterns of imagery. My own argument for the meaningfulness of Twain's ending finds a start in the statement of James M. Cox that "after Huck reached his unknown destination, the Phelps farm, the only terms on which he could exist were Tom's terms." Cox sees the ending as a "sad initiation" into respectable society ("Remarks on the Sad Initiation of Huckleberry Finn," *Southern Review* 62 [1954]: 389–405).

4. "The Relation between Point of View and Style in the Works of Mark Twain," *Style in Prose Fiction*, English Institute Essays: 1958 (New York: Columbia University Press, 1959), p. 165.

5. Compare Walter Blair, *Mark Twain and Huck Finn* (Berkeley: University of California Press. 1960), p. 60.

6. Blair, ibid., has demonstrated the relation of both novels to "the literary flux." Compare pp. 58–67, 111-30.

7. Henry Nash Smith, *Mark Twain: The Development of a Writer* (New York: Atheneum, 1967), p. 81.

8. In 1895 Twain wrote concerning Huck's decision in Chapter 16 not to betray Jim, "I should exploit the proposition that in a crucial moral emergency, a sound heart is a safer guide than an ill-trained conscience. I sh'd support this doctrine with a chapter from a book of mine where a sound heart and a deformed conscience come into collision and conscience suffers defeat" (Blair, *Mark Twain and Huck Finn*, p. 143).

9. *Life on the Mississippi* (New York: Signet, 1961), p. 267.

10. Smith, *Mark Twain*.

11. See ibid., chap. 5.

12. The parallels with *Don Quixote* were pointed out by Olin H. Moore, "Mark Twain and *Don Quixote*," *PMLA* 37 (1922): 337–38.

13. *Strains of Discord: Studies in Literary Openness* (Ithaca: Cornell University Press, 1958). p. 73.

14. *Life on the Mississippi*, p. 267.

15. I have elaborated this interpretation in "*Huckleberry Finn*: Journey without End," *Virginia Quarterly Review* 58, no. 3 (1982): 253–67.

16. Blair, *Mark Twain and Huck Finn*, p. 117.

17. Ibid., p. 229.

ROY HARVEY PEARCE

"Yours Truly, Huck Finn"

Huck Finn's closing words, as he is about to light out for the Territory, pose a dilemma not for him but for his reader.[1] Huck has been throughout a liar aspiring to be a shape-shifter, or vice versa. And he has not been altogether successful in either role. Moreover, as if his failure weren't enough, he is burdened—so one interpretive line has it[2]—with the failure of Mark Twain to invent for him in the final, the Evasion, chapters an action and a demeanor that will, from a reader's perspective, justify his special mode of credibility, his own way with the truth.

The problem centers on the ending of *Adventures of Huckleberry Finn*, to which in the end I shall come, in the hope of demonstrating that Huck has in fact, in the ironic rendering of his very factuality, wholly deserved that "Yours Truly," although at a great cost to us; and surely at a greater cost to Mark Twain. (Understanding this last would entail understanding the relationship between Samuel Clemens and Mark Twain—something beyond my competence.) For we must come to realize that rather than being possibly one of us—someone with whom, according to the canons of nineteenth-century realism, we might "identify"—Huck is exclusively a project of his own, Mark Twain-given possibility: in the end we must acknowledge the impossibility of his truth—all of it, and on its own terms—being ours. In the end we discover that we belong "realistically" at best with the Tom Sawyers

From *One Hundred Years of Huckleberry Finn: The Boy, His Book, and American Culture*, eds. Robert Sattelmeyer and J. Donald Crowley. © 1985 by The Curators of the University of Missouri.

of Huck's and our world, at worst with the Colonel Sherburns and the Dukes and the Dauphins—and, in a kind of merciful artistic transcendence, with the Mark Twains. But we also discover in the end that we are only possibly Tom Sawyers, Colonel Sherburns, Dukes and Dauphins, Mark Twains. Hope, for something better, defined with high irony, does remain. But not for those interpreters among us who want guarantees beyond hope. The hope of *Huckleberry Finn* is the hope of utopianism, but necessarily (because ours is the way of the world of Tom Sawyer, of Colonel Sherburn and the Duke and the Dauphin, of Mark Twain) a failed utopianism. *Huckleberry Finn* teaches us (we should not flinch at the phrase) that whereas utopianism is possible, utopians are not.

Huckleberry Finn, then, is the sort of book that becomes absolutely central to the experience of a reader, American or otherwise, who would try to understand his sense of himself as against his sense of his culture. Its domain is Western America, but its purview, as in its art it universalizes Huck's experience, is the whole world. Through Huck's account of his world and those who inhabit it, Mark Twain renders Huck for us too—Huck at once in his world and apart from it. This of course is the abiding pattern of most of the masterworks of nineteenth-century American fiction, which project for our experience and understanding the central problem for the American in the nineteenth century, and also in the twentieth: How, in Emerson's words, satisfy the claims of the self as against those of the world? How, in Whitman's words, conceive of the person who must exist simply and separately and also as part of the mass? The mass protagonists of nineteenth-century fiction before Mark Twain are put through trials and tribulations whereby they are readied for a return to a society whose integrity they, in seeking too fiercely to discover their own private identities, have somehow violated. At the end Hawthorne's Hester, Melville's Ishmael, and many others of their kind are ready to accommodate themselves to their society, and in their newfound knowledge of the complexities of relations between self and society are perhaps capable of contributing to the "improvement" of both. The tales told of them are open-ended, finally ambiguous, and problematic. Under such terminal conditions, they have earned their right to try out the future. They have come to be endowed with a sense of their own history.

None of this is true of Huck. Return and accommodation—above all, the capacity to be an agent of "improvement"—are quite beyond him. His function, it turns out, is to demonstrate the absolute incompatibility of the sort of self he is and the sort of world in which he tries so hard to live. He gains no sense of his own history and has no future. Nor, as I shall show, need he have. Unlike Hester, Ishmael, and their kind, unlike the kind of committed person whom Emerson and Whitman envisaged, Huck neither could nor should be one of us. He exists not to judge his world but to furnish us the means of judging it—and also our world as it develops out of his.

The means to the judgment are the superb comedy and satire deriving from Huck's quite immediate and lyrical accounts of his own person and from his resolutely deadpan rendering of the doings of those among whom he has his adventures. The lyrical accounts abound and almost always establish his consonance with the natural world, as opposed to the civilized:

> Miss Watson she kept pecking at me, and it got tiresome and lonesome. By-and-by they fetched the niggers in and had prayers, and then everybody was off to bed. I went up to my room with a piece of candle and put it on the table. Then I set down in a chair by the window and tried to think of something cheerful, but it warn't no use. I felt so lonesome I most wished I was dead. The stars was shining, and the leaves rustled in the woods ever so mournful; and I heard an owl, away off, who-whooing about somebody that was dead, and a whippowill and a dog crying about somebody that was going to die; and the wind was trying to whisper something to me and I couldn't make out what it was, and so it made the cold shivers run over me. (P. 20)

Against this tone, there is that of the witness to civilized falseness, foolishness, and cruelty to others. Here, Huck and Jim have taken on the Duke and the Dauphin and Huck has listened patiently to their outrageous stories about themselves:

> It didn't take me long to make up my mind that these liars warn't no kings nor dukes, at all, but just low-down humbugs and frauds. But I never said nothing never let on; kept it to myself; it's the best way; then you don't have no quarrels and don't get into no trouble. If they wanted us to call them kings and dukes, I hadn't no objections, 'long as it would keep peace in the family; and it warn't no use to tell Jim, so I didn't tell him. If I never learnt nothing else out of pap, I learnt that the best way to get along with his kind of people is to let them have their own way. (P. 166)

The range in style—from lyrical to matter-of-fact—delineates Huck's character. In the latter style, he can make judgments, but no judgments that lead to significant action. Above all, he is not one to change the world. What is important is that he be allowed at critical moments to be himself, so as to combine in that self the directness, naiveté, and often helplessness of a boy with the practical wisdom of a man, clever in the ways of surviving in towns and woods and on the river. His authentic self as Mark Twain develops it makes him essentially a witness, even when he is a participant. His is a vital presence. In the long run, what he does is altogether secondary to what he is.

It was, as we now know, Mark Twain's original intention to involve Huck all the way in the practical—and in effect radical—action of helping Jim achieve his freedom. Hence the opening words of Chapter 15 consolidate the action thus far: "We judged that three nights more would fetch us to Cairo, at the bottom of Illinois, where the Ohio River comes in, and that was what we was after. We would sell the raft and get on a steamboat and go way up the Ohio amongst the free States, and then be out of trouble" (p. [115]). It is in this chapter, too, that Huck's instinctive sense of Jim as a person becomes clear; he can even bring himself to "humble [himself] to a nigger" and not be sorry for it. In the next chapter, although he is conscience-stricken at realizing what helping Jim means, still he protects him. And then they discover that they have gone by Cairo, are still on the Mississippi in slave territory. If Mark Twain had let Huck and Jim find Cairo and the Ohio River, he would have realized his original intention and made Huck into the moderately "activist" type he first conceived him to be. Likely the story would have ended there. In any case, Mark Twain knew little or nothing about the Ohio River and almost everything about the Mississippi and would have been hard put to find materials with which further to develop the story. In his plotting he seems to have come to an impasse. For he stopped writing at this point, in 1876, not finally to complete *Huckleberry Finn* until 1883.[3] At the end of Chapter 16, a steamboat smashes the raft, and Huck and Jim, diving for their lives, are separated.

In the context of the Evasion episode, the fact of Mark Twain's impasse is worth pointing out, because the Huck of the rest of the book, although continuous with the Huck of the first sixteen chapters, is not confined to his own small world and the river, not just dedicated (but in an agonized way) to helping Jim achieve his freedom, but also made witness to the full panoply of people and institutions that, as we see even if he does not, would deny freedom not only to Jim but to themselves.

Between October 1879 and June 1883, while he finished *A Tramp Abroad* and *The Prince and the Pauper*, Mark Twain was able to write only Chapters 17–22 of *Huckleberry Finn*, for he still had not discovered the means of turning Huck's adventures with Jim into something of a wider compass. During the winter of 1882–1883, he was writing *Life on the Mississippi*, developing it out of a series of magazine articles, "Old Times on the

Mississippi," published in 1875. In preparation for that development he had revisited the Mississippi River and was depressed to see how much of all that he had so lovingly recalled in the magazine articles was disappearing. Indeed, his life during the period 1876–1883 had been difficult and too often personally disappointing. Traveling to Europe, he despaired of the development of those traditional free institutions that most of his contemporaries had persuaded themselves had been Europe's glorious gift to the world. Reading Dickens's *Tale of Two Cities*, Carlyle's *History of the French Revolution*, and Lecky's *History of European Morals*, he began to think of man's history as only confirming the view he (and his collaborator, Charles Dudley Warner) had taken of corruption in government and business in *The Gilded Age* (1873). Thinking about the Mississippi again, meditating the downward path from past to present, finding his increasingly desperate view of the human situation confirmed by his reading, he discovered his imagination empowered and vivified. It was as though he were compelled to finish *Huckleberry Finn*. He finished a draft of the book during the summer of 1883, spent seven months revising it, and saw it published in England in December 18 and in the United States in February 1885.

Despair, then, is, as antecedent and consequence, a prime characteristic of *Huckleberry Finn*. But in the book itself it produces mainly comedy and satire of a superb order. For counterbalancing the despair that went into the writing of the book, there is the abounding joy of Huck when he is most fully himself. In all his cleverness and dexterity, he is—except for what he does for Jim—essentially passive. He lives in the midst of violence and death; yet his only violence, if it can be called that, is the mild, ritualistic sort whereby when necessary he feeds himself. He hunts and fishes only when he has to. His joy is virtually private—to be shared, because instinctively understood, only by Jim. He is of course given no comic or satiric sense. He is given only his own rich sense of himself-richest when he is alone with Jim, on the river.

Comedy and satire derive from Huck's conviction that he must report fully what he sees—and further from the fact that it is he, capable of such joy, who does the reporting. Irony, a product of a tightly controlled point of view, is everywhere enforced for us by the fact that Huck, all unknowing, is its agent. He does not understand much of what he sees. Mark Twain's irony, however, lets us understand. What Huck is witness to again and again are doings of people who have contrived a world that distorts the public and private institutions—ranging from forms of government to forms of play—that just might make his sort of joy possible for all. His relationship with Jim—gained through his acceptance of the private guilt entailed by refusing to accept the injunction called for by public tradition and law—stands as a kind of utopian pattern for all human relationships. And we judge those in the book accordingly. Still, it is an appropriately primitive, even precivilized relationship; for Huck sees Jim not as a man with the responsibilities of a man but as one essentially like himself. This is his fundamental limitation, and yet the source of his strength. So long as that strength exists, so long as he exists, he can participate in the world only as a role-player, willing to go along with all the pretensions and make-believe that he witnesses. He accepts other names, other identities almost casually. Living them, he seems to "belong" in his world. But not quite. For always there is a certain reserve. Always there is the joy of his simple, separate self, to which he returns again and again as though to renew himself. Set against that self, the world in which he has his adventures can be constituted only of grotesque, marvelously distorted beings who are the stuff of comedy and satire.

In 1895, planning to "get up an elaborate and formal lay sermon on morals and the conduct of life, and things of that stately sort," Mark Twain defined Huck's situation in his world:

> Next, I should exploit the proposition that in a crucial moral emergency a sound heart is a safer guide than an ill-trained conscience, I sh'd support this doctrine with a chapter from a book of mine where a sound heart and a deformed conscience come into collision and conscience suffers defeat. Two persons figure in this chapter: Jim, a middle-aged slave, and Huck Finn, a boy of 14, ... bosom friends, drawn together by a community of misfortune....
>
> In those slave-holding days the whole community was agreed as to one thing—the awful sacredness of slave property. To help steal a horse or a cow was a low crime, but to help a hunted slave ... or hesitate to promptly betray him to a slave-catcher when opportunity offered was a much baser crime, and carried with it a stain, a moral smirch which nothing could wipe away. That this sentiment should exist among slave-holders is comprehensible— there were good commercial reasons for it—but that it should exist and did exist among the paupers ... and in a passionate and uncompromising form, is not in our remote day realizable. It seemed natural enough to me then; natural enough that Huck and his father the worthless loafer should feel and approve it, though it now seems absurd. It shows that that strange thing, the conscience—that unerring monitor—can be trained to approve any wild thing you want it to approve if you begin its education early and stick to it.[4]

Not only the distinction between heart and conscience but also the quite sophisticated notion of how culture, or society, or the world, forms conscience and so makes possible the death of the heart—these conceptions are central to the very structure of *Huckleberry Finn* as Mark Twain finally developed it, as is the fact that he gives Huck a sense of his own heart which, at however great a cost, persuades him that he can be in the great world only a player of roles.

At the beginning Huck tells us that this time, unlike the occasion of *Tom Sawyer*, he is going to speak out on his own and so correct Mr. Mark Twain in a few matters. His truth, in a consummate irony, is to be set against the conscience of even his creator. Huck now is letting himself be civilized and reports mildly on how it is. Yet at the end of the first chapter (in the first passage cited above), we know that he is in full possession of his truthful self. Assured of that fact, we can rest easy while he goes along with Tom Sawyer's complicated make-believe and even plays a trick on Jim. His sojourn in the Widow Douglas's world, as in Tom's, is throughout marked by role-playing and make-believe. And he can as easily adjust to his father's world, play his role there and sustain the make-believe, as he can to Tom's and the Widow Douglas's. Perhaps the patterns of make-believe in *their worlds* are harmless; no one is hurt much; everyone can make himself out to be aspiring to something better or nobler. But the pretenses and distortions of his father's world are dangerous and frightening; and Huck suffers accordingly—still managing, however, to record, in his frankness, his sense of his own truth. The make-believe and role-playing of Tom's boy's world are Huck's way into the make-believe and role-playing in the world of adults. The formal design is surely carefully contrived, allowing us easily to move with Huck from one world to the other, and demanding of Mark Twain that at the end of the adventures he arrange things so that Huck attempts to come back to his proper world, which, according to a proper pattern of conscience-directing institutions, must be a boy's world.

Indeed, the episodes of *Huckleberry Finn* evolve one into the other on Huck and Jim's trip downriver as so many exempla of the nineteenth-century American "conscience—that unerring monitor"—as it "can be trained to approve any wild thing you *want* it to approve if you begin its education early and stick to it." The murder of Pap, Jim's running away, Huck's information-seeking visit with Mrs. Loftus, their finding the wreck of the *Walter Scott*, Huck's cruel joke on Jim and the beginning of his sense of dedication and obligation to him, the separation, Huck amid the Grangerfords in all their distorted pride and nobility, his escape from the feud and reunion with Jim— these opening episodes, as we recall them, regularly involve Huck as either role-player or witness, or both. At their conclusion (at the end of Chapter 18 and the beginning of Chapter 19), Huck with Jim on his own, is his truest self:

> We said there warn't no home like a raft, after all. Other places do seem so cramped up and smothery, but a raft don't. You feel mighty free and easy and comfortable on a raft. (P. 156)

> Two or three days and nights went by; I reckon I might say they swum by, they slid along so quiet and smooth and lovely. (P. [157])

So it goes for the time being; and we are reassured. But almost immediately Huck and Jim are with the Duke and the Dauphin, consummate artists in those forms of make-believe that fool all of the people most of the tune, possessors of consciences distorted enough to make them (most of the time) masters of all whom they survey—including Huck and Jim. Again (in the second passage cited above), Huck is willing to go along. Or rather, he has no option but to go along.

The point is that he knows what he is doing, and accordingly we are reassured that his sense of his authentic truth will sustain him. He stands by—what else can he do?—while the Dauphin bilks a Pokeville campmeeting and the Duke takes over a print-shop and while they fleece the public with their promised obscene "Royal Nonesuch" show. Too, he is witness to Colonel Sherburn's denunciation of a small-town mob and his shooting-down of the town drunkard. There is no impulse to prevent any of this; this is beyond his capacities; and, after all, like the rest of the townspeople he too is fooled by the act of the comic drunk in the circus. Make-believe, all of it, and constant role-playing. Only with the attempt to fleece the Wilks girls does Huck's truth come to be powerful enough to bring him to act. Here, too, he acts by role-playing, but this time his role is set according to his truth. The failure of this attempt of the Duke and the Dauphin brings them to sell Jim. And there comes Huck's great crisis, in which truth once and for all triumphs over conscience, instinct over training, the self over society and all the good and needed things it offers.

The famous passage (in Chapter 31) begins:

> Once I said to myself it would be a thousand times better for Jim to be a slave at home where his family was, as long as he'd *got* to be a slave, and so I'd better write a letter to Tom Sawyer and tell him to tell Miss Watson where he was. But I soon give up that

notion, for two things: she'd be mad and disgusted at his rascality and ungratefulness for leaving her, and so she'd sell him straight down the river again; and if she didn't, everybody naturally despises an ungrateful nigger, and they'd make Jim feel it all the time, and so he'd feel ornery and disgraced. And then think of *me*! It would get all around, that Huck Finn helped a nigger to get his freedom; and if I was ever to see anybody from that town again, I'd be ready to get down and lick his boots for shame. That's just the way a person does a low-down thing, and then he don't want to take no consequences of it. Thinks as long as he can hide it, it ain't no disgrace. (Pp. 269–70)

This is the voice of conscience, and it torments Huck. He tries to pray but realizes he "can't pray a lie." For he knows he will sin against his conscience by continuing to try to help Jim. He goes so far as to write a letter to Miss Watson, telling her where Jim is, and feels "all washed clean of sin" (p. 271). But then he recalls his relationship with Jim and makes the great decision—to "steal Jim out of slavery again." And so he says, "All right, then, I'll go to hell" (p. 272).

But stealing Jim out of slavery, it turns out, is yet a matter of role-playing. At the Phelpses, Huck is taken for Tom Sawyer and thereupon enters the last of his adventures—once more by assuming the name and, in part, the conscience of another. Tom comes, assumes his brother's name, and plunges them both into the work of the Evasion. Fittingly, necessarily, Huck must be brought back into that segment of the society that is, by the world's standards, appropriate to him—a boy's world.

The complications of the Evasion episode, and also its detail and length, tend to put off many readers of *Huckleberry Finn*. They see it as Mark Twain's evasion of the moral implications of his story, especially when they learn that Jim has been free all along. Huck, they say, should have seen Jim all the way to freedom. It might well be that the episode is in fact too complicated and too long, overbalancing the end of the story. Still, in the necessary scheme of the novel, in the necessary contrast between Huck's assumption of various forms of conscience and the truth he constantly has within him—in that scheme, it is imperative that the book begin as it ends: in effect, with a grotesque and sardonic comment on the nature of the forms of make-believe, pretense, and distortion that set the life-styles of those whose consciences they shape. It is all in the end very stupid. Men have given up the authentic truth they might well have had as children for the falsifying forms of conscience that lead to the violence, destruction, and predation that transform their society into the enemy of the very men it should sustain and preserve. Tom Sawyer here as earlier patterns his play principally after the romances of Sir Walter Scott. For boys it is moderately harmless play, although Tom is slightly wounded in the final scuffle. Yet we recall the episode of the wrecked steamboat, itself called *Walter Scott*, and are forced to realize what will necessarily ensue when boyish make-believe and role-playing become the mode of life of mature men and women. Conscience will not let truth survive.

Indeed, in this world Huckleberry Finn cannot continue to exist. He says at the end that he will not return to St. Petersburg: "I reckon I got to light out for the Territory ahead of the rest, because Aunt Sally she's going to adopt me and sivilize me and I can't stand it. I been there before." The plan to go to the Territory is Tom's, of course, for whom it is another opportunity for "howling adventures," this time "amongst the Injuns." Huck will survive, that is to say, by playing yet another role in this make-believe, conscience-stricken world. Here, however, he speaks only as witness.

II

In the last chapter of *Huckleberry Finn*, Huck in fact speaks twice of going to "the Territory." The first time he is reporting Tom's plans, now that the Evasion has been managed successfully, "to slide out of here, one of these nights, and get an outfit, and go for howling adventures amongst the Injuns, over in the Territory." The second time he is speaking of his own plans: "I reckon I got to light out for the Territory ahead of the rest, because Aunt Sally she's going to adopt me and sivilize me and I can't stand it. I been there before" (p. 366).

I suppose that the obvious irony of the two passages has not been pointed out precisely because it is so obvious. The Territory is, of course, the Indian Territory, which was to become Oklahoma. From the 1820s on, it had been organized and developed as a region to which Indians could be safely removed away from civilized society, since their lands were needed for higher purposes than those to which they could put them. The cruelty and deprivation of removal were generally taken to be the inevitable price American society had to pay as it passed through its God-ordained stages of development. One part of this price was said to be the yielding of a certain amount of freedom or, to put it as an article of faith in Manifest Destiny, the surrendering of a "lower" for a "higher" freedom.[5] It seems fairly evident that the man who was to write "To the Person Sitting in Darkness" and other such pieces would be fully aware of the removal episode, with its justifications and consequences, and that he intended his readers to be aware of it too. Read in this light, what for Tom is yet another willful adolescent fantasy becomes for Huck a compelling actuality. Tom's willfulness effects a parody that points up some of the grotesqueness of the historically authentic pioneering, civilizing spirit. Huck's compulsion effects a satire that simply denies that that spirit is authentic, despite its historical actuality. Huck will seek the freedom of the Territory just because it is an uncivilized freedom. (A better word, perhaps, is *noncivilized* freedom.) It is, indeed, the only true freedom for the authentic human being Huck eventually comes to be—in spite of himself.

Yet there is more to the passages, particularly the second, than this. Huck, we recall, speaks of lighting out for the Territory "ahead of the rest." Here, at the end, Mark Twain introduces his own point of view, which, of necessity, is more encompassing than Huck's; as a result Huck is given more to say than he could possibly know.[6] From Huck's simple point of view, the allusion is to Tom's vague plans to go to the Territory; for Mark Twain, it is to the Boomer movement that was a prime factor in the taking over of Indian lands, "sivilizing" the Territory, and creating another American state. The effect is that Huck, all unknowing, is given a kind of prescience that his adventures at this point surely justify. No matter where he goes, he will be one step ahead not only of the Tom Sawyers of his world but also of the sort of people into whom the Tom Sawyers grow.

After the Civil War, there was constant agitation in Kansas and Missouri to open up the unsettled parts of the Indian Territory to whites. To this end, bills were repeatedly, if on the whole unsuccessfully, introduced in Congress. Pressures were put on the so-called Five Civilized Nations (Cherokees, Creeks, and Choctaws principally) to cede part of their lands in the Territory to be used as reservations for other Indians and, for due payment, to make them available for settlement by whites. In the late 1870s and into the 1880s, white incursions into the Territory were numerous enough to call for the use of troops to defend Indian rights. Moreover, in 1879 a court decision found that even those lands in the Territory that had been ceded to the government by Indians could not be settled by whites, since such lands had been ceded conditionally for future settlement by other Indians.

Inevitably, however, white incursions—by groups who came to be known as Boomers—increased in tempo and number. Invaders were not jailed but fined. When they could not pay the fines, they were simply escorted to the territorial border by soldiers. The economics of the situation were complex: railroads encouraged and propagandized Boomers; cattlemen, wanting to use the lands for grazing, opposed the Boomers, who were farmers, and defended Indian rights, which included the right to rent their lands for grazing. The story (one of confusion, broken promises, and violence—all in the name of "civilization") moved toward its resolution in 1889, when the government bought certain lands from Indians and opened them to settlement as the Territory of Oklahoma.[7]

Boomerism, then, was the most recent expression of the westering American spirit. In the words of an 1885 petition to Congress, drawn up by B. L. Brush and John W. Marshall in Howard, Kansas, on behalf of Boomerism:

> Resolved, That we are opposed to the policy of the Government in using the army to drive out or interfere with actual settlers upon any of the public domain, as being foreign to the genius of our institutions....
>
> Resolved, As this selfsame, bold spirit, that is now advancing to the front, has ever existed since the Pilgrim Fathers set their feet on Plymouth Rock, and will ever exist so long as we remain citizens of this grand Republic, that we, the citizens of Howard and vicinity, pledge ourselves to firmly support this grand element—the vanguard of civilization....
>
> Resolved, That we are opposed to the settlement of any more bands of wild Indians on the Indian Territory.[8]

Although I know of no direct allusion in Mark Twain's writings to the troubles in the Indian Territory, I think it likely that he was well aware of them, for they were widely publicized and debated and of great interest to Congress. A considerable amount of Boomer ferment developed in Mark Twain's—and Huck's—Missouri, although Kansas was a more important center. The summer of 1883, when Twain was writing the last part of *Huckleberry Finn*,[9] David Payne and his Boomers were particularly active in promoting their cause. One historian of Oklahoma reports that the general whose responsibility it was to turn Boomers back declared that in 1883 "the whole affair had become simply a series of processions to and from the Kansas line.[10]

Thus it would seem that in 1883, Mark Twain, now finally committed to a conception of Huck Finn whose fate it must always be to seek a freedom beyond the limits of any civilization, ended his novel by contrasting Tom's and Huck's sense of the Territory. Note that Huck is willing to go along with Tom, if he can get the money to outfit himself for those "howling adventures amongst the Injuns." Jim tells Huck that, now that his father is dead, he does have the money. However, he will have to claim it himself. The matter of the money and the "howling adventures" is then dropped. Since Tom is "most well" now, Huck says, there "ain't nothing more to write about." He will "light out for the Territory ahead of the rest." In one sense, perhaps, he simply means ahead of Tom and Jim; in a larger sense (so I think we must conclude) he means ahead of all those people whose civilizing mission Boomerism actualized in fact. The realities of the case are, as ever, contrasted with Tom's fantasies.

The Huck who seems willing to go along with Tom is, of course, not the Huck who, against the dictates of his conscience, has helped Jim in his quest for freedom. It is altogether necessary that this latter Huck must, alone, "light out for the Territory ahead of the rest." With the curious prescience that Mark Twain gives him, he knows that in antebellum days (as Mark Twain surely knew that summer of 1883), even in the Territory, he will be only one step ahead of the rest: Boomers, Dukes and Dauphins, Aunt Sallies, Colonel Sherburns, and Wilkses—civilizers all. Certainly we are not to assume that Huck self-consciously knows the full meaning (even the full moral meaning) of what he says here. Yet we cannot conclude that this allusion is simply a matter of Mark Twain speaking out in his own person. Huck's view and Mark Twain's, in a culminating irony, here become one. Huck's prescience is, within the limits of the narrative, a matter of intuition, forced into expression by his hardheaded sense that he has almost always been one step "ahead of the rest." He can say his final "Yours Truly" and yet must be willing to go to hell for saying it.

III

I think we must conclude that Huck is not meant to survive. He is so powerfully a being of truth as against conscience, self as against society, that he exists not as an actuality but as a possibility. In him Mark Twain projects the American's sense that somewhere, at some point—even if only in the imagination—it would indeed be possible to regain access to the truth, if only we could cut through the sharps of conscience and of the institutions that form and justify it. But in the present situation, Mark Twain despaired of that possibility and in Huck, his nature, and his history saw it only as impossible. Huck, then, is that ideal, perhaps never-to-be-attained type—in Wallace Stevens's phrase, an "impossible possible philosopher's man." Huck, then, stands as witness to his experience, totally unaware of the irony whereby it becomes at once an aspect and a function of our experience. In rendering the witnessing, Mark Twain makes us, if we but grasp the irony, the judge of that experience—Huck's and our own—and the world in which it is shaped. It is inappropriate to regret that Huck does not follow through on his own to free Jim. That is not Huck's proper role; for it would be the role of someone in whom conscience and truth were to a significant degree harmonious. Huck, for whom conscience always means role-playing, in whom the naked truth must finally be overpowering, stands, as I have said, not as possibly one of us but rather as our means of judging his world and Mark Twain's—and, along with it, ours.

We can take Mark Twain's preliminary "Notice" to *Huckleberry Finn* with the deadly serious levity with which it is meant: "Persons attempting to find a motive in the narrative will be prosecuted; persons attempting to find a moral in it will be banished; persons attempting to find a plot in it will be shot." "Motive" and "plot" are, however, not so much absent as negative. Huck's motive is to survive; and we know that the conditions of his life and of his society are such that survival is impossible. The plot of his *Adventures* lays out the pattern of the impossibility; Huck's is a history of whose meaning he cannot be conscious and still be his truest self. Above all, the story has no "moral." Rather it is an exercise in the use of such moral sensibility as remains with us. Knowing what Huck is, we can know what we have become and measure the cost and the worth.

F. Scott Fitzgerald wrote in 1935,

> Huckleberry Finn took the first journey *back*. He was the first to look *back* at the republic from the perspective of the west. His eyes were the first eyes that ever looked at us objectively that were not eyes from overseas. There were mountains at the frontier but he wanted more than mountains to look at with his restive eyes—he wanted to find out about men and how they lived together. And because he turned back we have him forever.[11]

The condition of his turning back, however, is that we cannot demand that he be one of us. He stands as witness, bound to his own truth, so that we might go forth and be likewise.

NOTES

1. This essay is a conflation and development of two previously published: "'The End. Yours Truly, Huck Finn': Postscript," *MLQ* 24 (1963): 753–56; and "Huck Finn in His History," *EA* 24 (1971): 783–91. I am grateful to the editors of those journals for allowing me to reprint material they have published. I dedicate this essay to Robert Elliott and John Isaacs: In Memoriam.

2. The major critique, of course, is Leo Marx, "Mr. Eliot, Mr. Trilling, and *Huckleberry Finn*," *ASch* 22 (1953): 423–40.

3. See Henry Nash Smith, *Mark Twain: The Development of a Writer* (Cambridge: Harvard University Press, 1962), pp. 113–37, and Walter Blair, *Mark Twain and Huck Finn* (Berkeley: University of California Press, 1960), for basic accounts.

4. Quoted in Blair, *Mark Twain and Huck Finn*, pp. 143–44, copyright 1960 by the Mark Twain Co.

5. See my *Savages of America* (Baltimore: Johns Hopkins University Press, 1965), pp. 56–61.

6. Smith, *Mark Twain*, pp. 134–37, points out that the Colonel Sherburn episode derives from Mark Twain's point of view and thus is intrusive, a "flaw" in the structure of Huckleberry Finn. I think, however, that one must argue for Huck as a "reporter" and in this and other episodes (particularly that of the Evasion) wherein he is in no position to participate in, or at least dominate, the action and so render it in terms wholly congruent with his sensibility and understanding. The question is: How much irony are we to allow Mark Twain? An incidental burden of this interpretation is that in the end we must allow him enough and demand only of his novel that it "contain" its elements of irony.

7. The story is best outlined in Roy Gittinger, *Formation of the State of Oklahoma, 1803–1906* (Norman: University of Oklahoma Press, 1939), pp. 68–157. On the Boomers, see Carl Coke Rister, *Land Hunger: David L. Payne and the Oklahoma Boomers* (Norman: University of Oklahoma Press, 1942).

8. Gittinger, *Oklahoma*, pp. 272–73.

9. Walter Blair, "When Was *Huckleberry Finn* Written?" *AL*, 30 (1958); 1–25.

10. Gittinger, *Oklahoma*.

11. I quote the statement from the original typescript, with the kind permission of its owner, Prof. Matthew Bruccoli. It has been previously printed in *Fitzgerald Newsletter* 8 (Winter 1960).

HAROLD BEAVER

Huck Adrift

'But I go a good deal on instinct ...' (ch. 32)

T.S. Eliot was right. 'Huck we do not look at', he declared, '—we see the world through his eyes.' Now we must try to turn the tables round. Instead of looking *through* Huck, we must try to look *at* Huck. We must look into those wary, curious, roving, matter-of-fact, anxious eyes.

By his own estimation, Huck is 'ignorant', 'so kind of low-down and ornery' (15/14). But he is not stupid. He takes pride in his practical intelligence. When Jim tells him 'bees wouldn't sting idiots', for example, he is sceptical. Because he has personal experience of bees. Because, he says, 'I had tried them lots of times myself, and they wouldn't sting me' (41/55). Nor is the chuckle in that sentence Huck's; the touchstone of his personal experience is absolute.

Yet even to a boy of his own age he can seem dumb. When Buck asks him the Moses riddle, Huck is stuck:

'I said I didn't know; I hadn't heard about it before, no way.'
'Well, guess,' he says.
'How'm I going to guess,' says I, 'when I never heard tell about it before?'[1]

From *Huckleberry Finn*. © 1987 by Harold Beaver.

Huck has severe limitations, even as an observer. If he has no previous experience of something, he is at a loss. He cannot make a guess. He just gives up. Even the nature of a riddle—the very concept of intellectual play— is beyond him.

> 'Well, if you knowed where he was, what did you ask me for?'
> 'Why, blame it, it's a riddle, don't you see?'

But Huck doesn't.

He is wholly empirical. His role, in the initial chapters, is to play Sancho Panza to Tom's quixotic imagination. Where Tom sees 'julery' and 'rich A-rabs', Huck sees only turnips and Sunday-school picnickers. Playboy Tom calls him a 'numskull' for his pains, a 'perfect sap-head'; devout Miss Watson a 'fool'. But, if a fool, he is a holy simpleton, a wise fool.

Take the opening paragraph of chapter 16, which originally introduced 'The Raftsmen's Passage' (lifted into *Life on the Mississippi*):

> We slept most all day, and started out at night, a little ways behind a monstrous long raft that was as long going by as a procession. She had four long sweeps at each end, so we judged she carried as many as thirty men, likely. She had five big wigwams aboard, wide apart, and an open camp fire in the middle, and a tall flag-pole at each end. There was a power of style about her. It *amounted* to something being a raftsman on such a craft as that.

Huck is always on the alert. He is always closely observant of detail. He has a quick, practical grasp. There is enough detail here to construct a model from his report. Of their own raft, which he knows from bow to stern, he can give the exact measurements: 'It was twelve foot wide and about fifteen or sixteen foot long, and the top stood above water six or seven inches' (44/60). One trusts such figures, such easy precision. Huck seems utterly reliable as witness. But he is more than a mere witness. His mind is charged with activity. He is always thinking and judging. Observation is backed by practical inference and rapid calculation. So 'we judged she carried as many, as thirty men, likely': around four men to each oar, that is, and: six to a wigwam.

His is a detective skill, moving from inference to observation as well as from observation (or reported observation) to inference. 'I knowed mighty well that a drownded man don't float on his back,' he comments on a corpse claimed to be his father's. Or on the origin of stars, with Jim arguing for creation and Huck for evolution:

I judged it would have took too long to *make* so many. Jim said
the moon could a *laid* them; well, that looked kind of reasonable,
so I didn't say nothing against it, because I've seen a frog lay most
as many, so of course it could be done.[2]

Huck is always logical, always reasonable on his own empirical terms.

What most impresses him, however, is 'style'. In this he is a true
Southerner. He loves to cut a dash. He adores a swagger, a hint of bravura, a
touch of class. (Twain allows a rare italic emphasis to the verb '*amounted*'.)
Huck is infallibly awed by style. But he, too, can put on panache. His own
'style' is stylish. Though mainly metonymic, in its temporal and local
sequences, it is capable of metaphoric flights: 'as long going by as a
procession'. The fact that the raft is 'monstrous long' and so almost literally
passing by—from flag-pole to oars to wigwams to camp-fire to wigwams to
oars to flag-pole—like a procession makes the simile peculiarly Huck-like.
For it evokes not only the details but also the exact *impression* produced. We
see, that is, as always through Huck's eyes.

For Huck is all eyes and hands and nostrils and ears. He *sees* things with
precision. He *handles* things experimentally. He *hears* things exactly:
'*plunkety-plunk*' (horses coming); '*k'chunk!*' (sound of an axe across water);
'*h'wack!*' (crack of thunder). He even *smells* the essence of night: 'Everything
was dead quiet, and it looked late, and *smelt* late. You know what I mean—...'
(32/42).

Or take his description of the parlour in the Grangerford house:

Well, there was a big outlandish parrot on each side of the clock,
made out of something like chalk, and painted up gaudy. By one
of the parrots was a cat made of crockery, and a crockery dog by
the other; and when you pressed down on them they squeaked,
but didn't open their mouths nor look different nor interested.
They squeaked through underneath. There was a couple of big
wild-turkey-wing fans spread out behind those things. On a table
in the middle of the room was a kind of a lovely crockery basket
that had apples and oranges and peaches and grapes piled up in it
which was much redder and yellower and prettier than real ones
is, but they warn't real because you could see where pieces had
got chipped off and showed the white chalk or whatever it was,
underneath.[3]

Huck not only studies all the ornaments on the mantlepiece, he touches
them and presses on them; and obviously picks them up to examine their

manufacture from underneath. He probes the world around him. He scrutinizes it. He tests it with his hands. Huck is the practical American boy, matching hand and eye. He exposes himself to experience. He plunges into water and into the woods. Much like Thoreau, his contemporary, another tramp in the woods. Like Emerson even, shorn of transcendentalism. For Emerson supplied the symbols. The very stuff of language, he argued, was revealed in hieroglyphs and puns. Hand and eye, research and rhetoric, life and letters are one. Meaning itself becomes transparent. The seeing 'eye' is transformed to 'I', the experimental 'hand' to 'and'. In the sequential handling of our world the 'I' is for ever linked to 'and'.[4]

Not that Huck would have cared. His problems are almost never semiotic; they are profoundly moral. As a contemporary American critic put it:

> What Huck really is ... is simply the usual vagabond boy, with his expected shrewdness and cunning, his rags, his sharp humor, his practical philosophy. The only difference between him and his type would be found in his essential honesty, his strong and struggling moral nature ...[5]

His characteristic trait is loyalty. He remains loyal, at heart, to Pap. He remains loyal to Tom. In all his confusion, he remains loyal to Jim. He is loyal to Sophia Grangerford. He even remains loyal, in the end, to the king and duke. His heart aches for reconciliation and love. It aches for the two tricksters, tarred and feathered, straddling a rail. He breaks down in tears at Buck's death and at the loss of Jim. This spontaneous overflow of feelings affects his relationship to almost all the characters. His sympathy extends to the Widow, who 'looked so sorry that I thought I would behave a while if I could'. To the gang aboard the *Walter Scott*: 'I begun to think how dreadful it was, even for murderers, to be in such a fix.' To the Grangerfords; 'I liked all that family, dead ones and all, and warn't going to let anything come between us.' To the circus 'drunk'. To victims of the king and duke. To Mary Jane Wilks: 'It made my eyes water a little, to remember her crying there all by herself in the night.' To Aunt Sally: 'I wished I could do something for her, but I couldn't, only to swear that I wouldn't never do nothing to grieve her any more.' Finally even to that 'poor old woman' (Miss Watson) and 'the poor old king'. Huck scorns self-conscious preaching ('all about brotherly love and such-like tiresomeness'), but he is no slouch himself at universal brotherhood; bidding this adieu to the king and duke:

> Well, it made me sick to see it; and I was sorry for them poor pitiful rascals, it seemed like I couldn't ever feel any hardness

against them any more in the world. It was a dreadful thing to see. Human beings *can* be awful cruel to one another.[6]

But his response is *all* feeling. It is solely by feeling. It is nothing but feeling. There seems to be no cohesion between Huck's sympathies and his actions. No intellectual awareness. No consistency between what he *feels* and what he *does* at all. That is why he has no sense of history, no active memory, no sense of time even. His very tenses wobble indeterminately between the past and historic present. Spatially Buck is always in control. Geographically each episode is explored with absolute precision. But the intervals between episodes are left vaguely adrift: 'Two or three nights went by'; 'Two or three days and nights went by; I reckon I might say they swum by'; 'Soon as it was night'; 'pretty soon'; 'One morning'; 'by-and-by'. In this context Tom's final revelation, that 'Old Miss Watson died two months ago', seems extraordinary. For all Huck ever registers is sequence.[7]

As the raft drifts, Huck drifts. He is hopelessly fatalistic. Now he is 'lazying around', now on the jump. One by one, things just happen. There are good signs; there are bad signs. There is good luck and bad luck. Huck lives in a predetermined world where 'the good and the bad are the things that happen to you, not the ways you choose to behave'.[8] In fact, there is a total lack of connection between Huck's actions and any ideas. All he realizes is that there is: (1) something wrong with Miss Watson's version of Christianity in general and the Grangerford version of Presbyterianism in particular; (2) something wrong with the conventions of morality as a system; (3) something wrong with slavery as an institution.[9] All he has is a negative conscience (THOU SHALT NOT) which is haphazard and wholly unpredictable in its spontaneous irruptions. As he concludes:

> it don't make no difference whether you do right or wrong, a person's conscience ain't got no sense, and just goes for him anyway. If I had a yaller dog that didn't know no more than a person's conscience does, I would pison him. It takes up more room than all the rest of a person's insides, and yet ain't no good, nohow.[10]

This undogmatic, drifting, spontaneous approach to life is what makes Huck so endearing, of course. His problems may be moral, but he does not confront them as moral problems. Not as complex and demanding issues. A 'thing that had some good in it' (like smoking) simply means something that makes him feel good. His is a wholly sensual register of 'right' and 'wrong'. It is all a matter of expedience. The questions are never remotely speculative but can be reduced, on their lowest terms, to: what makes Huck feel comfortable? What makes him feel uncomfortable? Conscience is such a 'yaller dog' because it invariably makes him feel uncomfortable. It is really this discomfort, rather than what is discreditable, that troubles him. This is why he tells himself (it is his major imperative) always to 'do whichever come handiest at the time'. What he asks himself on the key issue of betraying Jim is:

> would you felt better than what you do now? No, says I, I'd feel bad—I'd feel just the same way I do now. Well, then, says I, what's the use of you learning to do right, when it's troublesome to do right and ain't no trouble to do wrong, and the wages is just the same?[11]

Huck is a philosopher of a kind in that he likes to relax a good deal and smoke and meditate: 'I laid there in the grass and the cool shade, thinking about things and feeling rested and ruther comfortable and satisfied' (34/45). But he can only really think about what is in front of his nose. In the long run, he is pragmatic. He is a fatalist. In a word, a hedonist.[12] James M. Cox put it well:

> Freedom for Huck is not realized in terms of political liberty but in terms of pleasure. Thus his famous pronouncement about life on the raft: 'Other places do seem so cramped up and smothery, but a raft don't. You feel mighty free and easy and comfortable on a raft.'[13]

Or, again, he avoids tangling with the king and duke by observing: 'what you want, above all things, on a raft, is for everybody to be satisfied, and feel right and kind towards the others' (102/165).

Huck's ultimate principle, then, is the pleasure principle: lounging, 'talking, and singing, and laughing'. It is a wholly passive principle. It even affects his language. Huck has a trick of transforming adjectives, describing a passive state like 'lazy' or 'sad', into active verbs: 'And afterwards we would watch the lonesomeness of the river, and kind of lazy along, and by-and-by lazy off to sleep' (97/157). It is as if passivity, experienced deeply enough, can itself become an active principle. As if even to 'drift' might become an active verb. As if rafting were responsibility. Yet the raft inevitably drifts and cannot initiate action. For that reason Huck, despite his quick-change defence mechanisms, is such easy prey for active predators like Tom, or the king and duke.

Twain first published his thoughts on rafting in his book of German travels:

> The motion of the raft ... is gentle, and gliding, and smooth, and noiseless; it calms down all feverish activities, it soothes to sleep all nervous hurry and impatience; under its restful influence all the troubles and vexations and sorrows that harass the mind vanish away, and existence becomes a dream, a charm, a deep and tranquil ecstasy.[14]

There has been general jubilation all round among critics at the beauty of raft society and of raft relationships, especially of the relationship between Huck and Jim. But Jim, as it were, has been hijacked on to the raft. For him this raft-as-idyll is merely a means to an end: to safety and self-possession. Freedom for him can only mean political freedom. (Both Huck and the majority of his critics are peculiarly thick-skinned about this.) For Huck, of course, there is a charm, a dream, an ecstasy. This soothing of feverish activity, this calming 'all nervous hurry and impatience', is a kind of harmonious self-indulgence. It means, for a start, an emptying out of 'conscience'. That is his temporary bliss. He can now *both* help another *and* look out for him all the time, yet think continually about himself (which the Widow had expressly warned him against).

Such are the positive blessings for Huck in the drift; for Jim there are none. To that extent T. S. Eliot was right: 'Huck is the passive observer of men and events, Jim the submissive sufferer from them; and they are equal in dignity.' Or as Jonathan Raban more robustly phrased it: Huck 'tries to transfer this passive acceptance into situations which demand moral and intellectual discrimination'.[15] It leaves him singularly unprepared to meet crises. His reaction is to duck. He avoids confrontations wherever possible. When the king and duke, for example, board the raft, his main concern is to 'keep peace in the family':

> But I never said nothing, never let on; kept it to myself; it's the best way; then you don't have no quarrels, and don't get into no trouble ... If I never learnt nothing else out of Pap, I learnt that the best way to get along with his kind of people is to let them have their own way.[16]

To troubles which he cannot duck, he abjectly surrenders. When the king and duke unexpectedly reappear after the Wilks funeral, he just wilts. He never fights back. It is all he can do 'to keep from crying' (163/260).

In other tricky situations he blindly forges ahead. He simply trusts in 'Providence'. This confused and fatalistic residue of conflicting versions of predestination, as presented in the Watson–Douglas household, is his only resource. He has no other moral or intellectual map to guide him. At the critical moment, on approaching the Phelps farmhouse, he is without a plan, without an initiative, without a safeguard. He just goes right along, 'trusting to Providence to put the right words' in his mouth. It is a parlous predicament.

His empirical quick wits and acute observations are not much help, either. Huck is interested in *what* things are (how they work, how they are made), not in *why* they are there in the first place. As Huck lies in the cool shade of Jackson's Island 'thinking about things', the play of light catches his eye; the cause of those shifting, dappled sun-specks is the kind of 'thing' he thinks about:

> I could see the sun out at one or two holes, but mostly it was big trees all about, and gloomy in there amongst them. There was freckled places on the ground where the light sifted down through the leaves, and the freckled places swapped about a little, showing there was a little breeze up there.[17]

He is always observant, always inquiring. But his pragmatic mind stops short at practical questions. It can make certain deductions. It reasons from visible shifts below to an invisible breeze above. But that is all. It never probes this causal chain. It never pushes beyond immediate cause and effect. That is why Huck can so shrewdly observe society and still be taken in. As he is taken in by the Grangerfords. As he is taken in by the circus 'drunk'; and the ring-master as well:

> Then the ring-master he see how he had been fooled, and he *was* the sickest ring-master you ever see, I reckon. Why, it was one of his own men! He had got up that joke all out of his own head, and never let on to nobody. Well, I felt sheepish enough, to be took in so ...[18]

That is why Huck is so often a victim of events, or incompetent or ineffectual in his undertakings. However observant, his naïvely objective mind is naturally credulous. He notes that the fruit in the Grangerford parlour is fraudulent, artificial, made of plaster; but leaves us, his readers, to ponder the social and moral implications. He inspects and explores and tests his world, but he does not interpret it. He does not translate it. He does not read it. He is literate, but too literal-minded. So, unlike Tom, he is a halting rather than a habitual reader. Leafing through *Pilgrim's Progress* is a puzzling experience: 'I read considerable in it now and then. The statements was interesting, but tough' (83/137). Tough, that is, for someone without an instinctive symbolic imagination. Huck seems not even to recognize that this book 'about a man that left his family it didn't say why' might have symbolic implications for his own mysterious departure from Pap and St Petersburg.[19] But by his same literal standards he is impressed by Emmeline Grangerford's doggerel 'Ode to Stephen Dowling Bots, Dec'd'. 'It was very good poetry,' he asserts. It is his one unqualified critical judgement.

As Locke might have put it, Huck possesses sensibility, imagination and memory, but little power of reflection since he cannot compare ideas or reason abstractly.[20] So naturally he cannot grasp the abstract idea of fiction, only of the practical disguises (or fictions) by which he sustains his life. Introducing himself, oddly, as a reader (of a book) and a character (in that book), he is at once its most formidable critic:

> You don't know about me, without you have read a book by the name of 'The Adventures of Tom Sawyer', but that ain't no matter. That book was made by Mr Mark Twain, and he told the truth, mainly. There was things which he stretched, but mainly he told the truth.

The sole test of fiction for Huck is truth. He is no Pirandello-like character in search of an author. Decisively he *verifies* Mark Twain: 'he told the truth, mainly'. *The Adventures of Tom Sawyer*, he insists, 'is mostly a true book'; then again modifies the claim: 'with some stretchers, as I said before'. Untruths nag. When qualified to judge a text, he qualifies his critical judgement not aesthetically, not morally, but with the evidence of his senses, of his memory, with first-hand proof. Twain may be a literary author, that is, but Huck remains the living authority. Though often and easily fooled, especially by close friends, Huck never fools himself. He just fools others with his fictions.

A 'huckleberry', in contemporary parlance, was a person of no consequence. Huck, who is of 'mudcat' status like Pap, is basically a survivor. At a pinch he can mount a dramatic action. Just as Jim decisively left Miss Watson, so Huck planned his own very stylish and incontravertible murder. But his active interventions tend to misfire. For they tend to be based on the Sawyer model (his only model for dramatic action); and Huck is no Tom. Unlike Tom, for one thing, he never comes on 'ca'm and important, like the ram' (179/285). Unlike Sherburn, too, with a double-barrel gun on his porch roof: 'ca'm and deliberate, not saying a word' (118/189). He bungles the visit to Mrs Loftus. He bungles the boarding of the *Walter Scott*. He bungles disastrously with the dead rattlesnake; and even more disastrously in the attempt to locate the Ohio at Cairo.

Only at the Wilks funeral does he successfully initiate an action and energetically intervene. His participation there, though, is an exception that proves the rule; and even then it misfires. He is torn by puppy love. The rival claimants put in their appearance. He feels threatened, whichever way he turns, by the extraordinary rigmarole woven round him by the king. For once he has no idea what to say. He is hedged in by truth. He is hedged in by lies:

> here's a case where I'm blest if it don't look to me like the truth is better, and actuly *safer*, than a lie. I must lay it by in my mind, and think it over some time or other, it's so kind of strange and unregular. I never see nothing like it.[21]

Exposed to questioning, therefore, he is hopelessly out of his depth:

> Then the doctor whirls on me and says:
>   'Are you English too?'
>   I says yes; and him and some others laughed, and said, 'Stuff!' ... And by-and-by they had me up to tell what I knowed. The king he give me a left-handed look out of the corner of his eye, and so I knowed enough to talk on the right side. I begun to tell about Sheffield, and how we lived there, and all about the English Wilkses, and so on; but I didn't get pretty fur till the doctor begun to laugh; and Levi Bell, the lawyer, says:
>   'Set down, my boy, I wouldn't strain myself, if I was you. I reckon you ain't used to lying, it don't seem to come handy; what you want is practice. You do it pretty awkward.'[22]

Which is much what Mrs Loftus told Huck in drag: 'You do a girl tolerable poor, but you might fool men, maybe' (53/74). Still, he does outsmart the king and duke by hiding the gold in Peter Wilks's coffin. They reckon the 'niggers' stole it; and even when it turns up in the exhumed coffin they mutually suspect each other sooner than suspect Huck of outwitting them both.

It is ignorance, incompetence, powerlessness that bedevils Huck. That is why he is so overawed by the Grangerfords and the king; why he kowtows to Tom. For they are all endowed with a 'demonic force'.[23] Poor Huck is far from demonic. Leslie Fiedler called him 'the most non-violent of American fictional children'. Unlike Tom, he observes, he never fights with his fists: 'He runs, hides, equivocates, dodges, and, when he can do nothing else, suffers.'[24]

NOTES

1. *Huckleberry Finn*, ch. 17, p. 81/135.

2. ibid., ch. 19, p. 97/158.

3. ibid., ch. 17, p. 83/136–7.

4. To this wondering 'I' with wandering hands I shall return, for a full discussion of Huck's style, in Chapter 13.

5. Charles Miner Thompson, 'Mark Twain as an interpreter of American character', *Atlantic Monthly*, vol. 79 (1897), pp. 443–50. But I omit the racist conclusion: 'his strong and struggling moral nature, so notably Anglo-Saxon'. This adds a new twist to the debate surrounding the genteel reception of the book. See above, Ch. 3.

6. Huckleberry Finn, ch. 33, p. 182/290.

7. See Alan Trachtenberg, 'The form of freedom in *Adventures of Huckleberry Finn*', *Southern Review*, new series vol. 6 (October 1970), pp. 965–6.

8. Jonathan Raban, *Mark Twain: Huckleberry Finn* (London: Edward Arnold, 1968), ch. 1, p. 18.

9. Even this is arguable. His main worry at the end is why "Tom can act like a 'low-down abolitionist': 'I couldn't even understand, before ... how he could help a body set a nigger free, with his bringing-up' (227/358).

10. *Huckleberry Finn*, ch. 33, p. 183/290.

11. ibid., ch. 16, p. 76/127–8.

12. A 'lazy hedonism' was Lionel Trilling's phrase (1948).

13. James M. Cox, *Mark Twain: The Fate of Humor* (Princeton, NJ: Princeton University Press, 1966), ch. 7, p. 178.

14. Mark Twain, *A Tramp Abroad* (1880), ch. 15.

15. T.S. Eliot, introduction to *The Adventures of Huckleberry Finn* (London: Cresset Press, 1950), p. xi; Raban, *Mark Twain: Huckleberry Finn*, ch. 1, p. 17. 'Dignity' hardly seems an appropriate word for Huck; but even 'passive' seems to offend some critics. 'The very last word one should use to describe Huck is "passive",,' wrote Gilbert M. Rubenstein. 'He is no drifter but a plucky, lovable boy who, after painful self-examination, achieves an iron determination to help his friend Jim, reach free territory.' See 'The moral structure of Huckleberry Finn', *College English*, vol. 18 (November 1956), pp. 72–6, which is a reply to Lauriat Lane, Jr, 'Why *Huckleberry Finn* is a great world novel', *College English*, vol. 17 (October, 1955), pp. 1–5. Iron determination? To reach free territory? 'Passive' seems to alarm some readers as much as if one had called Huck 'queer'. See Leslie Fiedler's notorious essay, 'Come back to the raft ag'in, Huck honey!', *Partisan Review*, vol. 15 (June, 1948), pp. 664–71.

16. *Huckleberry Finn*, ch. 19, p. 102/165.

17. ibid., ch. 8, p. 34/45.

18. ibid., ch. 22, p. 120/194.

19. This may also be something of a private joke. Twain's own first book was entitled *The Innocents Abroad, or The New Pilgrim's Progress* (1869). Huck is yet another 'New Pilgrim', or Innocent Abroad.

20. John Locke, *An Essay Concerning Human Understanding*, ed. Peter Nidditch (Oxford University Press, 1975), p. 160.

21. *Huckleberry Finn*, ch. 28, p. 148/239.

22. ibid., ch. 29, pp. 157–8/252–3.

23. George C. Carrington, Jr., *The Dramatic Unity of 'Huckleberry Finn'* (Columbus, Ohio: Ohio State University Press, 1976), ch. 2, p. 55.

24. Leslie Fiedler, *Love and Death in the American Novel* (New York: Criterion Books, 1960; London: Paladin, 1970), ch. 13, pp. 426–7.

ANDREW JAY HOFFMAN

Huck's Heroism

Mark Twain's *Adventures of Huckleberry Finn* has left squadrons of uneasy critics. The novel's hero and the novel's ending seem so unsuited to one another that critics have been able to find no sure ground between them. Readers praising Huck Finn tremble at the formal confusion of *Huckleberry Finn*; readers moved by the novel's moral complexity doubt its hero's heroism. Understanding the novel as a whole, however, means seeing the hero in his story, and seeing him all the way through to the end, no matter how bitter. Few critics have demonstrated a comprehensive relationship between Huck and *Huck*, especially its ending. Early critics, such as Lionel Trilling and T. S. Eliot, lavished praise on Huck's courage in the face of a corrupt society, seeing him as a natural philosopher of the democratic virtues of equality and individualism. After Leo Marx knocked the stuffing out of this reading by pointing out in "Mr Trilling, Mr. Eliot, and *Huckleberry Finn*" that the last fifth of the novel was wholly inconsistent with it, modern critics looked for a moral structure for the novel which included the evasion sequence. George C. Carrington made the best and most comprehensive attempt in his *Dramatic Unity in "Huckleberry Finn."* He writes, "The highest meaning of the novel lies in the reader's outraged response to it, the central part of that response being the usual resentment of the ending. Without committing himself or forcing us, Twain allows us to identify contentedly

From *Twain's Heroes, Twain's Worlds.* © 1988 by the University of Pennsylvania Press.

with Huck; then he disillusions us, and we howl" (122). Carrington wisely reads the ethic of the novel as situational and Huck's growth not as moral development but as increased expertise in influencing the small dramas in which the situational ethic obtains. Like most later critics, Carrington gives Huck's heroism no quarter. Huck's moral heroism, like the "masochistic interest in Jim, is [the reader's] own creation, not Huck's" (123). Carrington finds a unity in *Huckleberry Finn* in part by denying Huck the kind of heroism most readers experience in the text.

I believe we can find this unity between the book and its narrator even closer to our experiential knowledge of the novel by looking first at Huck as hero. In the following chapters I will argue that we experience Huck as a hero in the novel because his story closely resembles models of traditional heroism. Other interpretations of Huck's heroism—as existential hero, as romantic hero, as nonhero—illustrate aspects of Huck's function in his world, but few account for both his character and behavior. Huck's traditional heroism is masked slightly by the transformations of oral storytelling literature makes—the transformation of royalty into rapscallions, for example—but reading Huck's story in the context of inherited tales makes the correspondence between the two startling. Huck closely fits our expectations of the traditional hero. This discovery answers one question for us and suggests an answer for the second: we see now why we view Huck as a hero, among the greatest creations of American literature, despite his failure at the end; and we begin to see why Huck has to fail. Twain has taken a traditional hero, a creature of oral tale-telling, by nature ahistorical, and put him in a fiction wholly unsuited to him. The context distorts and defrocks Huck as hero. He looks either foolishly romantic or helplessly unheroic, his heroic powers diminished, perhaps completely sapped, by his surroundings. It is at this point of dissonance that we find Carrington's "highest meaning of the novel," a juxtaposition poignant and disappointing. Mark Twain has created a comprehensive traditional hero and placed him in a world where his heroism cannot function, where the magic, the idealism, the integrity of the traditional hero have no power.

In the next chapter I will examine the sort of world the novel creates, a world which has the power to defeat a hero's magic. Finding this world poses as many difficulties and perhaps fewer rewards than Columbus' explorations. We must navigate Huck Finn's language to get to it, and Huck's talk resists the application of most critical tools beyond simple appreciation. Tense confusion makes separating Huck-the-writer from Huck-the-written-about nearly impossible. Diction and a flexible irony make separating Huck and Twain a matter of assertion, not proof. Huck's studied ignorance makes the readers' complicity in the novel's construction an integral part of the fiction.

Huck's language creates of *Huckleberry Finn* a text impervious to deconstruction, a sort of fun-house whose construction resists any understanding of its construction from within. To comprehend, critics must get above and look down into the novel. This movement reveals in the novel a special sort of reality, one based on a confluence of time and writing. Time—the measure of time, that is—and writing create history, and the world of the novel is an historically conceived one. Further, they defeat tradition, particularly the oral one where heroes exist out of time and where the rules of the world of experience no longer apply. Huck's heroism loses in the novel's end to nothing more—or less—than history.

That history, though, is not simply abstract. The history in *Huckleberry Finn* particularly concerns Jacksonian America. Huck is made to be more than a traditional hero; he is the hero of the age. Using the work of historians of the period, the third chapter reveals Huck as the emblem of the Jacksonian cultural goals of Nature, Providence and Will and the Jacksonian socio-political goals of equality, democracy and individualism. More, we see in looking into the journals and travelogues of the day just what everyday Jacksonian America looked like and find it looks exactly like the world the novel presents us. The tensions in the novel exist not only between an oral hero in a written world, the ahistorical powers of magic against the unstoppable flow of time and writing that is history, but also between the ideals of an age and its reality. Jacksonian Democracy braced itself with the twin concepts of individual freedom and political equality, but it stood on the twin abuses of slavery and Indian resettlement. The novel begins where *Tom Sawyer* ends, with Huck and Tom recapturing the money Injun Joe stole. It ends, as critics have always noted, in moral disarray, our hero's efforts to free Jim decimated by a culturally based romantic idealism, the last piece of Huck's crusade blown away by the unexplained whimsy of Miss Watson's death-bed manumission. This confluence of heroes and history, of Jacksonian ideals and Jacksonian life, produces new flashes of meaning in *Huckleberry Finn*.

*   *   *

Let us begin by clarifying the nature of Huck's heroism. Many critics argue for Huck's complete lack of heroism. Lawrence Scanlon's "Unheroic Huck," for example, finds a host of opportunities to make of Huck a traditional hero, opportunities Twain sets up and rejects to prove Huck's lack of heroism. Scanlon finds the novel's initial cave and barrel imagery reminiscent of the womb and writes, "Usually when womb imagery appears in literature, it is preparatory to the rebirth of the hero" (100), but in the novel Huck is not reborn from those wombs; he just surrenders himself to the Mississippi. For Scanlon, Huck's predeliction for passivity is the fundamental aspect of his character. The raft, controlled only by the river's flow, matches perfectly the nature of its inhabitant, and that is why Huck finds happiness on it. Huck's "lack of purposive action" (107) continues to the novel's conclusion where readers at last get frustrated with Huck. "By preferring passivity to action, fantasied death to active life, Huck turns the conventional notion of the hero upside down" (111). In making him a nonhero, Twain shows "that all forms of response to society as it presently constituted are alike impossible, if not insane" (113).

Scanlon's argument invites two fundamental questions. First, exactly what society has Huck refused participation in? Apart from the occasional manhandling by the King and Duke, characters his own actions brought into his life, nothing induces Huck to leave the river. Huck visits Mrs. Loftus because "it was getting slow and dull, and I wanted to get a stirring up, some way" (66). He begins the final portion of the novel with an extremely purposive action: "For a starter, I would go to work and steal Jim from slavery again; and if I could think up anything worse, I would do that too" (271). Even though Tom Sawyer dominates the evasion, Huck's actions form a necessary part of it. If Huck were an absolute devotee of inaction, there would be no book; he would never write one. Huck's conflicts with society come not from his attempts to escape its domination of him, but from his persistent will to self-determination when within society, a will that drives him to perform actions he knows society cannot approve. Taken from Huck's point of view, society is any group structure which disallows his freedom; a calculated lack of response to this society is impossible because the society itself only exists in contradistinction to his own actions.

Second, taking Scanlon's arguments on its own terms, what distinguishes a nonhero from a hero of a more definable sort? Scanlon writes, "If in this context a hero is defined as one who acts bravely and purposely on behalf of himself and others, a whole culture possibly, and an anti-hero one who acts similarly to destroy himself or his society, the non-hero does not act at all. His primary, and sometimes all-embracing, feature is passivity" (111). This passivity is not powerlessness, Scanlon insists. "Mark Twain through Huck's passivity has rendered an even more telling judgment on society than he could have with a frontal assault" (113). Other critics give other names to heroes performing the functions Scanlon ascribes to Huck. In "Huck Finn as Existential Hero: Making Sense of Absurdity," Arthur Asa Berger argues that "Huck functions as a *fool*," making "use of the humor of pattern and exaggeration, techniques used throughout the book" (13). A fool, Berger leaves his reader to gather, points out his own wisdom by exaggerating the patterned idiocy of society at large. Huck achieves this primarily through his pragmatism, that fundamental American characteristic. We first see Huck's pragmatism in his unsuccessful prayers for fish hooks; it reaches its peak in his subtle ridiculing of Tom by "letting on" picks and stairs are case knives and lightning rods, as long as Tom's plan will eventually free Jim. He tells Tom, "When I start in to steal a nigger, or a watermelon, or a Sunday school book, I ain't no ways particular how it's done, so it's done.... I don't give a dead rat what the authorities thinks about it, nuther" (307). According to Berger, Huck "is his own authority" (14). Counter to Scanlon's argument, Berger notes that, as a fool, Huck is not expected to act, only to represent. "Huck symbolizes man's possibilities for goodness and Huck's moral development is a demonstration of man's potentialities being realized" (15). At the same time, Berger's argument goes, Huck's alienation from society and his frequent adoption of other identities to cope with the alienation establishes Huck as an existential hero. "Huck Finn suggests ... what might be called an awareness of the possibility of error. This is important, for if we are aware of error then we can try to correct it" (17). Huck's heroism is of a moral nature, Berger implies; his inaction matters less than his ridicule of society on one hand and his moral awareness on the other. Being who he is, knowing what he knows, is Huck's heroic action. The whole book serves as prelude, Berger asserts, to Huck's final action, the mythic initiation of lighting out for the territory, a new land, which Berger equates with Mircea Eliade's Center of the World.

This somewhat incoherent presentation of Huck's heroism appears a bit closer to the Huck we experience in reading *Adventures of Huckleberry Finn* than Lawrence Scanlon's, but there remain several gaps and problems. First, Huck reaches his moral peak in famous Chapter 31, when he consigns himself to hell for his willingness to save Jim from further enslavement. Leo Marx points out in the influential essay "Mr. Eliot, Mr. Trilling, and *Huckleberry Finn*" that, while Huck does represent "the redemptive possibilities of the human race" (437), those possibilities remain only that. The failure of the novel's ending is the failure of Huck himself to make good on his moral promises. When he lights out for the territory ahead of the rest he leaves his betrayed readers' hearts behind. If this move west proves "Huck's authenticity," as Berger contends, then the move ought to elicit a sympathy for Huck's quest, not the coldness we do feel after 80 pages of Huck's participation as the erstwhile Tom Sawyer in the torture of his friend Jim.

Further, the very moral integrity upon which Berger bases his argument is suspect. A close look at Chapter 31 reveals an acceptance of society, not a refusal of it. Huck has "got to decide, forever, betwixt two

things, and I knowed it" (270): between following law and morality by
returning Jim to Miss Watson, or breaking law and morality by freeing him.
Huck perceives his choices as two: being socially acceptable, like Tom
Sawyer or the Widow Douglas, or being socially unacceptable, like Pap or
the King and Duke. Huck chooses to join his father and the royalty in hell,
a choice he makes in the very first chapter in response to Miss Watson: "She
told me about the bad place, and I said I wished I was there" (3). All Huck's
experiences have simply served to refine his determination to spend eternity
with the Devil. His first-chapter assertion grows out of his desire to "go
somewhere, all I wanted was a change, I warn't particular" (4), granting the
moral plane the same boundless feel as the West's Great Plains. By the peak
of his moral crisis, however, the range of possibility has narrowed to a choice
between social convention and hell. In case we miss the point Huck repeats
his claims to be "lowdown," "born to wickedness" and so on. Huck's
alienation from society is only an alienation from a part of it, the society
implied by the term 'society pages.' Huck identifies himself with Pap's class,
with Pap himself and with Pap's wholesale acceptance of the institutional
immorality we find in his "Call this a gov-ment" speech (33–34), an
institutional immorality against which we deeply want Huck to rebel.

Second, though Berger claims for Huck some traditional heroic
qualities, he does not make himself specific. Huck is cast as fool, he says, but
in the book itself Jim plays the fool in Huck's court; the conversations about
Solomon and the French language in Chapter 14 will prove that. Berger
alludes to the continuing death and rebirth of Huck but does not fit these
heroic attributes into a heroic model. His consideration of Huck's traditional
heroism is left at the level of allusion.

Several cogent arguments about the nature of Huck's traditional
heroism have appeared. The premier one, from Robert Regan's *Unpromising
Heroes*, examines Huck against the background of the well-articulated,
folktale-based type of the title. Regan finds in Mark Twain a pattern of
heroism stemming from youngest-child folktales. In these stories, stronger
but ill-willed older brothers serve themselves instead of their ailing fathers,
mothers or lovers. The disenfranchised, disdained, and dispossessed younger
brother performs the needed service, usually through a combination of
cunning, kindness, and magic, but is temporarily denied reward by the
actions of his jealous siblings. In time, though, he rises to kingship either
through marriage to a princess or inheritance of his father's throne, again
achieved through this same combination of cunning, kindness, and magic.
Regan maintains that this unpromising or unlikely hero theme underlies
most of Twain's heroes, Tom Sawyer, Hank Morgan, and David Wilson most
notably. Only rarely "Mark Twain could, by special effort, escape the narrow

confines of his most persistent theme, and produce, albeit painfully, as in *Adventures of Huckleberry Finn*, a hero who is motivated by impulses more exalted than the dream of glory" (14). Regan argues that Huck's character, and not plot exigencies, directs the novel in the end to pit Tom, Twain's conventional hero type, against Huck. Regan sees Huck's character much as Berger does, as a moral force for disengagement, a Bartleby on a raft, always preferring absolute inaction to social conformity and corruption. When forced to action by the strength of his conviction he discovers just how much trouble bravery and higher purpose can be. Tom, "still motivated in all he does by a neurotic impulse to make himself a hero" (158), Regan writes, "provides a conclusive dramatization of Huck's election of the anti-heroic— the genuinely heroic—life" (159). Temporarily tempted by Tom, Huck agrees in the novel's final fifth to an uneasy peace with his past, the romantic and artificial world of Tom and St. Petersburg. The compromise is rife with tension, though, and Regan sees the outcome of this conflict as beautifully represented by the question of identities: Huck only seems to become Tom, but "Huck of course never quite forgets his true identity" (160), the security of identity itself being Huck's only true claim to heroism.

Regan reads Huck convincingly. Sadly Huck lies outside the province of his study; Regan does not turn his folkloric eye on Huck himself and instead sees him only as a counter to his other, well-argued traditional type. He defines Huck primarily as not-Tom: antiromantic, inactive, inward-directed, asocial. Unfortunately he leaves a particular reversal unexplored, a reversal I will myself explore later: the picture of Huck Finn as a Promising Unhero, a positive definition of Huck's traditional heroism gone down in failure at the novel's end.

Other critics have found traditional heroic characteristics in Huck, many of which run counter to Regan's portrait-by-negation. Daniel Hoffman, in his classic *Form and Fable in American Fiction*, sees Huck's "moral eminence" in his stark contrast to Tom's romantic visions. Huck resists the bookish artifice of Tom and the con-men Duke and King, whom Hoffman sees in moral alliance with Tom, and instead goes to school with Jim, where he learns the hidden powers of Nature. Jim is more than Huck's fool, more than the traditional hero's also traditional strong and stout-hearted friend. For Hoffman, "If the river is a god, Jim is its priest.... Only when Jim is alone with Huck on the river island or drifting on the current is he so free from the corruption of civilization that he can partake of the river god's dark power" (335). Learn as he might, Huck's powers have boundaries. While in his easy assumption of alternative identities he "seems to remain true to the American folk concept of the metamorphic hero" (343), his "powers of transformation are not ... illimitably protean" (346). His attempts to be like

Tom only increase the danger to himself and Jim. Huck can survive "the threats to his identity of the retrograde Pap, of the avaricious slave-hunters, of the feuders with their courtly savagery and the lynch mob with its cowardly passions" (348), but among the quality against whom these vermin define themselves, a quality among whom Tom's artifice works superbly, Huck has no power and must flee. Huck's "classical pattern of death and rebirth of the hero" (343) places him outside of the real world's realm. In the real world, when operating smoothly at its most corrupt, Huck's powers do not work. The magical pairing of Huck and Jim does not represent a homoerotic deathwish, as Leslie Fiedler maintains in *Love and Death in the American Novel*. Instead, Daniel Hoffman writes, "the two themes" the regular pairing of white and nonwhite in American literature "exemplify are primitivism and egalitarianism" (349). In this sense, we can construe Huck's heroism as fitting a part of Scanlon's earlier definition of the hero: Huck represents virtue for the whole culture.

Some critics disagree with aspects of Hoffman's view of Huck. Warren Beck in his seminal "Huck Finn at Phelps Farm," the first extended attempt to resolve the conflict over the ending of the novel, writes that "Mark's conception of Huck was not superficially romantic but genuinely and deeply so. Huck is not a noble savage, existing with naive aplomb in an unmodified innocence; he transcends ignorance, step by slow step, as any man must, by taking upon his own shoulders the knowledge of good and evil" (27). More than a decade later, Alan Ostrom made Beck's "knowledge" more specific: "The sole continuing conflict in the novel, in fact, a conflict made manifest in every incident, every episode, is the conflict between the person-as-individual and the person-as-member-of-society. For if Huck is a Romantic youth figure, he is *not* a noble savage" (164). Individualism marks this romantic character. The contrast between Huck and Tom in the novel's end is not between socially approved and sophisticated romance and elitism on one hand and antisocial primitivism and egalitarianism on the other, these critics imply, but between a false, book-based romanticism and a true, self-based one. Following this, Neil Sapper views Huck as a Tocquevillian individualist. "Tocqueville has provided an archetypal image of Huck Finn" (37), Sapper claims, by defining individualism as "a calm and considered feeling which disposes each citizen to isolate himself from the mass of his fellows and withdraw into the circle of family and friends; with this little society formed to his taste, he gladly leaves the greater society to look after itself" (Tocqueville, *Democracy in America*, 506). As many critics have pointed out, most notably Robert Shulman in "Fathers, Brothers, and 'the Diseased': The Family, Individualism, and American Society in *Huckleberry Finn*," Huck and Jim form a family which "suggests the possibility of an individualism not at odds with the community" (327). It is in this family, most critics agree with Hoffman, that Huck acquires the knowledge that makes him a heroic force. Few critics have solved the problem of what transforms his heroism into a spent force when Huck reaches the Phelps plantation.

Two things remain consistent in these inconsistent critical appraisals of Huck Finn's heroism: Huck's heroism has traditional qualities; and no matter what form that heroism seems to take prior to Chapter 31, it comes out bruised and tarnished between that point and the end of the novel. I began this review of critical thinking on Huck's heroism with the comment that these two common observations remain insufficiently linked. The slippage between Huck's traditional heroism and his failure to act heroically (or between Huck as hero when alone and Huck as failure in society) invites deconstruction. But before I turn my attention to Huck Finn's language, which provides our best clue in solving this disjuncture, we must clarify our conception of these divided parts.

The nature of Huck's failure at the Phelps' farm seems clear: the pressure of this world prevents him from making good on the heroism promised earlier. This is why we find critics arguing first that Huck is a hero and then that he is not, or arguing that he is a noble savage or a romantic youth figure and then not. This formulation of the problem advances us towards a solution in the following way. Rather than assuming that the failure of Huck's heroism is narrative—that is, that Huck himself changes his character in the course of the book, or that Twain failed in keeping Huck consistent—this construct assumes that the book is *about* the failure of a hero. Other narratives of failed heroism must be told from the third person, because the hero dies, or involve comically small achievements, such as the failure of the hero in John Barth's *The Floating Opera* to kill himself. In *Huckleberry Finn* we have instead a true hero with worthy goals who, unaware of his failure or his heroism, tells his own tale. While the perspectives discussed above grasp aspects of Huck's heroism, none has laid hold of that heroism's very nature, something we must do in order to comprehend its failure. And as an expression of contemporary knowledge of the nature of heroism in fiction I know no better book than Lord Raglan's *The Hero*.

Not that Raglan's treatise comes without objection. In the fifty years since its publication, *The Hero* has sustained a nearly endless barrage of criticism. Almost all the resistance to the book comes down to its lack of rigor. *The Hero* in no way meets contemporary criteria for critical validity: Raglan was an amateur; he did most of his research in his own library; he often appears more concerned with wit than substance in his arguments. His choice as to what to include both in his book as a whole and in his particular construction of the hero's life seems purely arbitrary. His work reads more like pleasant fireside chat, fascinating but aimless, than a serious inquiry into important matters, a particularly painful scratch to dedicated scholars of folklore hoping to get their long-neglected discipline some deserved respect. Further, one significant point relies on the long-discredited premise that all folktales derive from a single point, an Ur-form.

But I do not use *The Hero* as I have used the Twain critics I have mentioned thus far. Criticism is secondary material; Raglan's work, whatever its flaws of rigor, is a kind of primary document. Whether or not what he writes meets disciplinary criteria for criticism matters less in this context than the text's expression of a cogent and popularly acceptable notion of the traditional hero. The book's continuation in print over more than half a century of critical disrepute indicates its wide use for just this purpose. I do not mean my use of it here to be an indication that either I or readers generally accept Raglan's premise that all the heroes which concern him derived from a single ritual drama performed in the lost past; our wider knowledge of history does not render Gibbon's *Decline and Fall of the Roman Empire* useless, but rather only qualifiedly useful. I do not mean Raglan to be taken as the complete or final expression of the hero. His arbitrary partiality does leave gaps, but that does not prove that what he does include is incorrect. And Lord Raglan's charm and humor has given his book and ideas a much longer life than more rigorous and less interesting scholars might have achieved.

Raglan attempts to prove in his classic work that the roots even of literate fiction lay in ancient ritual drama. In ritual drama, Raglan says, myth and ritual combine in a religious ceremony; a story of magical import is told and acted by the tribal kings and leaders as a sop to the gods or a satisfaction of some lost tribal need. In time the myth and the ritual become separate. Raglan does not say why; perhaps because the teller of the tale finds some benefit in telling his stories nonritually or because other raconteurs in the group appropriate aspects of ritual telling to their secular purposes—explanations of the tribal past, simple entertainment, whatever. The myths persist, coming down to literate culture as history or as fiction.

The view of myth as history grows from the belief that, within even the most outlandish and supernatural events of myth, there resides a kernel of historical fact. So: Hercules might not have swept out the stable, but he was a very great king, of massive strength, who came to rule by overcoming tremendous adversity. The savageness of the wise humor with which Raglan ridicules it testifies to how recently this view became discredited. Stories are not based on fact; instead, stories transform fact into a fiction that audiences find more believable. A preliterate culture, having a past but no history, tells its stories with more concern for truth than facts; facts cannot be verified without records, but truth relies only on the agreement of the audience. Raglan demonstrates how this habit of telling tales which transform facts survives the coming of writing. The differences between literate and preliterate cultures encourage the misappropriation of stories told in a lost context. For example, discussing the mythification of Henry V, Raglan writes that "those who composed the traditional stories about Prince Henry applied to him, in a more or less modified form, stories they had heard in a different but not dissimilar connection" (212). This fictionalization of history requires its Henry to have a riotous youth and a near indecent association with a man like Falstaff. "To Shakespeare's audiences the proper way for a budding hero to behave was to roister with a drunken buffoon" (213).

This willful neglect of the historical Henry, almost dour and rather staid as a prince, points to the limited interest storytellers or their audiences have in historical reality when creating a mythical hero. Literate peoples attribute mythical proportions to recent historical or even contemporary figures, as I will indicate later in regard to Andrew Jackson.

Heroes connected to history by invention rather than fact—for example the creations of modern fiction—have much less restraining their fulfillment of the traditional requirements of the hero. We would expect to find, then, a correlation between the attributes of a traditional hero and characters from contemporary fiction. But literate culture moves against the employment of types in its storytelling. Preliterate cultures have few ways to store knowledge; the apparent repetition of stories and types serves this end. I say apparent because pure repetition, repetition without variation, is impossible without the very tools that make a culture literate. This variation goes unnoticed—or if noticed is denied—by the members of the concerned tribe. These changes reflect the changing knowledge of the audience's world, but the audience's insistence that the story is pure repetition expresses the need to have a cultural link to the common knowledge which makes the audience a unified group. A culture of books and libraries, archives and museums, has no need to tie itself to its past; those ties are strong enough. Such a culture needs instead to differentiate itself from its past, to fight its past to achieve its needed change. The very notion of a supernaturally empowered hero contradicts literary tradition: the supernatural takes place out of time and is therefore highly resistant to the sort of change literature documents. Literary tradition seems to prefer heroes who are ordinary people in extraordinary circumstances; a thorough investigation of the heroes of this past century's fiction will produce few that follow Raglan's model of the traditional hero. Literate culture constantly develops new heroic patterns for its fiction; the existence of other hero types, such as the anti-hero, shows this. A quick review of Raglan's hero shows broad areas where the design of the traditional hero jars modern sensibility. Royal birth is, for the most part, out of the question in contemporary fiction. The mysticism and religiosity of the last eight points—the remarkable fit between this standard recitation of the traditional hero's death and the last days of Christ should both give pause to believers in Christ's historicity and proof to my point—appear awkward in the imagination of a scientific age. One part fits literate fiction; Raglan himself points out that the tradition of romance is "based on the central part of the myth" (191). That accounts only for points 10 through 13 in the Raglan's following model:

1.   The hero's mother is a royal virgin;
2.   His father is a king, and
3.   Often a near relative of his mother, but
4.   The circumstances of his conception are unusual and
5.   He is also reputed to be the son of a god.
6.   At birth an attempt is made, usually by his father or his maternal grandfather, to kill him, but
7.   He is spirited away, and
8.   Reared by foster-parents in a far country.
9.   We are told nothing of his childhood, but
10.   On reaching manhood he returns or goes to his future kingdom.
11.   After a victory over the king and/or giant, dragon or wild beast,
12.   He marries a princess, often the daughter of his predecessor and
13.   Becomes king.
14.   For a time he rules uneventfully, and
15.   Prescribes laws, but
16.   Later he loses favor with the gods and/or his subjects, and
17.   Is driven from the throne and city, after which
18.   He meets with a mysterious death,
19.   Often at the top of a hill.
20.   His children, if any, do not succeed him.
21.   His body is not buried, but nonetheless
22.   He has one or more holy sepulchres. (179–80)

A quick review of this sequence shows a tripartite structure. Points 1 through 8 recount the birth of the hero; 9 marks the sharp division between that story and the traditional romance of points to through 13. Point 14 establishes another break before the final third, the death of the hero. These three stories—birth, ascension to power and marriage, and death—are slung together to create a semblance of a whole life. These periods of dormancy are as telling for the traditional hero as the stories they link: it is almost as though the hero does not exist except when fulfilling the active requirements of heroism.

Despite the winds blowing against the possibility of a hero of modern fiction fitting into Raglan's heroic scheme, Huck Finn fits remarkably well. Without interpretive stretching, Huck fits half the provisions of the hero; interpretations modifying Raglan's scheme for modern American readers add several points of correspondence. The sequence of Huck's heroic acts does not match Raglan's, but, as I have noted, literariness encourages transformations of tradition. We do find in *Huckleberry Finn*, however, what Raglan found in his examination of traditional myth heroes: the same elements, though disordered. Because a written text needs to distinguish itself from previous written texts in ways unnecessary and unthought-of for oral tales, and because of the circumstantial need for variation in both oral and written cultures, we must expect many changes in contemporary renditions of traditional storytelling elements. These elements can be quite small, such as the national origin of adversaries, which in American war movies have changed from Japanese and German to Arab and Russian, or, as we see in *Huckleberry Finn*, quite large. Raglan writes that these elements change to suit the audiences' capacity for belief. We therefore cannot simply launch into an attempt to correlated Huck Finn and Raglan's construction of the hero. We must first explore how several modern readerly beliefs have affected the representation of traditional heroic actions.

I would like to review three aspects of the traditional hero and their transformations in *Huckleberry Finn*: the impermanence of death; the existence of kings; and the involvement of divinity or magic in real life. Contemporary America has an egalitarian, scientific ideology which allows little or no room for palingenesis, royalty or the supernatural, and yet these are vital ingredients in traditional popular stories. The democratic drive to include tales from the people in works of literature, perhaps best represented in the nineteenth century by Mark Twain, stems from the same ideology which actually makes aspects of those tales acceptable only as folklore, not as literature. To escape the identification of folktales with the quaint and arcane, storytellers must either transform these traditional elements or abandon them entirely.

Though Raglan does not explicitly include a round trip to the underworld in his hero pattern, he finds the Orpheus myth repeated and transformed for many heroes of tradition. Modern concepts of death preclude a true return from afterlife except in certain forms of reincarnation, but those beliefs have not eliminated the presence of palingenetic archetypes in contemporary fiction. Modern gothics often substitute coma for death, with the hero-victim often returning evilly empowered; Raglan notes that Christian-era holdovers from ritual drama play under the auspices of the Devil and that, in these holdovers, supernatural heroes become supernatural villains. Film, halfway between the elite novel and the gothic romance for realism, plays this theme often. Paddy Chayeffsky's and Ken Russell's 1980 film *Altered States* has its scientist-hero reach into the underworld of our genetic past and return, again evilly transformed. American fiction of this century has used this theme in many forms. John Barth's *The End of the Road* opens with its protagonist in a deathlike trance; he is analyzed and cured by a scientist. The planned confusion between characters named Quentin in William Faulkner's *The Sound and the Fury* creates the effect of death and return. In "The Aspern Papers" Henry James sends his unnamed narrator into the dusty death of the past and brings him back again. All of these renditions of the Orpheus myth of death and return work by transfiguring the nature of the death involved.

Sufficient critical attention has been paid to the presence of this theme in *Adventures of Huckleberry Finn*. No reader can help but notice the endless comparisons with and invocations of death in the novel. To bring Orpheus to bear in this book, Twain chooses a simpler solution than did his successors: he has his hero fake death. This simple solution meets the necessary criteria of creating out of something as incredible as palingenesis something more credible than the bungled romance of the evasion. It also provides opportunity for humor and elegance. Huck rigs his own death to escape Pap. For the next several chapters we receive pointed reminders of Huck's ambiguous position among the living: he witnesses attempts to find his body; he encounters Jim who, like everyone else, believes him to be dead; Mrs. Loftus speaks to Huck matter-of-factly about his murder. Chapter by chapter death appears. Before his own death, Huck "don't take no stock in dead people" (2) and he can not hide his disgust that Tom Sawyer's Gang "hadn't killed any people, but only just pretended" (14). But after Huck fakes his own death real death is everywhere: with the murderous bandits aboard the *Walter Scott*, in the floating house, at the Grangerford-Shepardson feud. Between acts leading to death, in moments of relative peace, Huck is so lonesome he wishes for death, or is imperiled by the elements, or takes on the identity of the mysterious dead baby Charles William Albright. His first encounter at the Phelps farm reminds us of the underworld nature of his journey. "I heard the dim hum of a spinning wheel wailing along up and sinking along down again: and then I knowed for certain I wished I was dead—for that is the lonesomest sound in the whole world" (277). When Huck is mistaken for Tom Sawyer "it was like being born again, I was so glad to find out who I was" (282). For the whole of the evasion Huck lives in the twilight world between life and death; being Tom is only *like* being born again. Only when Huck recovers his identity with the reappearance of Aunt Polly can he be said to reenter the living world completely. Like so much in *Huckleberry Finn*, death is more a matter of appearance than reality. Huck's death at his father's cabin convinces the good people of St. Petersburg; on the symbolic plane it convinces readers. The novel manages to incorporate the mystical qualities of palingenesis without straining contemporary readers' credulity.

Raglan believes traditional heroes of folktales are kings because the central figure in ritual drama was a king whose primary kingly responsibility was the ritual drama. "If folktales were really composed by the folk, we should expect them to deal with subjects with which the folk are familiar— matters of village courtship and marriage, of quarrels and revenges, of seedtime and harvest, of plenty and dearth, of hunting and fishing— ... but we should be disappointed. It is very seldom that peasants appear in the tales at all" (139). Instead, folktales concern either royalty or talking animals, which are in Raglan's view disguised royalty. In America, this presents a problem: we have no royalty. American fictions have solved this lack by replacing royalty with the rich and powerful. Prime-time soap operas dwell interminably on this class, as do movies; even the extraordinary *Ordinary People* documents a very well-to-do family. We interpret the determination not to write about royal-equivalents as political, as in the works of Richard Price or Marge Piercy. Earlier writers of the lives of plain folk have had to defend their choices with political or aesthetic manifestos: Norris and Dreiser championed naturalism, Dos Passos and Steinbeck a whole America. But lives of the socially advantaged do not require a political or aesthetic philosophy to be written: James and Fitzgerald wrote of almost no one else.

Not so Mark Twain. *Huckleberry Finn*'s low-life sensibility so offended high-brow Concord that the town banned it from their library. Though the novel contains little of the cultural elite, it is almost overloaded with a certain sort of royalty: the Duke and the King. After noting that "All kings is mostly rapscallions," Huck says "Sometimes I wish we could hear of a country that's out of kings" (201). America might be out of inherited royalty, but in Twain's construction we have picked up another kind. America's kings, like Huck's and Jim's unwelcome companions, get their crowns by bilking the public.

This is a sort of backhanded praise of America: we invert the traditional political hierarchy, putting the people on top and the royalty on the bottom. So long as the King and Duke and Pap and others of "his kind of people" (165) remain inversions of the social code, they will rule their particular underworld. Royalty dominates *Adventures of Huckleberry Finn*, the story of two unfortunates on the outs with conventional society. Huck, born into this inverted royalty, at first rejects it but later apprentices and becomes a "valley" to it. In his paradoxically moral stand of freeing Jim and going to hell, Huck rejoins the class to which his blood entitles him membership. He sets himself, as did the King and Duke and Pap, against society from within it, not from outside it. Twain has found a place for royalty in America, logically in opposition to the conventions of their democratic world.

Magic plays a fundamental role in the life of the hero. "Against the hero with the magic weapons the monster is powerless; he falls at the first blow. That is because the hero is a ritual personage using ritual weapons to deliver a ritual blow" (147). Magic acts play like miracles in drama, Raglan argues, and miracles have the following traits: they are performed by superhumans, their results are appropriate for superhuman acts, and they can only come out of ritual acts. In *The Tempest*, he writes, Ariel can appear and disappear miraculously, but in the plays of Prince Henry, Falstaff cannot. The relative positions of the hero and fool are the same in these plays, but the audience's acceptance of the miraculous has changed because of the conditions of the drama. Conditions in modern America disallow the miraculous. As a rule, narrative miracles need to be couched as science, as in science fiction, presented as the conscious deception of a public on the part of a confidence man, or imagined in metaphor, the magic of words. In Hemingway, for example, miracles become metaphors, plain and obvious symbols, such as the diverging railroad tracks in "Hills Like White Elephants." In this construction of the miraculous, the author himself becomes the supernatural force determining the shape of the fictive universe; this sort of magical transformation forms the core of metafiction. Con artists gratify the need for the supernatural by the creation of alternative realities; when we read fictions about them we see and accept both the narrative reality and the artificial ones they create within it. And science fiction allows anything to happen, especially the supernatural, so long as it is accompanied by an explanation that has the look and feel of science. Twentieth-century America looks askance at miracles and shapeshifting. It demands in their place the power of metaphor, the dodge of science fiction or the artifice of con artistry.

Twain himself, often called the father of American Realism, resists the miraculous. In his hilarious dismemberment "Fenimore Cooper's Literary

Offences," Twain writes that one of the "nineteen rules governing literary art in the domain of romantic fiction" requires "that the personages in a tale shall confine themselves to possibilities and let miracles alone; or, if they venture a miracle, the author must so plausibly set it forth as to make it look possible and reasonable" (*Unabridged*, 1242). In *Huckleberry Finn* he observes the rules of realism by rendering the miraculous commonplace. Conventional religion, the common residence for modern-day belief in the miraculous, is usurped from the first chapter on: Miss Watson's description of heaven only makes us laugh; the feuding families are called Shepherdson and Grangerford; the King milks religious sentiment at a revival meeting. Religion has no magic powers in the novel except in limited metaphors: we hear of "Moses and the Bulrushers" only to illuminate Huck's role as liberator. If we are looking for magic and miracles in *Huckleberry Finn* we will have to look outside conventional religion.

Outside religion we find superstition, the term we give substandard beliefs. Before Huck ventures into the underworld, superstition afflicts everyone in the novel, but most particularly Huck and Jim. Twain ridicules these beliefs more savagely than he ridicules conventional religion, showing us that Jim's "superstitions, like the hagiolatry of the ignorant peasants in *The Innocents Abroad*, are the manacles upon his soul" (Hoffman, 331). Jim's transformation of Tom Sawyer's prank in Chapter 2 into worldwide witch travel derides both Jim and superstition. But then, on Jackson's Island, "the nature of Jim's superstitious belief undergoes a change" (Hoffman, 332). Jim reads rain in the birds and the future in almost anything. He becomes a magus of Nature, and the satire of superstition transforms itself into a sort of respect. Granted Huck believes Jim only skeptically, and granted too that Huck's river-rat ignorance allows the reader to retain some distance from even that skeptical belief, but still, the early chapters' ridicule has become something closer to wonder. The belief in superstition gains some authority by the novel's end. Jim says "Signs is *signs*, mine I tell you; en I knowed jis' 's well 'at I 'uz gwineter be rich agin as I's a stannin' heah dis minute!" (361). He predicted when on Jackson's Island that he would be rich and he is: not only with Tom's forty dollars, but with himself—a discovery he also made on the island.

In place of the more traditional shapeshifting, the novel gives us artifice, which also grows in power and value in the course of the book. In the initial chapters, before Huck's death, Tom, the master of artifice, receives nothing but mockery for his creations, not only from Twain but in time from Huck too. Huck, it seems, has even less patience than the reader for Tom's vision of Sunday School children as bewitched Arabs. But Huck enters the underworld via Tom's sort of artifice and once in the underworld not only indulges in artifice with astonishing regularity but also sees Tom's expertise at it as praiseworthy. His first thought after his faked murder is of Tom: "I did wish Tom Sawyer was there, I knowed he would take an interest in this kind of business, and throw in the fancy touches. Nobody could spread himself like Tom Sawyer in such a thing as that" (41). Huck's hedged enthusiasm in that passage—I find it easy to read ironically—gives way in the course of the novel to a less grudging version. Huck goes from derision of artifice with Tom Sawyer's gang to wholehearted practice of it as he adopts new life after new life, becoming in the end Tom himself. The presence of the Duke and King remind us that Huck is not employing any magic to achieve his shapeshifting; Huck just practices the con-artists' game.

We can see in these contextual considerations of Huck's traditional heroism the clear retention of myth. Without straining our credulity, Twain includes magic, royalty and palingenesis. We learn to expect a hero who can employ the powers of this transformed tradition, who needs the help of Jim, the traditional wise-fool sidekick, who has the vision to see a quest in the random events witnessed and experienced by two outcasts floating down a river on a raft. We get Huck Finn, a hero whose story runs surprisingly close to Raglan's 22-point model.

Even if we include knowledge gained from *The Adventures of Tom Sawyer*, a questionable practice made allowable by the reference to the earlier novel in the latter's first chapter, we can still say nothing to several of Raglan's points, such as 1) the hero's mother is a royal virgin, 3) often a near relative of the (father), or 4) the unusual circumstances of conception. In the special way noted above, though, 2) Pap is a king. If, as Daniel Hoffman says, the river is a god, simple metaphor makes 5) Huck the son of a god: the river gives him birth in too many metaphorical ways to index here. We can give Huck half a point for his supernatural origins. 6) His father does attempt to kill him, though not at birth, and 7) he is spirited away, and 8) reared by foster parents. Whether or not the widow's place in St. Petersburg can be considered "a far country" from Pap can be debated; Pap, not Huck, has gone away. But the distance between Pap and proper society, the very distance that makes a certain sort of king of him, is immeasurable, being simply the same as the distance between two sides of a single coin. 9) We are told nothing of his childhood.

10) On reaching his manhood he goes to his future kingdom. With this point we enter the romance part of the traditional hero's narrative and for Huck the essence of his story, which is in formal terms a picaresque *Bildungsroman*. Huck's escape from his father through death is his entry to manhood, and the idyllic colors in which he paints Jackson's Island leave little doubt that the island is his kingdom. It takes Huck most of the novel to

achieve his 11) victory over the king, in this case the King and Duke, who stand in for Pap. Unless we want to accept Leslie Fiedler's thesis on the submerged homosexuality between Huck and Jim, I can find no candidate for 12) the princess he marries, except Mary Jane Wilks. In the artifice the King has created, Mary Jane, though not his daughter, is the King's niece. Huck writes of her:

> In my opinion she had more sand in her than any girl I ever see; in my opinion she was just full of sand. It sounds like flattery, but it ain't no flattery. And when it comes to beauty—and goodness too—she lays over them all. I hain't never seen her since that time that I see her go out that door; no, I hain't ever seen her, since; but I reckon I've thought of her a many and a many million times, and of her saying she would pray for me; and if ever I'd a thought it would do any good for me to pray for *her*, blamed if I wouldn't have done it or bust. (244)

There is no marriage here, but Huck and Mary Jane cry together and have an emotional future, at least in Huck. This is worth a remark, but not worth a point. I have already noted the ways in which Huck 13) becomes king in his morally ambiguous stand on freeing Jim. It is by this act that he finally accepts of himself that he is one of Pap's people, and we never see him drop this self-interpretation the remainder of the book.

Raglan acknowledges that "every literary community has certain types of story outside which none but exceptional geniuses can venture" (143). I have no need to argue for Twain's exceptional genius; the very existence of this study and the hundreds like it give testimony. I must note that Twain's manipulation of the hero-pattern's death sequence in *Adventures of Huckleberry Finn* adds to his reputation for genius. As should be clear from the earlier discussion of death and return in the novel, Twain lays the final third of the hero's life over the whole of the story. The death of the hero occurs simultaneously with his life. Huck Finn's death does not come at the end of his reign as king but rather throughout his entire narration, and Huck's continued reference to death not only reminds us that we are reading his journey through the underworld but also outlines for us the experience of death. This experience chills us and we fear for Huck's life, paradoxically, of course, because we know emphatically that Huck will not die: Huck is telling the story. The novel splinters the story of the hero. Huck knows he is telling us the romance; he does not know he is telling us his death. This is possible because we actually experience two Hucks: Huck-the-written-about and Huck-the-writer. We do not actually hear from Huck-the-written-about;

everything we know about him comes to us through the recollections of Huck-the-writer. Huck-the-writer makes clear throughout the book he knows he is telling us a story, the subject of which is the romantic history of an earlier version of himself. The framing presence of Twain enables us to recognize that, while Huck-the-writer tells about the other Huck, he also tells a story about himself of which he has no consciousness, the story of his death and rebirth.

In the next chapter I will explore the relationships between the two Hucks, Twain and the reader more fully. For the purpose of seeing how Huck fits the model of the traditional hero, knowledge of this division between the teller and the told of is sufficient. This interpretive tool makes Twain's genius manifest: Huck 14) for a time reigns uneventfully while he composes the book we read. The equivalence of writing to 15) prescribing laws is too obvious to dwell on. Readers of novels are both its subjects and gods, with whom Huck 16) loses favor as Huck-the-written-about participates in the torture of Jim and Huck-the-writer allows Tom to dominate his story. Attempts to "sivilize" Huck 17) drive him from his kingdom, which is to say outside of the society entirely, as opposed to his royal position in it but against it. His 18) death, suspended as it is over nearly the whole length of the novel, is mysterious. Huck-the-writer dies like any narrator, when he has written his last word. This takes place at the Phelps farm, which while not described explicitly as occupying 19) the top of a hill leaves that impression; a quick look at E. W. Kemble's drawing to head Chapter 32 (276) confirms that. 21) Huck's body does not get buried, because Huck-the-writer has no corporeal form. 22) He has an uncountable number of holy sepulchres: every copy of *Huckleberry Finn*, "a trouble to make" but an enduring temple to his status as mythic hero.

Huck Finn's heroism plainly suits the traditional model; the points of correspondence between his story and the model often exceed the number found between the model and the heroes Raglan used to assemble it. This discovery in part answers why readers sympathize so strongly with Huck. We construct our heroes to carry our hopes for us, and I will explore what hopes we ask Huck to carry later. But just from the argument above, we see that Huck's heroic shoulders ought to be strong enough to carry whatever burden we place on them. They are not, of course: Huck ceases to be a hero, traditional or otherwise, when we reach the novel's end. The evasion seems to readers too long, too showy, too baroque, too burlesque, and all this it may be. But if Huck is a hero of traditional power the world that defeats him will need something equally powerful to overmatch him. Complaints aside, we must all agree the evasion does overmatch Huck, both in his morally questionable participation in what amounts to Jim's long torture and in his narratively questionable retirement to the position of Tom Sawyer's comrade. The next chapter will investigate the power that allows *Huck* to defeat Huck.

DAVID E.E. SLOANE

Huck's Moral Reasoning as Heroism

The climax of the novel, the point at which it becomes truly an American classic, is Huck's decision to go to hell to save Jim in chapter 31. The action from chapter 29—the wrapping up of the Wilks episode—through chapters 30 and 31 leads directly to this climax. Huck's "Judas" speech foreshadows it, and after this point, Huck is largely helpless in relation to events, even though they are events which he set in motion. Tom Sawyer's reentry into the novel will bring finality to Huck's diminished power in normal society. Huck is passive in the actions of chapters 29 and 30, as events outpace his plans. Nonetheless, Providence is developed in the action in a way that suggests belief, not skepticism, and the Wilks episode concludes with its climactic acknowledgment by Mary Jane and the recapture of the raft by the Duke and Dauphin. All that remains is the full coming to moral manhood by Huck. He does so in terms which are consistent with a Victorian vision of morality, suggesting the superficiality of the reading given *Adventures of Huckleberry Finn* by its critics in Concord. *The Royal Path of Life* is one of many sources that give a contemporary basis for the nature of Huck's decision, and study of that manual of social life throws light on Huck's radicalism. Twain, himself, never fully reconciled his ideas with this solution, and it ultimately became the pessimism of *What Is Man?*

Upon the appearance of the "opposition line," the Duke and Dauphin's

From *Adventures of Huckleberry Finn: American Comic Vision.* © 1988 by G.K. Hall & Co.

fortunes lead, naturally, to their eventual tar and feathering. Late in chapter 29 Huck is complimented by Levi Bell the lawyer as being pretty awkward at lying; a natural outcome of the situation, the comment is suggestive of the reversals surrounding Huck. A lynch mob forms around the pairs of Wilks claimants. Business about the tattoo on the dead man's chest takes the entire town to the graveyard for a melodramatic disinterment during an oncoming thunderstorm, and the crescendo of events provides the climax for Huck's involvement with the Duke and Dauphin. Huck escapes as the townspeople lunge forward—as we know crowds do from the Boggs–Sherburn incident—to look at the spectacle of the gold on the dead man's chest.

Huck's escape embodies emotional climaxes built on three important elements. First, as he runs through the darkened and deserted town, he sees the light go on in Mary Jane's window, meaning that he has returned as agreed to help Huck. He is rescued from feeling "sorry and disappointed" and his heart "swelled up sudden, like to bust," with the same rapidity as the steamboat that overran the raft, "and the same second the house and all was behind me in the dark, and wasn't ever going to be before me no more in this world." Huck is talking in the language of ultimates, even though the action need not be ultimate; a sense of absolute finality surrounds Huck's moral actions. Second, Huck returns to the raft, is knocked overheard by the sight of Jim as King Leer (*sic*) and a drownded A-rab, and they flee: "It *did* seem so good to be free again and, all by ourselves on the big river and nobody to bother us." The theme of the river and freedom and security from society is reechoed only to be destroyed in the third important component of this passage; the Duke and the Dauphin are heard rowing across the river and Huck "wilted right down onto the planks, then, and give up." This series of turns and reversals provides us with a climax reestablishing Huck and Jim, but within a paragraph sweeps away our relief, in a tragic reinvasion by the mock royalty, grown more like Pap Finn. The usurpers have gained their freedom, and Jim and Huck and the raft are recaptured. The king even begins to shake Huck and threatens to drown him, placing him essentially in the same jeopardy that caused him to flee from Pap Finn. Important themes of security, kindness, and resolution are mingled in the concluding defeat for Huck and Jim. By the end of the chapter, the two rapscallions lie drunkenly and lovingly in each other's arms, "as thick as thieves again," while Huck and Jim are reduced to the level of auxiliaries.

Chapter 31 is a purposefully weakened return to the river in which Twain shows the two thieves falling back on their shallow resources, faking dancing schools and yellocution lessons with the facility of Artemus Ward's pet kangaroo—a standing joke of the literary comedian Ward in the 1860s for the fraudulent representation of moral and uplifting entertainment, based on Barnum's Museum. Huck is at his most dryly Twain-like distance from the two rogues as the raft journey continues. A lowered level of intensity from the events of the Wilks episode corresponds to the conspiratorial whisperings of the Duke and Dauphin in the wigwam. When the Duke and Huck discover the king drunk in a village "doggery," Huck flees to the raft and finds that Jim has vanished. For the second time in this part of the novel, Huck talks of crying, and this time actually does—he only does so twice in the novel. He will shortly learn that Jim is at the Silas Phelps farm twelve miles down the river, sold as an escaped slave by the king for the money to get drunk on. Huck will then encounter the Duke and give him ten cents, as he had done with his own Pap before—echoing that relationship from the early part of the novel—and pretend to strike for the back country. The actual effort to free Jim will be the anticlimax to the moral climax of the novel which occurs in this chapter.

Huck's moral decision proceeds by reversals and contrasts when Huck sits down in the wigwam on the raft to think—which he does until he wears his head sore. His reasoning is based, as in the Wilks episode, on loyalty through kindness. He criticizes the Duke and the Dauphin "after all this long journey, and after all we'd done for them ... all come to nothing" because they had the "heart" to trick Jim and "make him a slave again all his life, and amongst strangers, too, for forty dirty dollars." The Duke and the Dauphin, of course, were just as eager to sell the Wilks' slaves to strangers, so this particular level of unfeeling is characteristic of them. However, Mary Jane and her sisters and Huck have all had in common the regard for slaves being kept among their own people. Perhaps more compelling is the idea of the forty dirty dollars, close enough to the thirty pieces of silver of Judas's betrayal of Christ to carry that resonance of cosmic ugliness of spirit. Huck's thinking in this paragraph is a summary of everything that the Duke and the Dauphin demonstrated in relation to the Wilks girls, but here it has come home to himself and Jim. He had already combatted their actions once; now his problem will be to combat them at a still larger level of action which he will have to reason out through the tortuous reversals of ethics which Miss Watson's Christianity imposes on his purer and simpler "sound heart but deformed conscience."

For all the melodramatic excitement of the events of the novel up to this point, the greatest event of the book takes place as Huck's internal monologue; the monologue represents one of the truly great moments in American fiction. The moment had as much importance to the readers of 1885 as it retains for modern critics, perhaps even more. To suggest the nature of Huck's courage as a Victorian ideal, we might refer to a moral self-instructor, such as *The Royal Path of Life*, subtitled "Aims and Aids to Success and Happiness," written by T. L. Haines A.M. and L. W. Yaggi, M.S.[21] It has not been demonstrated that Twain owned or read this particular volume, but it is so representative of a variety of such books that embodied the ethics of his generation of Americans that it provides a vital touchstone for his and his readers' emotional demands on Huck if Huck is to rise to true greatness in representing their highest ethical impulses. *The Royal Path's* statements on "Courage" describe fully Huck Finn's ultimate heroism within the life of the book. First, we must accept Huck's realistically portrayed world as one of small rather than noble actions—a point consistent not only with literary realists, but also with pragmatic moralists and, at the plot level, for those readers already disliking Tom Sawyer's style.

The Royal Path states: "To lead the forlorn hope in the field of course requires less nerve than to fight ignobly and unshrinkingly the bloodless battle of life. To bear evil speaking and illiterate judgement with equanimity, is the highest bravery. It is in fact the repose of mental courage" (216). Huck is the self-effacing hero of this ideal. As well, the quotation describes the Duke and the Dauphin's relation to Huck, for their Shakespeare demonstrated their lack of literary judgment, only superseded by the lowness of those they cheated. Huck's tears were for despair over Jim; his manner has indeed been to fight the "bloodless" battles—and at present, he has lost, for Jim has been taken back into slavery far from home. *The Royal Path* elaborates: "Physical courage, which despises all danger, will make a man brave in one way; and moral courage, which despises all opinion, will make a man brave in another. The former would seem most necessary for the camp, the latter for council; but to constitute a great man, both are necessary" (216). Huck has just endured physical danger—the threats of a lynch mob— while attempting to bring forth good for Mary Jane in secret. His courage has been suggested by the ultimate terms he uses in treating his relationship to her. The moral courage which despises all opinion is suggested by the fact that only she knew of his goodness, a powerful foreshadowing of his further seeking in private for Jim's good. Huck abandoned interests he might have had in aiding the Duke and Dauphin, thus becoming irrelevant to them. Twain had already used Colonel Sherburn to disparage the courage of men in an army. Thus most of the elements of the textbook definition of personal courage are played out before the reader's eyes.

The Royal Path continues in the same vein:

> No one can tell who the heroes are, and who the cowards; until some crisis comes to put us to the test. And no crisis puts us to the test that does not bring us up alone and single-handed to face

danger. It is nothing to make a rush with the multitude even into the jaws of destruction. Sheep will do that. Armies might be picked from the gutter, and marched up to make food for powder. But when some crisis singles one out from the multitude, pointing at him the particular finger of fate, and telling him, "Stand or run," and he faces about with steady nerve, with nobody else to stand behind, we may be sure the hero stuff is in him. When such a crisis comes, the true courage is just as likely to be found in people of shrinking nerves, or in weak and timid women, as in great burly people. It is a moral, not a physical trait.... A good cause makes a courageous heart.... Though the occasions of high heroic daring seldom occur but in the history of the great, the less obtrusive opportunities for the exertion of private energy are continually offering themselves. With these, domestic scenes as much abound as does the tented field.... It rescues the unhappy from degradation, and the feeble from contempt. (216–17)

Huck is a low rather than a heroic figure. His setting is domestic, especially as developed in the Wilks episode, rather than chivalric. Most important, he and Jim have been the powerless feeble in the face of the authority of Duke and Dauphin and townspeople, alike, as demonstrated by the recapture of the raft by royalty and of Jim by the local bounty-seekers. The ethic proposed is romantic democracy at its highest, relying on the individual, no matter how low; true to the beliefs of the founding fathers, as well, it distrusts collective man as a mob. In fact, it embodies the dominant formative beliefs of American culture as opposed to the beliefs of communist and collectivist cultures even today.

Six paragraphs comprise Huck's highest moral statement, climaxing in his decision to "steal Jim out of slavery again," and if he can think of anything worse to "go the whole hog." Huck begins by considering the disgust of people toward himself and Jim for trying to escape. He advances to his sense of Providence punishing him, and continues to seek help in prayer and in a letter to Miss Watson to free himself from "sin." Reminiscences of the raft journey lead to personalizing rather than moralizing, and he reverses his plan of action and decides to follow out Jim's wishes and his own human sense of feeling the true "right" thing, rather than the demands of his conscience.

Huck thus sits down to think, not on the tented field but in the wigwam of the raft. He cannot write to Tom Sawyer because Miss Watson will be disgusted at Jim's "rascality and ungratefullness" and sell him down the river again. As readers, we have no difficulty in detecting this obvious irony of the naif. Crushingly, as with any government, the worst punishment comes for trying to rebel, and it comes by guaranteeing the event that caused the rebellion. Selfishness from Huck, as with Joanna, also figures in this level of reasoning. Huck protests the disgrace falling on "*Me!*" for helping "a nigger to get his freedom." The emphasis on slavery and freedom is such that no reasonable reader could help developing allegiance with the other side of Huck's reasoning, as yet not emerged. The word "freedom," in fact, puts the reader emotionally ahead of Huck in the reasoning process.

The ironic reversals of moral purpose continue in the most intense passages in the novel. Huck has just noted how heartless it was for the Duke and Dauphin to betray Jim. Consequently, the reader is immediately prepared for Huck's reasoning as he, in his own turn, considers the betrayal of Jim, either for Jim's own good or for Huck's good through conscience-cleansing. As prepared for in the Wilks episode, the turn to microcosmic personal experience is a crucial determiner of moral action. As Huck sees "Jim before me, all the time, in the day, and in the night-time," he conjures up a brief history of the warmest moments of the protectiveness of Jim. In opposition to the loneliness of his room at the widow's or in the face of even his admired leader Tom, Huck remembers "we a floating along, talking, and singing, and laughing." Huck cannot "strike no places to harden me against him." The hardness of feeling versus its opposite kindness becomes the means by which Twain allows the heart to overcome the conscience. Huck even gives the reader a reprise of events: Jim standing watch, the fog, the feud and the swamp reconciliation, Huck's lie about the smallpox when Jim called Huck his "best friend old Jim ever had in the world, and the *only* one he's got now." The language of this last sentence is again the language of ultimates—the world, the isolation of the two in their joined purpose. It is language which establishes the basis for Huck's response at an equally ultimate and universal level.

Huck's rightness of heart is also equated to religion by Twain, establishing the antimoral antagonist to personal goodness: abstract moral training. Abstract ideology identified Jim as an "ungrateful nigger." Huck feels boot-licking shame from hiding the disgrace of doing a "low-down thing." Notably, Twain does not name Huck's specific sin other than "to help a nigger get his freedom." As Huck studies the matter, "my conscience went to grinding me." Finally, Huck comes to the ultimate moral abstraction and declares that "the plain hand of Providence" is slapping him for his "wickedness." The crime is now specified: "stealing a poor old woman's nigger that hadn't ever done me no harm." Twain is at his best in using dramatic irony here; each term of Huck's self-reproach is intuitively—subconsciously and consciously—felt by readers to be false. Miss Watson was not a poor old woman, she was a lean old maid with goggles on. She was not someone who never harmed Huck; first she made him feel lonely and restricted; second, she initiated the dispatch of Huck to hellfire, even sending Tom with him. *We*, the readers, know that Huck is reasoning a wrong position. When the "One" scares Huck and Huck confronts himself with going to Sunday school, readers of *Tom Sawyer* will remember the fraudulent collection of Bible study tickets; readers of *Huck Finn* will review the scepticism toward Sunday school in the early part of the book and the travesty of religion portrayed in the Grangerford feud.

Huck's attempt to "pray a lie" is given its own paragraph. It demonstrates again the emotional mystification that corrupt social religion has worked on Huck. Why can't he pray, Huck asks himself—and answers, because "my heart warn't right." Huck's heart is committed by daily life to Jim and to the events that have made the raft seem its own separate world; his heart is more involved and refined than those of the Duke and Dauphin. All the reverse morality of Pap Finn and the robbers on the *Walter Scott*, and all the implications of Jim stealing his own family from the rightful owners, and all the implications of Huck offending against the people of his hometown by stealing a "poor old woman's nigger" lie behind the dramatic irony of this confusion worked on natural instinct by social precept. The passage taps into the deepest concerns of civilized man—the perception of self in relation to moral action.

Twain appeals not only to our concepts as observers of society through literature, and not only to our satisfaction with the working out of image and form in the literary work; here he appeals also to the needy child in readers hidden behind the coolly self-denying façade of adulthood.[22] Huck's debate with himself exemplifies Twain's contention that he showed a boy with a sound heart but a deformed conscience working out the problems of life. Huck's recognition that only his mouth is saying he will do the "right thing," ironically reversed, triggers in readers an enthusiasm for reversal; the reversal of Huck's saying that he wished he would go to hell to Miss Watson has already established the basis for its repetition and expansion to a wider moral field of action. Another deft abstraction by Twain has Huck refer to writing to "that nigger's owner." Naming a legal entity rather than a person reemphasizes the tension between an individual's feelings and social-legal rights. When Huck says that "He knowed it,"—God knows he is lying—the cosmic irony of his dilemma is complete.

It is not clear that God has taken the opposite side, of course, only that he sees Huck's actions; it is Huck who imputes evil to himself. Huck writes a note to Miss Watson and then feels himself "washed clean of sin for the first time I had ever felt so in my life." Where this statement might have a positive power, the camp meeting sequence has undercut this sort of ideology already. Huck's good feeling is held for a moment with no reason given—and none is needed other than the reader's demand for a resolution to the ironic constraints that baffle satisfaction—and then Huck "went on thinking." His thinking is composed of the last great reprise of the raft journey, with each of the moments on board designated as a happy one filled with immediate personal love demonstrated through affection. All the emotions of loneliness overcome and violence escaped from—the negative force of the book—and all building up of personal affection between Huck and Jim—as fully activated in Huck's responsive aid to Mary Jane Wilks—the positive force of the book—focus in the most intense moment of the novel. Huck, leaping again to the language of ultimates, proclaims, "it was a close place.... I was a trembling because I'd got to decide, forever, betwixt two things and I knowed it." Huck decides to go to hell; Huck decides in favor of the will to freedom by his friend Jim.

Huck's decision to go to hell is his greatest moment. It confirms the reader's rejection of the irony which Twain has created. It has the power of Ahab's rejection of heaven, even though the "tore it up" completing action is minuscule. The particularity of the moment and its privacy is the fulfillment of the ultimate act of moral heroism as identified in *The Royal Path*. In the realist's world of social, political, and industrial might, the turn to private individual action is the response of the isolated man. Huck's finest hour has with it the futility of its individuality. Endorsed as it is by the textbook moralists of *The Royal Path*, it is not the ethic of power. Couched in the language of self-denial—the truly Christian sense of sinful unworthiness—Huck's planning establishes an underlayer of acceptance in his choice for the later submission to Tom Sawyer which some critics find so perplexing. Yet this psychoreligious level of the novel's action as fully supports Tom Sawyer's reentry as does Huck's repeated wishing that he could have carried out Tom Sawyer effects to complete several plot events.

Huck's abandonment of the idea of reform fulfills his decision to go to hell and also foreshadows his relinquishing of power to Tom. He declares that he will take up wickedness, separating himself from Tom and others in society, even though he had also been happy to hear Miss Watson say that Tom would go to hell. The language of ethics has become the ironic language of the character's own moral reasoning. His upbringing is part of thinking, and as Miss Watson and Pap were primary landmarks in that experience, some further denial of that upbringing is in order. His declaration that he would not only steal Jim out of slavery satisfies the demands of readers—Nook Farmers and all—that slavery be denied as an evil. Huck's determination to go "whole hog" even reechoes the commentary on hogs going to church and the maltreatment of hogs in the river town of Bricksville. Huck's ultimate choice is a choice of hoggishness as complete in its individualization as Pap's drunkenness—his was the hand of a hog, after all—but with such an incalculably higher object that readers must thrill in response to the final irony, as deftly sophisticated as any reflected image in American fiction. It is small wonder that, despite its importance, analytic readers feel restive during the conclusion of the novel which follows, comprising almost a fifth of the book's length.

Twain's optimism manifests itself in Huck Finn's action. In a private act of conscience, a person's kindness responds to kindness and guarantees ultimate human rights. For Twain, this truth is the highest law. Trowbridge, in *Cudjo's Cave* in a somewhat different context, had established the same hierarchy of values. He has a young German-American lad, Carl, refuse to honor a contract with a slaveholder, only to be reassured by the blind minister Mr. Villiers that "sometimes people do wrong from a motive so pure and disinterested that it sanctifies the action" (206). American culture had the moral machinery in place as fiction for twenty years by the time Huck Finn took his stand on the front porches of Twain's subscribers. Later, in *What Is Man?* (1906), Twain gave a more pessimistic view of the same kind of action. Contemplating Hamilton's duel with Burr, he proposes that Hamilton was driven by "public standards of honor." He continues that when standards of "love" seem to apply, however, they merely serve "to secure his personal comfort." Huck's thinking does indeed coincide with this model. Conscience is a thing which twists in order to gratify self-approval in both Huck's case and in Twain's later pessimism. The moment is elevated in *Huckleberry Finn* by its focus on the good outcome, parallel with the democratic philosophy. Late in his life, Twain withdrew from that external solace.

In a number of ways the novel seems to end here. The Duke and Huck are finally separated, with Huck performing an act like he had performed with his own Pap, giving the Duke ten cents. The Duke, starting to tell the truth, reverses himself and lies to Huck, thus completing their separation. He went to "studying," just as Tom will do shortly in betraying Huck and Jim to his own fantasy fun. The Duke, part way between a feeling of sympathy and a threateningly "ugly" look of violence, in effect plays into Huck's plan by threatening Huck and sending him away. The chapter closes, in the original edition, with a picture of the back of Huck as he heads into the country—the perfect visual statement for an ending.

However, Huck has plans to get shut of that kind. He will further his own general plan at the Phelps farm, finally concluding his adventures with Tom and Jim. The great moral decision has been made, however. The moral triumph of the raft ethic is complete in terms of the great river. Now, it will be transmuted and diminished to the reality of the shore—and of Twain's realistic view of society.

NOTES

21. Published in 1876 by W. C. King and Co. of Springfield, Massachusetts, and by the Western Publishing House of Chicago; the 1881 edition is cited here.

22. See Alice Fisher's *The Drama of the Gifted Child*, R. D. Laing's *The Politics of Experience*, and Sigmund Freud's *Civilization and Its Discontents* for elaboration of these psychological issues.

TOM QUIRK

The Realism of
Huckleberry Finn

"Hast seen the White Whale?" gritted Ahab in reply.

"No; only heard of him; but don't believe in him at all," said the other good-humoredly "Come aboard!"

"Thou are too damned jolly. Sail on. Hast lost any men?"

"Not enough to speak of—two islanders, that's all; but come aboard."

        —*Moby-Dick*, chapter 115, "The *Pequod* Meets the *Bachelor*"

"It warn't the grounding—that didn't keep us back but a little. We bowed out a cylinder-head."

"Good gracious! anybody hurt?"

"No'm. Killed a nigger."

"Well, it's lucky; because sometimes people do get hurt."

        —*Adventures of Huckleberry Finn*, chapter 32

I

The second of these passages, too familiar to require much commentary, is frequently instanced as a dramatic rendering of much that is noteworthy about *Huckleberry Finn*: the centrality to the novel's purpose of questions of racial prejudice; the transparent irony disclosed in Aunt Sally's anxious question and her genuine relief that no "people" were injured; the canniness of Huck himself, who, though perplexed by this sudden relative who calls

---

him "Tom," knows enough about human nature to invent yet another fictional experience and to adopt yet another persona on the instant, but who is totally unaware of the satire, irony, or humor of his own remark. Huck knows his audience *inside* the novel; time and again he sizes up his situation in an antagonistic adult world and plays to the several desires, fears, and biases of those who confront or question him. However (despite his amiable introduction to us in the opening paragraph, his final summary complaint about the "trouble" he has had telling his story, and his closing adieu, "YOURS TRULY, HUCK FINN"), Huck is often indifferent to or ignorant of his effects upon an audience *outside* the book, which is to say us as readers.

If realism depends upon a certain consensual understanding of the world, an understanding, that is, of what Henry James said we cannot, one way or another, "not know," then the realism of *Huckleberry Finn* stands in peculiar relation to other realist works. As Michael Davitt Bell has shown, Twain's attachment to the announced principles of literary realism is tenuous at best,[1] and what is true for Twain is even more true for his young narrator. For Huck not only does not knowingly participate in this consensus understanding, but he also is supremely unqualified to render it in his narrative. Time and again, Huck proves that he can readily adapt to the moves of the game, but no one has taught him the logic of it. The origins of feuds, the behavior of pirates and robbers, the decor of the Grangerford house, the prerogatives of royalty, all these remain obscure and mysterious to him, but he quickly sizes up the situation and plays his part as best he can.

The first passage comes from as famous a book. Yet so far as I know this exchange and its coincidentally parallel expression in *Huckleberry Finn* have gone virtually unnoticed. There may be several explanations for this. Among them, and one perhaps worth exploring, involves the difference between the romanticism of *Moby-Dick* and the realism of *Huckleberry Finn*. That difference may be as simple as the distinction between motive and action, the difference, that is, between quest and escape—between the pursuit (all defiant of necessity and contingency, fixed upon some insane object and driven by some overruling passion) and the "scrape" (the unanticipated event somehow managed, eluded, or negotiated). Ahab bends the will of his crew to his purpose and dispenses with genial observances and courtesies; Huck caters to whim and courts favor, always with an eye to the nearest exit. The unmarried captain of the *Bachelor*, as with most of Melville's bachelors, is an emblem of moral complacency and lavish good humor, in command of a full cargo and homeward bound. Aunt Sally is a type, an equal mixture of Christian goodwill, blind bigotry, and doting affection, glad to receive the boy whom she takes to be her nephew. *Moby-Dick* is characterized by its symbolic trappings, its metaphysical inquiries, its lyrical spontaneity, its

Shakespearean "quick probings at the very axis of reality," as Melville said in "Hawthorne and His Mosses."

But *Huckleberry Finn* works by other means: It subverts the same high drama that promotes its episodes (Boggs's drunken swagger, for example, results in his murder, but the dramatic emphasis is upon the town's perverse fascination with his dying; a distempered gang calls for the lynching of Colonel Sherburn, but what they receive is an upbraiding lecture on mob cowardice). It indulges on the happiest terms in reflective moments through the benign auspices of folklore, superstition, and enviable credulity. Ishmael's crow's-nest reverie is blasted by the anxious recognition that he hovers over "Descartesian vortices," but Huck and Jim argue the origins of stars—the moon must have laid them after all—and no one gets hurt. *Huckleberry Finn* displays much less of the Melvillean interest in an "Anacharsis Clootz deputation" of humanity than in the solidarity of two, a "community of misfortune" as Twain would later describe the partnership of Huck and Jim. In the above cited passages, Melville's is a throwaway line, Twain's an epitome of vernacular realism.

Huckleberry Finn, like *Moby-Dick*, is a storyteller's story. In both books the teller and the tale vie for our attention. Ishmael, the yarn-spinner, is intent on chasing to their dens the significances of his experiences, though it is seldom the case that we as readers feel that these adventures are existentially his at all. Huck, too, is a receptacle of impressions, but they are filtered through a distinctively adolescent consciousness—quick to perceive, slow to comprehend.

But there are two "authors" of *Huckleberry Finn*, Mark Twain and Huck Finn, and there are also two distinct fictive worlds established by them. Twain presents us with a world that must be judged, Huck with a world that must be inhabited. If both authors are realists, however, their realism is of different orders of experience. Huckleberry Finn's story is primarily a record of feeling, not cognition, and as Twain once remarked, "emotions are among the toughest things in the world to manufacture out of whole cloth; it is easier to manufacture seven facts than one emotion."[2] The "quality of felt life" that Henry James claimed is central to the realist aesthetic is fulfilled in Huck's story; the deadly satirical thrusts of a man slightly outraged by life are largely the result of Twain's management of that same narrative.

The difference between Mark Twain's realism and Huck Finn's may be seen at a glance in comparable passages from *Life on the Mississippi* and *Huckleberry Finn*:

> I had myself called with the four o'clock watch, mornings, for
> one cannot see too many summer sunrises on the Mississippi.
> They are enchanting. First, there is the eloquence of silence; for

a deep hush broods everywhere. Next, there is the haunting sense of loneliness, isolation, remoteness from the worry and bustle of the world. The dawn creeps in stealthily; the solid walls of black forest soften to gray, and vast stretches of the river open up and reveal themselves; the water is glass-smooth, gives off spectral little wreaths of white mist, there is not the faintest breath of wind, nor stir of leaf; the tranquility is profound and infinitely satisfying. Then a bird pipes up, another follows, and soon the pipings develop into a jubilant riot of music.... When the light has become a little stronger, you have one of the fairest and softest pictures imaginable. You have the intense green of the massed and crowded foliage near by; you see it paling shade by shade in front of you; ... And all this stretch of river is a mirror, and you have the shadowy reflections of the leafage and the curving shores and the receding capes pictured in it. Well, that is all beautiful; soft and rich and beautiful; and when the sun gets well up, and distributes a pink flush here and a powder of gold yonder and a purple haze where it will yield the best effect, you grant that you have seen something that is worth remembering.[3]

In chapter 19, Huck and Jim watch "the daylight come":

Not a sound, anywheres—perfectly still—just like the whole world was asleep, only sometimes the bull-frogs a-cluttering, maybe. The first thing to see, looking away over the water; was a kind of dull line—that was the woods on t'other side—you couldn't make nothing else out; then a pale place in the sky; then more paleness, spreading around; then the river softened up, away off, and warn't black any more, but gray; you could see little dark spots drifting along, ever so far away—trading scows, and such things; and long black streaks—rafts; sometimes you could hear a sweep streaking; or jumbled up voices, it was so still, and sounds come so far; and by and by you could see a streak on the water which you know by the look of the streak that there's a snag there in a swift current which breaks on it and makes that streak look that way; and you see the mist curl up off of the water, and the east reddens up, and the river, and you make out a log cabin in the edge of the woods, away on the bank on t'other side of the river, being a wood-yard, likely, and piled by them cheats so you can throw a dog through it anywheres; then the nice breeze springs up, and comes fanning you from over there, so cool and fresh, and sweet to smell, on account of the woods and the flowers; but sometimes not that way, because they've left dead fish laying around, gars, and such, and they do get pretty rank; and next you've got the full day, and everything smiling in the sun, and the song-birds just going it! (156–57)

Disclosed here are the obvious differences to be expected between a genteel and a vernacular narrator, or more properly between an adult and a child. Twain's passage is deliberate—shaped by rhetorical motive, organized logically in homogenous time and space, varied in diction, consistent in tone, and obedient to the terms of its announced purpose. Descriptive detail corroborates the preordained sentiment; the hushed silence, the creeping mists, the massed color and softening light contribute to, even validate, the "enchantment" of the scene.

Huck's description moves by statement and correction—there is "not a sound," he says, "but only sometimes"; the air is "sweet to smell" but "sometimes" there is a dead gar laying around. There is in Huck's passage the unembarrassed monotony of phrasing—the word *streak* is used three times in the same clause. And Huck dispenses with explanatory remark. Twain's river is a mirror in which are to be found the reflections of wood and shore; but when Huck says "and the east reddens up, and the river" there is no authorial indication that the river reflects the red of the sky, for his world need not answer to the laws of optics. The phenomenon is local to his perception; it would not occur to him that the scene is an "effect." Huck's river at dawn is shifting impressions first and only incidentally a world of objects—the "little dark spots," we are told by way of an appositive, are trading scows; the "dull line," the woods; the "long black streaks," rafts. His world is populated by things, but they don't authorize his experience. And he does not belabor the mental corrections necessary to make such a world.

Twain's description is a "composition," a self-conscious act of language so constructed that we may grant that the scene is "worth remembering." Whether or not his depiction is memorably phrased, it stands as admiration of a natural event whose picturesque existence is independent of his rendering. Huck's scene is merely recalled, and one feels that without his consciousness to sustain it, the world itself might dissolve. For all that, however, Huck's landscape is the more tolerant; it admits the coexistence of the duplicity of cheats and stench of rotting fish with the music of birds. Huck is ever alert to treachery and snare, yet without condemning, he delivers an undiminished natural scene and exults in a privileged moment. Twain, by contrast, aims at a universal sentiment that is tonic relief from the "worry and bustle of the world."

Twain's presence pervades *Huckleberry Finn*, but with few exceptions, he is loyal to the terms of the book and favors Huck's unmediated world of feeling over his own often angry conviction.[4] That is, however strong Twain's own sentiments, he typically recognized that his first artistic responsibility was to a rendering of the authenticity of Huck's adolescent sensibility. The realism of *Huckleberry Finn* is disclosed alternately by the thread of Huck's consciousness, not yet come to full awareness of how fully implicated in events it is, and by the palpable events that seem randomly strung upon it, which is to say by the narrative itself. These are inevitably interwoven, and often tangled, but it is well to take up the teller and the tale separately.

II

One of the things to be observed about the realism of *Huckleberry Finn* is that Huck's voice functions much like Whitman's multivalent "I" in "Song of Myself"—he is the narrator of his chronicle and the author of his book; he is the chief witness of events and, emotionally at least, the principal victim of them; he is ruled and to a degree protected by the laws of the republic and the customs of place, but only accidentally a citizen of and never a voice in the dominant culture that so mystifies him.

Both as "author" and as narrator, Huck typically forgoes representational depiction. He himself has seen the Aunt Sallys of the world before, and he is far less interested in disclosing her character than in dealing with the situation. Huck's own considerable experience in the world (the result of having fended for himself most times, not of playing the detached observer of life), as remarkable as it is regrettable in a fourteen-year-old child, outfits him for his adventures. In this sense, the realism of the quoted passage above, and dozens of others like it, is presupposed in the telling itself.[5] Unlike Ahab, Huck takes the world on its terms, not his own, and experience has taught him how to best navigate its treacheries and to delight in its beauties.

Huck's wary canniness is frequently the source in *Huckleberry Finn* of the sort of narrative detachment so often associated with realist writing; it is also the source of a special pathos. When Huck sees the king and the duke tarred and feathered, men who "didn't look like nothing in the world that was human," he is incapable of hardening himself to their plight. Huck finally concludes, "Human beings can be awful cruel to one another" (290). This familiar scene is moving not because it effectively dramatizes Twain's attitudes toward the damned human race, nor for that matter because it serves as moral pronouncement (these two con men are scalawags through and through and deserve the sort of treatment they at long last receive). Nor, I believe, does it signal Huck's moral development, or as Leo Marx would have it, "a mature blending of his instinctive suspicion of human motives with his capacity for pity."[6] Instead, it is the unlooked for and disquieting revelation, somewhat surprising in a boy as familiar with the world as Huck is, that gives the moment force.

For Huck has witnessed earlier far greater and more disturbing cruelty than this: the murderous treatment of Jim Turner on the *Walter Scott*; the killing of Buck Grangerford, which still troubles his sleep; Boggs's gasping out his last breath under the weight of a family Bible; not to mention the thievery and calculated deceptions of the king and the duke themselves. What he hasn't before recognized, indeed does not fully recognize even as he speaks his sad conclusion, is the universal human condition of cruelty. Nor has he yet developed the righteous, which is to say the "civilized," indignation that would serve as defense against his own spontaneous impulses.

Huck and Tom have no opportunity to help these con men, and they go on home. But Huck is feeling "kind of ornery and humble," not so brash as before, even though he knows he hasn't done anything to cause the event he has just witnessed. Only two chapters earlier, in his famous decision to tear up the letter to Miss Watson and to "go to hell" and to help Jim, Huck's sympathies had prevailed against his training. Twain once observed in reference to a similar internal struggle in chapter 16, that this is a chapter "where a sound heart and a deformed conscience come into collision and conscience suffers defeat." His analogous moral decision in chapter 31 is a temporary triumph, however; as Harold H. Kolb, Jr., has remarked, "Huck never defeats his deformed conscience—it is we [as readers] who do that—he simply ignores it in relation to Jim."[7] When he sees the punished king and duke, however, Huck finds that a conscience, deformed or otherwise, has little to do with whether you do right or wrong or nothing at all. And precisely at that moment conscience moves in on him: "If I had a yaller dog that didn't know no more than a person's conscience, I would pison him. It takes up more room than all the rest of a person's insides, and yet ain't no good, nohow" (290).

Perhaps Huck is never so vulnerable as at this moment. His unwanted recognition, followed hard and fast by voracious conscience, has its inverted equivalent in *Moby-Dick* when Ahab realizes his quest is self-destructive but that he must press on nevertheless, and he drops his tear into the sea. For in Huck's response to the frenzied throng of townspeople exacting their revenge on these rapscallions and the image of the pair who do not look human, he concludes upon the human condition. Ahab is driven by interior impulses that extinguish all "natural" longings and lovings; but Huck, just as relentlessly, and simply by virtue of being alive and growing up, is being drawn into this inhuman, human world.

Robinson Jeffers, in "Shine, Perishing Republic," would have his children keep their distance from the "thickening center" of corruption:

> And boys, be in nothing so moderate as in love of man, a
> clever servant, insufferable master.
> There is the trap that catches noblest spirits, that caught—
> they say—God, when he walked the earth.

This is a belated wisdom, reduced to fatherly advice, that, boys being boys, will likely go all unheeded. But Twain (or Huck rather) dramatizes his troubled understanding at the moment of its birth; his conclusion is the unstudied remark, not yet a conviction, no longer a perception. For Huck, corruption has no center but spreads out evenly before him, just as he has left it behind in the wake of his flight; it presents no scrape to be mastered or outlived but the general human condition. And Huck is not yet wise; his insight yields instantly to vague, unaccountable feelings of guilt. And this, too, is a dimension of the realism of the book, for he is a boy more ruled by feeling than sober reflection.

Huckleberry Finn has sometimes been described as a picaresque novel without the picaro. This may be a meaningful statement if our understanding of the genre is qualified by the variations of it Cervantes accomplished in *Don Quixote*, a novel Twain read several times, Tom Sawyer at least once, and Huck not at all. Still, Huck is not quite an idealist, not yet a rogue. His mischievousness is typical of a boy his age, and it is combined with a special, sometimes ridiculous tenderness.

Huck is often capable of pseudomoralizing, citing his Pap as authority for lifting a chicken or borrowing a melon. This is also true when, in chapter 22, he dodges the watchman and dives under the circus tent: "I had my twenty-dollar gold piece and some other money, but I reckoned I better save it.... I ain't opposed to spending money on circuses, when there ain't no other way, but there ain't no use in *wasting* it on them" (191). Once inside, though the audience is hilarious, Huck is "all of a tremble" to see the danger of the drunken horseback rider. When, at length, he recognizes that he has been taken in by this performer, he is so admiring of him and the bully circus itself that he claims if he ever runs across it again, "it can have all of *my* custom, every time" (194).

In this relatively slight episode are compactly blended the multiple functions of Huck as author, character, narrator, and comic device. As author, he tries to make the circus scene vivid to us, but he is not equal to the task. His rendering of the performance is notable for its descriptive flatness. The passages are sprinkled with a few vernacular metaphors, but unlike his disturbing description of his Pap in chapter 5, Huck's language here is indefinite and vague. The men are dressed in their "drawers and undershirts," he says, and the ladies have lovely complexions and are "perfectly beautiful." What is vivid, however, is his faltering speech, his slightly breathless excitement. As narrator, he gropes for adjectives and falls into abstractions and platitudes. Huck is mastered by the spectacle, which is simultaneously his experience and his subject matter. But as boy, he is true to childlike enthusiasm and typically replaces descriptive detail with hyperbolic affidavits of his rapt attention: it was "the splendidest sight that ever was"; the women looked like "real sure-enough queens"; it was a "powerful fine sight"; "I never see anything so lovely"; "they done the most astonishing things" (191–92). At length, he becomes the straight man to his own joke. So pleased is he with the sight that he promises the circus can have his business any time, evidently unaware of the humor of the remark, that his "custom" has in no way damaged his purse.

Huck is worldly wise but never jaded, as this episode dramatizes, but the significance of his pranks are defined less by youthful motive than by the terms of the adventure. The charm of what Neil Schmitz calls his "Huckspeech" (speech "written as spoken, talked into prose")[8] can be, and is, radically redefined by narrative context. There is prankishness involved, for example, when Huck plays his joke on Jim after they have been separated in the fog, but he receives a tongue-lashing that so cuts him that he "humbles himself to a nigger." Huck's manufacture of his own murder in order to escape the potentially lethal abuse of his Pap is grotesque to be sure, but it is highly dramatic too, and Huck regrets that Tom is not handy to throw in "the fancy touches" (41). He laments Tom's absence as well in an episode that is a mixture of romantic escapade and existential urgency when, in chapter 12, he and Jim undertake to save Jim Turner from certain death. The same may be said for his efforts to preserve the Wilks girls' fortune from the hands of the king and the duke.

As humorist Huck is humorless, as hero he is only accidentally heroic, and as narrator he seems never quite to know where to place the accent. He is constitutionally incapable of distilling from his supposed experience either the ultimate conditions or the deeper significance of his adventures. Huck never doubts the existence of the "bad place" and the "good place"; in fact, he believes them to be all that Miss Watson has told him. However, while he can imagine the fires of hell and the monotony of playing harps and singing forever, he scarcely comprehends eternity and has little interest in it. His famous declaration "All right, then, I'll go to hell" (271) is not accompanied with an exclamation point. The statement is matter-of-fact and to be taken literally, for Huck is a literal-minded boy. He is temperamentally suited to the bad place (wickedness is in his line, he says), and he will give up trying to achieve the other place. But his decision is also the resignation of self-acceptance, a declaration, that is, of the acceptance of the world's judgment upon him, not the resolution to abide by some higher moral authority, as is sometimes claimed. It is just this quality that gives the scene its special pathos. Huck is not built right, and the fact that he is social and moral refuse is hardly arguable.

Huck is caught between stern rebuke ("Don't scrunch up like that, Huckleberry"; "Don't gap and stretch like that") and enforced social acceptance ("Pray every day, Huckleberry"; "Chew your food, Huckleberry"). But he remains the same boy the town allowed to sleep in a hogshead, stay away from school, and make do for himself. Caught on the horns of this dilemma, there is nevertheless a strong undercurrent of self-affirmation; Huck is filled with self-recrimination and self-condemnation, but never self-loathing: When Jim is bitten by the rattlesnake, he curses himself as a "fool" for not remembering that the mate was apt to join the dead one he had placed in Jim's blanket; he is sorry for the outcome and his stupidity but not the impulse. Huck devoutly tries to admire Emmeline's poetic "tributes" and drawings because he accepts the Grangerford family faith that she was a saint; he even steals up into her room and browses through her scrapbook when he begins to "sour" on her. He often regrets that Tom Sawyer is not around to throw some style into his plans, but Huck never fully accepts the world's corrections or refusals of him. And this same realistic disclosure of a young boy's self-consciousness, in the hands of Mark Twain, becomes a satirical vehicle as well.

Twain often employs a satirical strategy in Huck that he seems to have observed in himself and to have dramatized in *A Tramp Abroad*. The narrator of that book does not condemn violent alien customs (most particularly the revolting German student duels) but instead curses himself for failing to comprehend the wisdom of received tradition. The same is true of countless occasions in *Huckleberry Finn* where Twain's intent, as opposed to Huck's, is to expose sham, pretense, and outright silliness: Huck is perplexed that the widow makes him "grumble over the victuals" even though there is nothing wrong with them; he takes it on faith that Emmeline Grangerford's pictures are "nice," but they always give him the "fan-tods"; he goes to church with the Grangerfords and hears a sermon about brotherly love and "preforeordestination," and everyone agrees it was a good sermon, and it must be so because, for Huck, it proved to be "one of the roughest Sundays" he had ever run across.

Tom Sawyer variously describes Huck as a lunkhead, an idiot, or a saphead for failing to comprehend the observances required of pirates, robbers, or royalty. Huck never disputes Tom's basic superiority or his own cultural and moral ignorance; after all, Tom is "full of principle" (307). In fact, Huck is flabbergasted that Tom is willing and eager to help him free Jim, and he regrets his own betrayal of his friend for not insisting that he not sink so low:

> Here was a boy that was respectable, and well brung up; and had a character to lose; and folks at home that had characters; and he was bright and not leatherheaded; and knowing, and not ignorant; and not mean, but kind; and yet here he was, without any more pride, or rightness, or feeling, than to stoop to this business, and make himself a shame, and his family a shame, before everybody. I *couldn't* understand it, no way at all. (292–93)

As a realistic portrayal of one boy's concern for another, the statement is touching; as satire, it is deadly—all the more so when we learn that Miss Watson has already freed Jim in her will and that Tom knows it.

Twain once astutely remarked that, unlike *Tom Sawyer*, *Huckleberry Finn* is not a book for boys but for those who used to be boys. It is not altogether clear Twain recognized this distinction at the time of writing the novel, so strong was his identification with his created character, but the instinctive decision to have an unwashed fourteen-year-old outcast tell a story ultimately meant for readers whose own innocence was behind them proved to be an enabling one. As a character or narrative consciousness, Huck is pure possibility—his future casually spreads out before him, luxuriant in meandering adventures and antics, freedom and easiness. But he is doomed as well—for every adult reader knows (though because we are adults we are often reluctant to admit it) that his delightful caginess and high jinks depend less on moral purpose than on youthful energy; his escapes and accommodations are destined to become evasions and compromises in the end.[9] Huck does not know this, he hasn't even considered the issue; but we his grown-up readers do, and every vile specimen of humanity surveyed in this rich cross section of America confirms it. Huckleberry Finn set out to tell a story and did the best he could. By degrees, it became apparent to Mark Twain that the boy was writing a novel.

NOTES

1. "Mark Twain, 'Realism,' and Huckleberry Finn," in *New Essays on "Huckleberry Finn,"* ed. Louis J. Budd (Cambridge: Cambridge University Press, 1985), 35–59.

2. *Life on the Mississippi* (New York: Viking Penguin, 1986), 228–29.

3. Ibid.

4. Twain does speak his own mind from time to time—most obviously when he has Colonel Sherburn scold the mob in chapter 22, and perhaps most interestingly when he chooses to speak through Jim about the benefits of industry and progress in parts of chapter 14.

5. Shaped as he is by experience, however, Huck remains innocent in an important way. Unlike Colonel Sherburn, say, who has traveled in the North and lived in the South and is therefore able to proclaim on the cowardice of the "average" man (190), Huck's perspective has not frozen into an attitude. Not only is the narrative point of view of this novel presexual, as has so often been observed, but it is also prepolitical, even preideological. Huck, in his efforts to help Jim, may worry that he may become a "low-down Abolitionist," but the quality of that anxiety is rather more like a thousand childhood myths—e.g., the worry children have that, having made an ugly face, it will "stick."

6. "Mr. Eliot, Mr. Trilling, and Huckleberry Finn," *The American Scholar* 22 (Autumn 1953): 423–40.

7. Twain, quoted in Walter Blair, *Mark Twain and Huck Finn* (Berkeley and Los Angeles: University of California Press, 1960), 143; Kolb, "Mark Twain, Huck Finn, and Jacob Blivens: Gilt-Edged, Tree-Calf Morality in the *Adventures of Huckleberry Finn*," *The Virginia Quarterly Review* 55 (Autumn 1979): 658.

8. *of Huck and Alice: Humorous Writing in American Literature* (Minneapolis: University of Minnesota Press, 1983), 96.

9. Twain knew this, too; in a cranky moment, he predicted that Huck would grow up to be just as low-down and mean as his Pap.

Character Profile

Huckleberry Finn is the proverbial free spirit, choked when forced to wear shoes and proper clothes, to abide by societal customs, and to be "sivilized." He is most at ease when afloat on his raft, left lying naked on his back to cogitate, smoke, and co-exist with nature. He appeals to us not only because of his fierce independence but because he has heart, nerve, a desire to do what is right, and the ability to grow. In *The Adventures of Tom Sawyer* Huck is subordinate to Tom Sawyer, but in *The Adventures of Huckleberry Finn* Huck shines as the actual narrator of his own richly developed story.

In *Huckleberry Finn*, Huck is just under fourteen years old. He largely is a social outcast. (At the time, "huckleberry" was the word used to describe a person of no consequence.) Huck's mother is dead and his father insists that the boy not attend school or church; Pap, as Huck calls him, is drunk nearly all of the time, leaving Huck to scavenge for his own food, a place to sleep, and other necessities. Huck apparently has no other relatives and is living in a small town in Missouri on the Mississippi River.

Huck shows his craftiness throughout the book, notably when he plans ahead to escape from his father's cabin and creates an elaborate fake death for himself so his father will not hunt him down. When Huck later encounters the slave Jim, who becomes his runaway companion, he explains how he faked the death. Huck tells us that Jim calls him "smart." He [Jim] said, "Tom Sawyer couldn't get no better plan than what I had." But Tom Sawyer does not view Huck as smart. Even though Tom is not in a large portion of this book, he refers to Huck's lack of intelligence more than once, with comments such as, "Shucks, it ain't no use to talk to you, Huck Finn. You don't seem to know anything, somehow—perfect saphead." It is curious that Tom makes similar comments later in the book, at the very point when he has designed the most unintelligent plan to free Jim—when Huck actually has the more intelligent plan.

Yet despite his track record, Huck sees himself in a poor light as well, calling himself "so ignorant, and so kind of low-down and ornery." Later when he starts to question whether he should help keep Jim from being captured, he again shows his low opinion of himself, saying, "...and I see it warn't no use for me to try to learn to do right; a body that don't get *started* right when he's little ain't got no show—when the pinch comes there ain't nothing to back him up...." This quote shows not only Huck's view of his ability to learn but also his acceptance of the belief that one will forever struggle if one's upbringing is poor. It is also part of his longer contemplation on wanting to do right and to know what right is. This young boy, who is looked down upon by almost all in the book, actually is the most concerned with true morality, not only here and at other points but most notably in the climactic chapter where he decides to help Jim escape.

We see Huck as having sympathy not only for Jim but also for other characters throughout the book. We see him as emotional, also, since he cries or says he is about to cry at several points. While these characteristics might make him seem weak, at the same time he is bold and never gives up. We see this when he cannot rely on nature alone for his needs but must interact with people. He lies numerous times and fabricates stories when in very tough situations. Not only is he admirable for his mettle in these situations but also for his on-the-spot ingenuity. Even when he decides he must save Jim, there is spontaneity to many of his actions. He writes, "I went right along, not fixing up any particular plan but just trusting to Providence to put the right words in my mouth when the time come; for I'd noticed that Providence always did put the right words in my mouth if I left it alone." This description is curious because once again Huck refuses to give himself credit, attributing his gift for talking his way out of jams to a higher being. Not only can he do it, but he also likes to practice, for even when he isn't in trouble, fabrications that are in some cases enormously involved or detailed flow from his lips.

It seems almost unbelievable that in the beginning of the book Huck appears lacking in imagination. This appears to be the case when Tom Sawyer explains to Huck and others about their responsibilities in their robber gang and describs grand stories of elephants, genies, and diamonds. Huck remains quite the literal thinker at that point, and only later do we see where his imaginative talents blossom. But even at the point very early in the text when Huck questions Tom about the genies, Huck's inability to accept subservience and captivity is clear. Tom explains the genie's role and Huck puts his own spin on it:

> "They belong to whoever rubs the lamp or the ring, and they've got to do whatever he says. If he tells them to build a palace forty miles long out of di'monds, and fill it full of chewing-gum, or whatever you want, and fetch an emperor's daughter from China for you to marry, they've got to do it—and they've got to do it before sun-up next morning, too. And more: they've got to waltz that palace around over the country wherever you want it, you understand."
>
> "Well," says I, "I think they are a pack of fatheads for not keeping the palace themselves 'stead of fooling them away like that. And what's more—if I was one of them I would see a man in Jericho before I would drop my business and come to him for the rubbing of an old tin lamp."

Huck's response is most fitting for a boy who needs to live his life his own way, outside of society. And ultimately it is fitting for this boy who though believes he may be condemned to eternal damnation for his action, is intent on freeing a runaway slave.

Contributors

HAROLD BLOOM is Sterling Professor of the Humanities at Yale University and Henry W. and Albert A. Berg Professor of English at the New York University Graduate School. He is the author of over 20 books, including *Shelley's Mythmaking* (1959), *The Visionary Company* (1961), *Blake's Apocalypse* (1963), *Yeats* (1970), *A Map of Misreading* (1975), *Kabbalah and Criticism* (1975), *Agon: Toward a Theory of Revisionism* (1982), *The American Religion* (1992), *The Western Canon* (1994), and *Omens of Millennium: The Gnosis of Angels, Dreams, and Resurrection* (1996). *The Anxiety of Influence* (1973) sets forth Professor Bloom's provocative theory of the literary relationships between the great writers and their predecessors. His most recent books include *Shakespeare: The Invention of the Human* (1998), a 1998 National Book Award finalist, *How to Read and Why* (2000), *Genius: A Mosaic of One Hundred Exemplary Creative Minds* (2002), and *Hamlet: Poem Unlimited* (2003). In 1999, Professor Bloom received the prestigious American Academy of Arts and Letters Gold Medal for Criticism, and in 2002 he received the Catalonia International Prize.

LIONEL TRILLING was a distinguished American literary critic. He was Professor of Literature and Criticism at Columbia University and a prolific writer and editor. Among his works are *The Opposing Self*, *The Experience of Literature*, *Freud and the Crisis of Our Culture*, and books on Matthew Arnold and E.M. Forster. Additionally, he was a contributor to numerous books and periodicals and has his work in many anthologies.

T.S. ELIOT is one of the most renowned poets of the twentieth century. He won the Nobel Prize in Literature and in addition to his poetry wrote criticism, essays, and plays. He was the founder and editor of the *Criterion*, a literary journal, and probably is most known for his poems "The Waste Land," "The Love Song of J. Alfred Prufrock," and his work *Old Possum's Book of Practical Cats*, which became the basis for the highly successful Broadway musical *Cats*.

LESLIE A. FIEDLER taught at the State University of New York at Buffalo. A scholar of American literature, he published *End to Innocence*, *The Inadvertant Epic*, and other books.

RICHARD POIRIER has been a Professor at Rutgers University, New Brunswick, N.J. He is the author of such works as *Poetry and Pragmatism*, *Robert Frost: The Work of Knowing*, and *Trying It Out in America: Literary and Other Performances*.

MILLICENT BELL is Professor Emerita of English at Boston University. Her works include *Edith Wharton and Henry James: The Story of Their Friendship*, *Marquand: An American Life*, and many articles on English and American literature.

ROY HARVEY PEARCE has been Professor of American Literature at the University of California, San Diego. He is the author of *The Savages of America*, *The Continuity of American Poetry*, and *Historicism Once More*. He is the editor of works by Hawthorne and of *Experience in the Novel*.

HAROLD BEAVER has held the Chair of American Literature at the University of Amsterdam. His essays on American literature are collected in *The Great American Masquerade*, and he has edited works of Melville and Poe.

ANDREW JAY HOFFMAN teaches at San Diego Mesa College. He has written *Inventing Mark Twain: The Lives of Samuel Langhorne Clemens* and *Writing Choices*.

DAVID E.E. SLOANE is Professor of English at the University of New Haven and has also been director of their Master of Arts in Humanities program. His books include *Mark Twain as a Literary Comedian*, *Student Companion to Mark Twain*, and Sister Carrie: *Dreiser's Sociological Tragedy*.

TOM QUIRK teaches at the University of Missouri in Columbia, Missouri. He is the editor of a book of Twain's and also of *Mark Twain: A Study of the Short Fiction*. He is the author of *Nothing Abstract: Investigations in the American Literary Imagination* and the joint editor or joint author of other works as well.

Bibliography

Altschuler, Mark. "Motherless Child: Huck Finn and a Theory of Moral Development," *American Literary Realism* 22, no. 1 (Fall 1989): pp. 31–42.

Barnett, Louise K. "Huck Finn: Picaro as Linguistic Outsider," *College Literature* 6 (1979): pp. 221–31.

Beidler, Gretchen M. "Huck Finn as Tourist: Mark Twain's Parody Travelogue," *Studies in American Fiction* 20, no. 2 (Autumn 1992): pp. 155–67.

Berger, Arthur Asa. "Huck Finn as an Existential Hero: Making Sense of Absurdity," *Mark Twain Journal* 18, no. 2 (1976): pp. 12–17.

Blair, Walter. *Mark Twain and* Huck Finn. Berkeley: University of California Press, 1960.

Blakemore, Steven. "Huck Finn's Written World," *American Literary Realism* 20, no. 2 (Winter 1998): pp. 21–29.

Bloom, Harold. *Huck Finn*, New York: Chelsea House, 1990.

Budd, Louis J., ed. *Critical Essays on Mark Twain, 1867–1910*. Boston: G.K. Hall, 1982.

———. *New Essays on* The Adventures of Huckleberry Finn. Cambridge and New York: Cambridge University Press, 1985.

Camby, Henry Seidel. *Turn West, Turn East: Mark Twain and Henry James*. Boston: Houghton Mifflin, 1951.

Camfield, Gregg. *Sentimental Twain: Samuel Clemens in the Maze of Moral Philosophy*. Philadelphia: University of Pennsylvania Press, 1994.

Coard, Robert J. "Huck Finn and Mr. Mark Twain Rhyme," *Midwest Quarterly* 10 (1969): pp. 317–29.

———. "Huck Finn and Two Sixteenth Century Lads," *Midwest Quarterly* 23, no. 4 (Summer 1982): pp. 437–46.

Dawson, Hugh J. "The Ethnicity of Huck Finn—and the Difference It Makes," *American Literary Realism* 30, no. 2 (Winter 1998): pp. 1–16.

Delaney, Paul. "The Genteel Savage: A Western Link in the Development of Mark Twain's Transcendent Figure," *Mark Twain Journal* 21, no. 3 (Spring 1983): pp. 29–31.

Dolmetsch, Carl. "Huck Finn's First Century: A Bibliographical Survey," *American Studies International* 22, no. 2 (1984): pp. 79–121.

Fishkin, Shelley Fisher. *Was Huck Black?: Mark Twain and African-American Voices*. NY: Oxford University Press, 1993.

Fox, Maynard. "Two Primitives: Huck Finn and Tom Outland," *Western American Literature* 1 (1966): pp. 26–33.

Frank, Albert J. von. "Huck Finn and the Flight from Maturity," *Studies in American Fiction* 7 (1979): pp. 1–15.

Freedman, Carol. "The Morality of Huck Finn," *Philosophy and Literature* 21, no. 1 (April 1997): pp. 102–113.

Gale, Robert L. *Plots and Characters in the Works of Mark Twain*. Hamden, Conn.: Archon Books, 1973.

Hart, John E. "Heroes and Houses: The Progress of Huck Finn," *Modern Fiction Studies* 14, no. 1 (1968): pp. 39–46.

Inge, M. Thomas. *Huck Finn Among the Critics: A Centennial Selection*. Frederick, MD: University Publications of America, 1985.

Knoenagel, Axel. "Mark Twain's Further Use of Huck and Tom," *International Fiction Review* 19, no. 2 (1992): pp. 96–102.

Kohli, Raj K. "Isabel Archer and Huck Finn: Two Responses to the Fruit of Knowledge." Mukherjee, Sujit and Raghavacharyulu, D. V. K. *Indian Essays in American Literature*. Bombay: Popular Prakashan, 1969: pp. 167–78.

———. "Huck Finn and Isabel Archer: Two Responses to the Fruit of Knowledge," *Banasthali Patrika* 11 (July 1968): pp. 73–82.

Liljegren, Sten Bodvar. *The Revolt Against Romanticism in American Literature as Evidenced in the Works of S. L. Clemens*. NY: Haskell House, 1964.

Mandia, Patricia M. *Comedic Pathos: Black Humor in Twain's Fiction*. Jefferson, NC: McFarland, 1991.

Manierre, William R. "Huck Finn, Empiricist Member of Society," *Modern Fiction Studies* 14, no. 1 (1968): 57–66.

Margolis, Stacey. "Huck Finn: Or, Consequences," *Publications of the Modren Language Association of America* 116, no. 2 (March 2001): pp. 329–34.

Marks, Barry A. "The Huck Finn Swindle," *Western American Literature* 14 (1979): pp. 115–32.

———. *Mark Twain's* Huck Finn. Boston: Heath, 1959.

Mason, Ernest D. "Attraction and Repulsion: Huck Finn, 'Nigger' Jim, and Black Americans Revisited," *College Language Association Journal* 33, no. 1 (September 1989): pp. 36–48.

McKay, Janet Holmgren. "Going to Hell: Style in Huck Finn's Great Debate," *Interpretations: A Journal of Ideas, Analysis and Criticism* 13, no. 1 (Fall 1981): pp. 24–30.

McKethan, Lucinda H. "Huck Finn and the Slave Narratives: Lighting Out as Design," *The Southern Review* 20, no. 2 (Spring 1984): pp. 247–64.

Mensh, Elaine. *Black, White, and Huck Finn: Re-imagining the American Dream*. Tuscaloosa: University of Alabama Press, 2000.

Oehlschlaeger, Fritz H. "Huck Finn and the Meaning of Shame," *Mark Twain Journal* 20, no. 4 (Summer 1981): pp. 13–14.

Olan, Levi A. "The Voice of the Lonesome: Alienation from Huck Finn to Holden Caulfield," *Southwest Review* 48 (1963): pp. 143–50.

Opdahl, Keith M. "'You'll Be Sorry When I'm Dead': Child-Adult Relations in *Huck Finn*," *Modern Fiction Studies* 25 (1979–80): pp. 613–24.

Ostram, Alan. "Huck Finn and the Modern Ethos," *The Centennial Review* 16 (1972): pp. 162–79.

Papp, James. "How Huck Finn Was Red: The Communist and Post-Communist Condition of Mark Twain," *Essays in Arts and Sciences* 27 (October 1998): pp. 83–93.

Pearce, Roy H. "Huck Finn in His History…," *Etudes Anglaises* 24 (1971): pp. 283–91.

Rusch, Frederick L. "Res Privata versus Res Publica: Huck Finn as Unconscious Henry Thoreau," *Journal of Evolutionary Psychology* 9, nos. 1–2 (March 1988): pp. 154–63.

Prioleau, Elizabeth. "'That Abused Child of Mine': Huck Finn as Child of an Alcoholic,'" *Essays in Arts and Sciences* 22 (October 1993): pp. 85–98.

Raban, Jonathan. *Mark Twain*: Huck Finn. London: Edward Arnold, 1968.

Robinson, Forrest G. ed. *The Cambridge Companion to Mark Twain*. Cambridge, England; NY: Cambridge University Press, 1995.

Sapper, Neil. "'I Been There Before': Huck Finn as Tocquevillian Individual," *Mississippi Quarterly* 24 (1971): pp. 35–45.

Sidnell, M. J. "Huck Finn and Jim: Their Abortive Freedom Ride," *The Cambridge Quarterly* 2 (1967): pp. 203–11.

Simpson, Claude M. Jr. "Huck Finn after Huck Finn." Brack, O. M., ed. *American Humor: Essays Presented to John C. Gerber*. Scottsdale, AZ: Arete, 1977.

Sloane, David E. E., ed. *Mark Twain's Humor: Critical Essays*. NY: Garland Publishing, 1993.

Staebler, Warren. "Huck Finn—Boy or Man?" Kalaga, Wojciech and Slawek, Tadeusz, eds. *Discourse and Character*. Katowice, Poland: Universytet Slaski, 1990, pp. 85–95.

Talbott, Linda H. "*Huck Finn*: Mark Twain at Midstream," *The Nassau Review* 1, no. 5 (1969): pp. 44–60.

Tenney, Thomas A. "An Annotated Checklist of Criticism on *The Adventures of Huckleberry Finn*, 1884–1984," Inge, M. Thomas, ed. *Huck Finn Among the Critics: A Centennial Selection*. Frederick, MD: University Publications of America, 1985.

Tulip, James. "Huck Finn—the Picaresque Saint," *The Sydney Review* 2 (1965): pp. 13–18.

Wall, Carey. "The Boomerang of Slavery: The Child, the Aristocrat, and Hidden White Identity in *Huck Finn*," *Southern Studies* 21, no. 2 (Summer 1982): pp. 208–21.

Zmijewski, David. "Busting His Way to Freedom: Huck Finn's Escape through Violence," *Southern Studies: An Interdisciplinary Journal of the South* 6, no. 1 (Spring 1995); pp. 75–98.

Acknowledgments

"Huckleberry Finn" by Lionel Trilling. From *The Liberal Imagination*: 104–117. © 1948 by Holt, Rinehart, & Winston. Reprinted by permission.

"An Introduction to *Huckleberry Finn*" by T. S. Eliot. From *The Adventures of Huckleberry Finn*, by Samuel L. Clemens: vii–xvi. © 1950 by The Cresset Press. Reprinted by permission.

"*Huckleberry Finn*: Faust in the Eden of Childhood" by Leslie A. Fiedler. From *Love and Death in the American Novel*: 575–91. © 1960 by Criterion Books, Inc. Reprinted by permission.

"Transatlantic Configurations: Mark Twain and Jane Austen" by Richard Poirier. From *A World Elsewhere: The Place of Style in American Literature*: 175–207. © 1966 by Richard Poirier. Used by permission of Oxford University Press.

"*Huckleberry Finn* and the Sleights of the Imagination" by Millicent Bell. From *One Hundred Years of Huckleberry Finn: The Boy, His Book, and American Culture*, edited by Robert Sattelmeyer and J. Donald Crowley: 128–145. © 1985 by the Curators of the University of Missouri. Reprinted by permission of the University of Missouri Press.

"'Yours Truly, Huck Finn'" by Roy Harvey Pearce. From *One Hundred Years of Huckleberry Finn: The Boy, His Book, and American Culture*, edited by Robert Sattelmeyer and J. Donald Crowley: 313–324. © 1985 by The

Curators of the University of Missouri. Reprinted by permission of the University of Missouri Press.

"Huck Adrift" by Harold Beaver. From *Huckleberry Finn*: 92–103. © 1987 by Harold Beaver. Reprinted by permission.

"Huck's Heroism" by Andrew Jay Hoffman. From *Twain's Heroes, Twain's Worlds*: 3–25. © 1988 by the University of Pennsylvania Press. Reprinted by permission.

"Huck's Moral Reasoning as Heroism" by David E. E. Sloane. From Adventures of Huckleberry Finn: *American Comic Vision*: 114–123. © 1988 by G. K. Hall & Co. Reprinted by permission of The Gale Group.

"The Realism of *Huckleberry Finn*" by Tom Quirk. From *Coming to Grips with* Huckleberry Finn: 83–96. © 1993 by The Curators of the University of Missouri. Reprinted by permission of the University of Missouri Press.

Index